New Insights into Foreign Language Learning and Teaching

Foreign Language Teaching in Europe

Edited by Pamela Faber/Wolf Gewehr/Manuel Jiménez Raya/Terry Lamb

Vol. 9

PETER LANG
Frankfurt am Main · Berlin · Bern · Bruxelles · New York · Oxford · Wien

Kees van Esch/Oliver St. John (eds.)

New Insights into Foreign Language Learning and Teaching

PETER LANG
Europäischer Verlag der Wissenschaften

Bibliographic Information published by Die Deutsche Bibliothek
Die Deutsche Bibliothek lists this publication in the Deutsche Nationalbibliografie; detailed bibliographic data is available in the internet at <http://dnb.ddb.de>.

ISSN 1437-3157
ISBN 3-631-52639-3
US-ISBN 0-8204-7322-7

© Peter Lang GmbH
Europäischer Verlag der Wissenschaften
Frankfurt am Main 2004
All rights reserved.

All parts of this publication are protected by copyright. Any utilisation outside the strict limits of the copyright law, without the permission of the publisher, is forbidden and liable to prosecution. This applies in particular to reproductions, translations, microfilming, and storage and processing in electronic retrieval systems.

Printed in Germany 1 2 3 4 6 7

www.peterlang.de

TABLE OF CONTENTS

INTRODUCTION 7

PART I
Sociocultural Theory and Second and Foreign Language learning
An Overview of Sociocultural Theory
JAMES P. LANTOLF 13

What Does SCT Research Reveal about Second Language Learning?
HOWARD GRABOIS 35

Cultural historical activity theory and the object of innovation
STEVEN L. THORNE 51

PART II
Communicative Language Teaching

Language, Identity, and Curriculum Design:
Communicative Language Teaching in the 21st Century
SANDRA J. SAVIGNON 71

Research Insights and Communicative Language Teaching
DIANE MUSUMECI 89

Communicative Foreign Language Teaching Through
Telecollaboration
CELESTE KINGINGER 101

PART III
Intercultural Communicative Competence in Foreign Language Education

Intercultural communicative competence in foreign language education.
Integrating theory and practice.
LIES SERCU 115

Researching the acquisition of intercultural communicative competence
in a foreign language. Setting the agenda for a research area.
LIES SERCU 131

The acquisition of intercultural communicative competence.
Some guidelines for better results on the 'intercultural competence'
level.
LIEVE DE WACHTER & ANNEMIE DECAVELE 157

PART IV
Learner Autonomy in Foreign Language Education

Learner Autonomy in Foreign Language Learning and Teaching
EUS SCHALKWIJK, KEES VAN ESCH, ADRI ELSEN & WIM SETZ 169

Effecting Change: research into Learner Autonomy in Foreign
Language Learning and Teaching
KEES VAN ESCH AND ADRI ELSEN 191

Learner Autonomy in Initial Foreign Language Teacher Education
SOCRATES LINGUA LEARNER AUTONOMY GROUP 219

Introduction

This book aims to offer insights into cognitive, sociocultural, communicative and pedagogical aspects of foreign language learning and teaching. It bears the fruit of collaboration between researchers and practitioners on both sides of the Atlantic and, therefore, offers a variety of perspectives.

The book is divided into four parts, focusing on the following four areas of research: sociocultural theory, communicative language teaching, intercultural competence and learner autonomy.

The first chapter of each part focuses on theoretical issues by outlining the origins and development of a theory and explaining its core concepts. In the second chapter, theoretical, empirical and applied research is reviewed, and the implications for foreign language learning and teaching are discussed. The third chapter of each part is devoted to the application of the theories in focus. It presents either an example of a research project or an application of the theory in terms of developing materials and/or giving suggestions for good practice in the foreign language classroom.

Part I Sociocultural Theory

Part I of this book is dedicated to sociocultural theory, which has its origins in the writings of the Russian psychologist and psycholinguist Vygotsky. The first chapter, written by James Lantolf, explores the philosophical and psychological origins of Vygotsky's ideas and examines their impact on psychology and education. It subsequently explains core concepts of sociocultural theory such as mediation, internalization, inner and private speech, imitation, the zone of proximal development and activity theory. By relating these concepts to each other, Lantolf provides insight into the impact of sociocultural theory on thinking and learning. His conclusions emphasize this theory as a theory of mind in which culturally constructed, concrete and symbolic artifacts are essential aspects.

In the second chapter, Howard Grabois considers how sociocultural theory research can inform second language learning and our approach to second language research methodology. In search of answers, he focuses on three areas: the notion of tool-and-result, the basic unit of analysis for consciousness and the discussion of Vygotsky's roles as methodologist and psychologist. Grabois examines research into central aspects of sociocultural theory, such as the zone of proximal development and the relation between language and the construction of self. In his conclusion, he underlines the holistic orientation of sociocultural theory as a broader theory of cognition and mind, and points to perspectives this theory affords in relation to methodological and theoretical issues of research in second language learning.

In the third chapter, Steven Thorne applies sociocultural theory in a research project. He starts with a brief introduction to Vygotsky and cultural activity theory in which Vygotsky's models of mediated action and of activity systems are explained. He then describes an action research project on expert-novice interaction in foreign language learning carried out by student teachers. In his discussion, he presents activity theory as an opportunity to deepen our understanding of the 'process' and 'product' in language education – one with potential to transform educational practice.

Part II Communicative Language Teaching

Part II is about communicative language teaching. In the first chapter, Sandra Savignon defines the central concept of communicative competence as the expression, interpretation and negotiation of meaning. She summarizes important principles of communicative language teaching and the five components of the communicative curriculum, for example, the preparation of learners to use their new language in the world beyond the classroom. In the second part of the chapter, she discusses sociolinguistic issues, such as the classroom as social context with different roles of teachers and learners. She ends the chapter with a 'tour' of different parts of the world where curricular reforms and teacher education have moved towards communicative language teaching.

In Chapter two, Diane Musumeci reviews research insights related to communicative language learning. From a psycholinguistic perspective and in the context of immersion classes in the Canadian-French area, she sheds new light on the role of comprehensible input and the place of form-focused instruction in successful second and foreign language acquisition. She discusses research on error correction and feedback which suggests the limited effects of explicit grammar instruction. She also refers to empirical evidence for possible developmental sequences in spite of this instruction and to evidence regarding Swain's output hypothesis about meaningful interaction in the second language. From a sociolinguistic perspective, she summarizes research into the effects of learners' use of the language in meaningful tasks on their communicative performance. Her conclusion is that the communicative approach in language teaching is important for classroom practice at all the levels of the curriculum, depending on intervening factors, such as goals, resources as well as local situations and expertise.

The third chapter is Celeste Kinginger's. She explores some of the components of communicative language teaching in projects on foreign language learning through telecollaboration, i.e. applying electronic networks and tools. The rationale for her approach is grounded in the history of intercultural exchange in language teaching and she relates this approach to communicative language teaching issues, such as authenticity, the role of the classroom in fostering language awareness and learning language as culture. She explains how telecollaborative language courses are designed and how three of the components of communicative language teaching – personal language use, language with a purpose and language analysis – can be applied within telecollaborative approaches. Her concrete examples of projects carried out with English-speaking classes learning intermediate or advanced level French in the United States, paired with French-speaking classes studying English in France, illustrate the challenges of this new approach.

Part III   Intercultural Competence

Part III discusses intercultural competence - a relatively new aspect of language learning. In the first chapter, Lies Sercu starts by looking at the notion of culture and its history in foreign language learning. She introduces a new perspective on the knowledge, skills and attitudes needed for interaction between speakers with different linguistic and cultural backgrounds. This perspective involves a contrastive approach, in which the foreign language learner has to learn to negotiate in intercultural situations according to a new system of (inter)cultural standards as well as linguistic and pragmatic rules. Describing the different 'savoirs' as important constituents of what she calls intercultural communicative competence, she argues that the acquisition of this capacity involves the development of interlanguage, intercultural competence and learner autonomy. She ends by elaborating these 'savoirs' and proposing criteria to select content, tasks and approaches in teaching culture.

The second chapter, also written by Lies Sercu, is an overview of research concerning the central concepts and the acquisition of intercultural competence in foreign language education. She examines how culture in foreign language has been viewed over the three or four last decades, and concludes that such views have developed from static to dynamic, that language and culture have become increasingly integrated. She reviews applied research on the development of teaching procedures in the acquisition and teaching of intercultural communicative competence by focusing on a number of variables: the setting, the teacher, the learner, materials and assessment.. At the end of the chapter she sets a research agenda for the future.

The third chapter focuses on the language teacher in multicultural classrooms. Based on the theoretical notions outlined in the first chapter of this part, especially the 'savoirs', Lieve De Wachter and Annemie Decavele stress the important role of the language teacher in the learner's process of becoming interculturally competent. They propose Gardner's Multiple Intelligence Theory as a way to understand the process of learning and teaching language and culture. Insights into the multiple intelligence profile of both teachers and learners are essential conditions for developing intercultural competence. They explain possible restraints in the foreign language classroom and underline the importance of the affective component, interactive communication and appropriate language and culture materials. They end by offering some strategies to break through these possible restraints.

Part IV Learner Autonomy

Part IV is about learner autonomy. In the first chapter, written by Schalkwijk, Van Esch, Elsen and Setz, the origins and backgrounds of learner autonomy are explored from three different perspectives. The first is the philosophical perspective that brings into focus the role of human agency and personal autonomy. The second is the sociological perspective that distinguishes different culture orientations and, consequently, different views on self-determination and personal autonomy. The third perspective stresses the importance of the affective, social and cognitive dimensions of learning and teaching in relation to learner autonomy. The last section discusses aspects of learner autonomy in foreign language education, such as ideals and everyday practice, new roles of learners and teachers, and other implications for foreign language education and teacher training.

The second chapter, written by Kees van Esch and Adri Elsen, is about research on learner autonomy in foreign language learning and teaching. The first section is about theoretical research and focuses mainly on the political and ideological dimensions of learner autonomy discussed in the previous chapter. In the second section, research on the application of different aspects of learner autonomy is reviewed. This includes problems and conditions related to the application of learner autonomy, the role of motivation and learner strategies. In the third section, the relationship between learner and teacher autonomy is discussed and implications for initial and in-service foreign language teacher training are considered. The chapter ends with suggestions for further research in different areas of learner autonomy.

The third chapter consists of a brief description of a Socrates Lingua-A project on learner autonomy in which notions and principles of learner autonomy are applied to initial foreign language teacher education. It has been written by some of the project participants. The chapter starts with a metaphor illustrating the complexity of learning processes, followed by an explanation of a four-stage learning model that serves as a theoretical framework for the teacher training modules developed during this project. Pedagogical principles for applying learner autonomy in the foreign language classroom are illustrated by sample objectives, structures, procedures and tasks taken from the project modules.

The aim of this book has been to make the four different perspectives it explores – sociocultural theory, communicative language teaching, intercultural communicative competence and learner autonomy – accessible to readers interested in these issues. We hope that the reader will not only enjoy reading this book, but will also acquire the new insights promised in the title. We also hope these new insights may contribute to impetus for developing new theoretical concepts, for carrying out new research projects and for translating deeper understanding of foreign language learning and teaching into practice. Then, and only then, will the aim of this book have been achieved.

Kees van Esch
Oliver St. John

Part I

Sociocultural Theory and Second and Foreign Language Learning

An Overview of Sociocultural Theory
James P. Lantolf, Pennsylvania State University, USA

1. Introduction

This chapter outlines the core statements of sociocultural theory, which inform the discussion in the respective chapters by Grabois and Thorne.

Sociocultural theory has its origins in the writings of the great Russian psychologist and psycholinguist L. S. Vygotsky. Despite his short life (he was born in 1896 and died in 1934 from complications arising from tuberculosis) and the brief ten-year span of his scholarly productivity, Vygotsky has had a remarkably profound and growing impact on psychology and education inside and outside of the former Soviet Union. By most accounts (see Valsiner & van der Veer, 2000, Lantolf & Appel, 1994, Homskaya, 2001) Vygotsky burst onto the psychology scene as a consequence of a paper he presented at the Second All-Russian Congress on Psychoneurology held in Leningrad in 1924. Although there is not agreement among scholars as to which of two possible papers Vygotsky actually presented on the Congress, there is clear documentation that Vygotsky's performance was nothing short of spectacular.[1] In his intellectual biography, A. R. Luria (1979, p. 38) remarks that when the then twenty-eight-year-old Vygotsky arose to deliver his speech that was to leave a lasting impact on those who were attempting to build a Marxist psychology, he spoke "with no printed text from which to read, not even notes. Yet he spoke fluently, never seeming to stop and search his memory for the next idea." His presentation, in which he began to lay the foundation for what was to become a theory that "regards mental processes as derivatives of cultural and historic development" (Homskaya 2001, p. 20), was all the more impressive, because Vygotsky at that point had not had advanced education in psychology, although he had pursued university courses in psychology along with courses in medicine, law, philosophy, education, and above all in his first love, literature. Indeed, his attraction to psychology emerged from his literary interests, in particular his fascination with the emotional responses people experienced upon reading a work of literature or viewing a piece of are (Valsiner & van der Veer 2000, p. 330). In Luria's (1979, p. 38) own words, "it is no exaggeration to say that Vygotsky was a genius" and the "more than five decades in science I never again met a person who even approached his clearness of mind, his ability to lay bare the essential structure of complete

---

[1] Some scholars believe the paper was entitled "Consciousness and the Subject of Psychology," while others, including his colleague and life-time disciple, A. R. Luria, claim that the lecture's title was "The Methods of Reflexological and Psychological Investigation."

problems, his breadth of knowledge in many fields, and his ability to foresee the future development of his science."

Not long after his presentation at the psychoneurology congress, and there is controversy regarding the exact events (see Prawat 2000), Vygotsky moved from the small Byelorussian town of Gomel, where he had been teaching literature and history in area schools (Valsiner & van der Veer 2000, p. 333), to the Institute for Psychology in Moscow. There he produced his Ph.D. dissertation *The Psychology of Art* and eventually joined the Institute's subsection for Pedology and Defectology. According to Prawat (2000), Vygotsky teamed up with N. K. Krupskaya, Lenin's wife, and along with several other colleagues, they undertook a sweeping reform of the Soviet educational system, most especially through the polytechnical schools. At the time, these schools emphasized training in "purely mechanical skills at the expense of broad knowledge," and so the aim of the reform was not only to train workers but to empower them "lift themselves through education" (Prawat 2000, p. 673).

Vygotsky's enterprise was not only to build a new psychology, but to build a new psychology that had practical relevance for the education and development of the new Soviet society. Tragically, the reforms that were emanating from group headed up by Krupskaya and Vygotsky, were short lived. Stalin and his cronies soon got into the act and Vygotsky and his group were censored and eventually blacklisted for ostensibly adopting a non-materialist stance that was heavily influenced by bourgeois views (e.g., Dewey, Piaget, Janet, the Bühlers, Yerkes etc.) on language, mind and education. Vygotsky's argument that thought and language are separate but dialectically intertwined features of higher forms of consciousness was especially singled out for attack. Stalin, laid claim to being a linguist, insisted that it was impossible for thoughts to be independent of a material "language shell" (Prawat 2000, p. 691). Indeed, as Prawat (ibid.) notes, it was to Stalin's advantage to adopt such a stance, because if he could control "what people said he could control what they thought." Some have speculated that Stalin's condemnation of Vygotsky may have contributed to his early demise. Prawat, citing a work by Yaroshevsky, Vygotsky's biographer, reports an incident following Stalin's attacks, in which Vygotsky's assistant recalls his running through a clinic saying "I do not want to live any more, they do not consider me a Marxist" (Prawat 2000, p. 691).

As it turns out, and to our great benefit, Vygotsky had the last laugh. Following Stalin's death, his works, banned for nearly two decades, were resurrected and published not only in their original Russian, but also in an increasing number of the world's languages (see Elhammoumi 1997). In what follows, I offer a necessarily brief overview of Vygotsky's theory. I will focus on the foundational statements of the theory and will leave the interested reader to explore the details and some of the controversies that have developed over the course of the 80 years that have passed since Vygotsky ascended onto the stage of psychology (see Vygotsky 1987, Wertsch 1985, Cole 1996, Newman & Holzman 1993, Valsiner & van der Veer 2000, Kozulin 1990, van der Veer & Valsiner 1991). The topics to be addressed are the following: mediated mind and higher forms of consciousness, which forms the basis of Vygotsky's theory; internalization, private and inner speech, which, along with the important, and under-explored concept of imitation, account for the inseparable and dialectic link between the social world and psychological activity; the zone of proximal development, the performative space where learning leads development and where the social and the psychological meet; the unit of analysis for the study of mind, perhaps along with activity theory, the concept that has generated the lion's share of controversy in the sociocultural literature; and finally, activity theory, arguably for many scholars, the contemporary instantiation of Vygotsky's theory.

2   Mediated Mind

The core concept of sociocultural theory is that the human mind is *mediated*. Basing his argument on Marx's writings on tool use in labor activity, Vygotsky proposed that higher forms of mental activity in humans, including planning, voluntary attention, intentional memory, rational thinking, and learning, are mediated by symbolic artifacts. Just as with physical artifacts, symbolic artifacts, including numbers, graphs, and above all speech and writing, are culturally constructed and are passed on and appropriated, often in modified form, from one generation to another. As with physical tools, symbolic artifacts establish an indirect, or mediated, relationship between ourselves and the world. Instead of digging a hole with our hands, we can use a shovel, which imbues us with the capacity to more efficiently dig a hole. Symbolic artifacts, among other things, enable us to plan the kind of hole we want to dig before engaging in the physical activity itself. The task of psychology, according to Vygotsky, is to understand how human social and mental activity is organized through culturally constructed symbolic artifacts. Vygotsky conceived of the human mind as a functional system in which the capacities of the natural, or biologically specified, brain are organized into a higher, or culturally shaped, mind through the integration of symbolic artifacts into thinking: "the cultural development of any function ... consists of a person's developing a series of artificial stimuli and signs in the process of mutual living and activity" (Vygotsky, 1997b, p. 154).

To appreciate the significance of Vygotsky's theorizing, it is helpful to recognize that his goal was to develop a unified psychology – one which overcame the Cartesian mind/matter dualism that had effectively fractured psychology into various subdisciplines (see Vygotsky 1997a). In a nutshell, the conundrum of the so-called "two-worlds model" (Bakhurst 1991) was to account for how it was possible for the human mind to acquire knowledge of the material world. The two dominant solutions to the conundrum were both reductive. One, essentially a Kantian turn, argued that the human mind/brain imposed structure on the world by virtue of (innately specified) mental representations. The difficulty with this position was that if the mind *"creates* the object of cognition as a representational entity" how can the subject ever grasp "how an object is 'in itself' by disentangling from its representation of the object those features that the mind itself contributes" (Bakhurst 1991, pp. 206-207). On the other hand, the empiricist solution, which argued that the mind reflected the world, immediately ran up against the problem of explaining how something without representational content could be comprehended by the mind, which operates representationally.

While the Cartesian dualism arose as a philosophical problem, it had consequences for the derivative discipline of psychology, breaking it into a branch that focused on the inner workings of the mind and a branch that concerned itself with purely the external behavior of people. In Vygotsky's view, both positions were reductive and as such were unable to account for uniquely human forms of mentation. He sought to overcome the dualism by arguing for a necessary dialectic connection between the external (socially constructed) world and the genetically endowed organ, the brain, which we use to think. According to Vygotsky, in the early stages of ontogenesis, children's mental activity is predominantly determined by their natural biological endowment. Thus, phenomena such as memory and attention are *directly* impacted by events in the world. Hence, a young child is compelled to attend (non-reflectively) to a loud noise or a flashing light. Once children begin to appropriate the language of their social environment, mental processes undergo a profound change in which purely organic processes are moved to the background as children begin to subordinate these processes to their own will. Thought begins as a natural, biologically endowed process – a process which humans share with other animals – and develops into a uniquely human form of semiotically mediated thinking or what Vygotsky referred to as higher forms of consciousness. Thus, not only does language permit humans to interact symbolically with other humans, but as a consequence of this interaction, they develop the ability to gain control over and regulate their own thinking processes. As Vygotsky put it: *"I only want to say ... that without man [sic] (=operator) as a whole the activity of his apparatus (brain) cannot be explained, that man controls his brain and not the brain the man* (Yaroshevsky, 1989, p. 230).

Importantly, Vygotsky realized that in order to construct a genuinely Marxist theory of psychology – a theory that would indeed surmount the dualism that plagued psychology, it was not enough to assign a central role to language (i.e., speaking and writing activity). Marxist theory is grounded in historical materialism, which means that it insists that humans, unlike any other species, create the circumstances of their own existence through their purposeful and coordinated concrete practical actions in the material world. With this principle in mind, Vygotsky proposed that human speaking, or indeed any symbolic activity was always linked to practical activity. Without this necessary and dialectic connection, the theory would be unable to overcome the two-worlds model and instead of the downward reductionism of neurobiological explanations of mind, we would be confronted with the upwardly reductive stance typical of current social-constructionist models (see Valsiner & van der Veer, 2000 and Jones, 1999).

The significance of Vygotsky's insight is brought out forcefully in the argument for idealization of the material world proposed by E. V. Ilyenkov, considered by many to be the most important Russian interpreter of Marxist theory (Bakhurst 1991). Ilyenkov understood that the human mind is incapable of accessing the concrete world as it is; "something must be added to the object" in order for humans to perceive it (Bakhurst 1991, p. 207). What is added is representational content, but unlike Kant, Ilyenkov suggested that this property "originates not in the mental but in object-oriented activity" and it is assumed to be a "property of the physical object itself" (Bakhurst 1991, p. 208).

Clearly, however, Ilyenkov is not making the claim that object-oriented activity is mindless; on the contrary, the mind is very much implicated in this activity, and it is implicated through symbolic mediation. To try to understand this important point, I will consider an example presented in Bakhurst (1991).

While a table as a physical object "holds no mysteries for the scientist," it cannot be fully understood in "purely natural-scientific terms," because "such an account fails to express the difference between being a *table* and being a *lump of wood*" (Bakhurst 1991, pp. 181-182). According to Ilyenkov, the difference can only be explained by "appeal to human activity" (Bakhurst 1991, p. 182). This activity gives new form and function (or said in another way, new form that entails a specifically human function) to natural objects, such as a lump of wood. Human activity is thus embodied, or objectified, in the natural object referred to in English as *table*. Although the activity of converting a lump of wood into a table requires concrete activity on a material object, it also entails a mental component in that the person who constructs the table also constructs an plan prior to building the table. This plan is carried out through the symbolic mediation afforded by language, frequently in conjunction with other culturally constructed artifacts such as paper and pencil. According to Ilyenkov (1977) such plans are idealizations, but importantly, these idealizations are not formulated independently of the physical properties of the natural object (wood, in this case). The activity of bringing a table into being must of course entail material activity, for mental activity alone cannot in itself change the physical world, but the symbolically formulated idealized plan is also an integral part of table-building activity. That is, "the use of words in planning cannot be artificially counterposed to activity, since it *is* activity," but activity on the representational rather than on the physical plane (Jones, unpublished manuscript).

To explain this point further, consider the case of an architect who designs a house. The architect develops a set of plans, which entails activity carried out

17

not only inside the head but also the activity of making marks on a piece of paper with a pencil. As a consequence of this activity, an actual concrete object is created – blueprints. This concrete object is the house in its ideal form, but "its ideality is a function of its role within the house-building process as a systemic whole uniting the activities of the architect and builder, the use of pencil and paper and brick and trowel" (Jones, 1999, p. 288). The unity of ideal and real comes about when "the plan is concretized (modified, altered, etc.) as it is realized" in social production (ibid.). The blueprints themselves only have meaning as they are used in the activity of building the house, at which point they are converted "into the real thing" (ibid.). As Jones (1999, p. 296) points out, words as acoustic waves in the air or as light waves emanating from a piece of paper are concrete objects, but when they function within social activity they are ideal in that they represent objects in the real world or in a future world. As with the architect's plans, their meaning arises as a consequence of their function within specific practical social activity.

Speech activity, for Vygotsky, then indeed has causal power, but not in the physical world of objects; rather in the representational world of planning (Jones, unpublished manuscript). It is important to recognize in this regard, however, that it is not speech that has power over humans, but it is humans who exercise their power through speech activity with each other and with themselves as they undertake concrete practical activities in the material world (ibid.).

Vygotsky argued that in the early stages of ontogenesis activity takes precedence over speech. This was robustly documented in Vygotsky's own research as well as that of colleagues such as A. R. Luria (1982). Both researchers noted that in young children egocentric speech, or private speech, as it was later called by Flavell (1966), generally followed or coincided with children's physical activity, as when they were playing with such objects as puzzles or drawing pictures. This research revealed, for example, that when drawing with paper and pencil, young children initially make random designs and only later do they label these as a specific object (Vygotsky, 1997b). As children mature, however, Vygotsky showed that speech eventually precedes children's practical activity and in so doing takes on its uniquely human planning function: "This dialectical transformation of action makes all human activity dependent upon the word and other ideal forms, a dependence which is not in itself the rule of mystical abstractions over people ... but an expression of the power of the human collective objectified in special symbolic form" (Jones, unpublished manuscript). Thus, at some point, children state what they intend to draw before actually setting out to draw the object.

Words play a central role not only in planning concrete practical activity, but in Vygotsky's theory they are the basis of concepts and conceptual thinking. For Vygotsky there is "no conceptual thinking outside of the special activity of mastering the symbolic form" (Jones, unpublished manuscript). Thus, concrete practical activity carried out by humans in the material world is planned, organized and coordinated through speech activity. This activity ultimately structures the material world in specifically human ways. This in turn enables humans to know the material world through the symbolic representations they create to plan, coordinate, and talk about the outcome of their activity. Humans therefore come to know the material world through their concrete, symbolically mediated, practical activity in it; that is, they know the material world as a consequence of understanding what their activity contributes to natural objects as they are formed into purposeful cultural artifacts (Ilyenkov, 1977).

3   Internalization and Inner Speech

The process that Vygotsky proposed for connecting the symbolically mediated concrete activity of humans in the material world with their mental activity is *internalization*. Indeed, internalization is the process through which the specifically human forms of thinking, what Vygotsky refers to as higher forms of consciousness, are created. As Kozulin (1990, p. 116) notes, "the essential element in the formation of higher mental functions is the process of internalization." In the words of A. R. Luria (1979, p. 45), "it is through this interiorization of historically determined and culturally organized ways of operating on information that the social nature of people comes to be their psychological nature as well." [2] According to Gal'perin (1967, pp. 28-29), through internalization what is originally an external and non-mental form of activity becomes mental; thus, the process "opens up the possibility of bridging this gap" [between the non-mental and the mental].

It is important to emphasize that internalization does not mean that something literally is "'within the 'individual' or 'in the brain'", but instead "refers to the subject's ability to perform a certain action [concrete or ideal] without the immediately present problem situation 'in the mind'" (Stetsenko, 1999, p. 245) and with an understanding that is derived from, but independent of, "someone else's thoughts or understandings" (Ball, 2000, p. 250-251). Thus, on this view, mental activity is carried out "on the basis of mental representations, that is, independently of the physical presence of things" (Stetsenko, 1999, p. 245). According to Frawley (1997, p. 95), the Russian term very much implies the emergence of "active, nurturing transformation of externals into personally meaningful experience." Again, to cite Stetsenko, the formation of intrapersonal processes "is explained as the transition from a material *object-dependent* activity (such as the actual counting of physical objects by pointing at them with a finger

---

[2] Frawley (1997, pp. 94-95) notes that the original Russian term, which has been translated into English as "interiorization" is *vrashchivanie*, which means "ingrowing." In Frawley's words, "the dynamic and developmental character of the notion is lost by the English nominal translation" (p. 95).

in the initial stages of acquiring the counting operation) to a material *object-independent* activity (when a child comes to be able to count the objects without necessarily touching them or even seeing them)" (1999: pp. 245-255).

Consider the difference between the expert and novice pool player, as discussed by Wertsch (1998). In order to determine what the result of a particular shot is likely to be, the novice must actually play the shot and rely therefore on the external material support of the cue stick, the balls, and the table. The expert, on the other hand, is able to determine the outcome of the shot before actually playing it. In fact, the expert need not even be in the presence of pool playing equipment to make such a determination. He or she can "visualize" the shot on the psychological plane. This is so because the expert has "internalized" what was at one time the external material support provided by the cue stick, balls and table.

Given that the theory holds that higher forms of thinking are culturally derived, it should come as no surprise that different cultures are not only likely to engage in particular form of practical activity, but are also likely to manifest different forms of mediated thinking activity as well. This is because different cultures produce and reside in different material circumstances. Luria's (1976) well known study of the effects of collectivization and educated literacy on thinking processes in Uzbek culture supports this position (see also Scribner & Cole, 1981; Lucy, 1992; Ratner, 1991). In a case study of an Ethiopian immigrant to Israel, Kozulin (1998, p. 113) reports that when asked if musical instruments could be grouped in a way other than by those instruments that are played together on particular social occasions, the immigrant failed to respond because the question was meaningless. For the Ethiopian there was no other conceivable way of grouping musical instruments (e.g., wind instruments, strings, percussion, etc.). Kozlin points out that as far as we know, all humans are capable of classifying objects, which may well be a biologically specified ability. However, not all humans classify objects according to the same schema. In some cultures, classification of objects is based primarily on the objects' functional role in everyday practical activity, while in others they are classified according to formal schema internalized in school. Thus, while biology provides a foundation for classification, the concrete schemata deployed by individuals to classify entities in their world is culturally constructed. This means that attempts to ground explanations of mental development in the individual as an entity separate from sociocultural history are inadequate.

4   Private Speech

Internalization as a concrete activity unfolds as a communicative process – a communicative process in which there is a shift from social dialogue to self- or private dialogue. Vocate (1994) argues that, as with social talk, self-talk is dialogic, but instead of an "I" talking to a "You," private speech entails an "I" that makes choices on what to talk about and a "Me" that interprets and critiques these choices. The interaction between I and Me "allows us to adapt ourselves mentally, physically, or both before we think or act further" (Vocate, 1994, p. 12). The selection and interpretation process carried out jointly by I and Me "is accompanied by entropic reduction and change" because "the adaptation process that increases the organization of the organism requires adjustments in either the individual, or the items to be ingested [i.e., internalized], or both" (Vocate, 1994, p.12). Cognitive adaptation, according to Vocate, is common in a variety of human interactional activities, including the instructional process. On the one hand, "concepts and principles have to be restructured to facilitate internalization by the student" and this is done "by simplifying relationships and using language that the student can understand," and on the other, "the student too must adjust (subroutine of accommodation) by remaining open-minded and by attempting to understand the material" (p. 12). A similar process also occurs through intrapersonal communication, but in this case, instead of interaction between teacher and student, the interaction is between the I and the Me. This means that people are capable of mediating their own learning on the intrapersonal level, but they do it in ways that reflect their interpersonal experiences as sanctioned by their sociocultural environment (e.g., the values and forms of knowledge prescribed in a particular setting).

Private speech is marked by the "abbreviation of interactive social speech into audible speech to oneself, or *private speech* and ultimately silent speech for oneself, or *inner speech*. Social dialogue condenses into a private dialogue for thinking" (Frawley, 1997, p. 95). As speech moves from social to private to inner, it becomes increasingly elliptical in form and condensed in meaning. Private speech is potentially understandable to someone "eavesdropping." Inner speech, on the other hand, if it were somehow to be audibly projected, because of its formal and semantic condensation, would be "incomprehensible to a listener" (Dance 1994: 200). Once private speech becomes inner speech, of course, it is no longer observable in terms of its specific form and content. Vygotsky theorized, however, that because of the genetic link between private and inner speech (that is, private speech, itself derived from social speech, is the precursor to inner speech), mental development can be studied, at least in part, through analysis of private speech. The research program of Vygotsky and his colleagues, focused on the ways in which children developed the ability to use private speech to regulate their own mental and even physical activity as they carried out concrete, culture-specific tasks (see Vygotsky 1987 and Luria 1982). Through the study of private speech, then, it is possible to observe, at least at the pre-inner speech level, human mental activity as it is being formed in situated practical activity.

In a revealing series of studies, Wertsch (see summary in Wertsch 1985: chapter 6) showed that in learning to solve certain cognitive tasks, such as reconstructing a wooden puzzle according to the specifications of a model, the behavior of young children (ages 2 to 7) initially was under the mediational control of the child's parent. Gradually, control passed from parents to children as they appropriated the language used by their parents as a means of mediating their own mental and indeed physical activity. At this point, the children's speech also shifted from an exclusively social to a shared psychological function, but as in the case of the novice pool player, the psychological function was still linked to the specific external circumstances in which the puzzle-solving occurred. The children's speaking activity, therefore, was in some respects social in that it occurred in the presence of the other person, but it was importantly psychological to the extent that it was not directed at the other person; rather it was oriented to the children themselves as they instructed themselves in selecting the appropriate piece from the pieces pile, placing the piece in the puzzle, and in evaluating the correctness of their moves.

The self-directed language attested in Wertsch's research and numerous other studies (see Diaz & Berk 1992), takes on an elliptical quality. That is, it most often consists of utterances that are not fully syntactic. In fact, self communication often looks like one half of a dialogue between individuals with a close personal relationship. For instance, utterances such as the following are frequently attested in self-directed speech in English: "What ?" "Next, an orange one," "Wait," "No," "I can't..." "Done," etc. This speech, in which we ask ourselves questions, answer these questions, tell ourselves to interrupt a particular activity, tell ourselves we are wrong or that we can't do something, and that we have completed a task, is generally referred to as *private speech*; that is, speech that has social origins in the speech of others but that takes on a private or cognitive function. As cognitive development proceeds, private speech becomes subvocal and ultimately evolves into *inner speech*, or language that at the deepest level loses its formal properties as it condenses into pure meaning. According to Vygotsky, it is in the process of privatizing speech that higher forms of consciousness arise on the inner plane and in this way our biological capacities are organized into a culturally mediated mind.

Once mental processes grow inward and private speech evolves into inner speech, mental activity need not remain, and for most people, they do not remain, as exclusively internal mental operations. In the face of difficult tasks, and here difficulty is ultimately determined by the individual, these processes can be re-externalized as the person attempts to regain control over them in performing the task. Frawley and Lantolf (1985) refer to this process as *re-accessing* earlier stages of development. If a task is especially difficult, and if the person decides that it is important enough to persist in the task, the person has the option of seeking help from other people. In this way, psychological processes once again become social as the person seeks out other mediation. Alternatively, the person may seek assistance not in some other person, but in particular artifacts made available by the culture. Hence, the person may decide to consult a book, use a calculator or computer, or even a horoscope as a means of obtaining needed mediation.

5 Imitation

Fundamental to internalization is the process of *imitation* (Vygotsky, 1987, p. 210). Contrary to what many developmental psychologists espouse (see Lightbown & Spada, 1993), imitation "is a critically important developmental activity because it is the chief means by which in early childhood human beings are related to as other than, and in advance of, who they are" ... it "is aimed at the future and not at copying the past. It is development because "something new is created out of saying or doing 'the same thing'" (Newman and Holzman, 1993, p. 151). Tomasello (1999) argues that imitation, unlike exposure, stimulus enhancement, mimicking and emulation, is a uniquely human form of cultural transmission. In imitative learning, "the goal or intention of the demonstrator is a central part of what they [children] perceive, and indeed the goal is understood as something separate from the various behavioral means that may be used to accomplish it" (Tomasello, 1999, p. 30). Lightbown and Spada (1993) argue that in child language imitation has its roots in behaviorist theories of (language) learning. They claim that while imitation, which they define as "word for word repetition of all or part of someone else's utterance" (p. 2), is attested among children, most children imitate less than 10% of what they hear around them. Importantly, however, they point out that "children's imitation is selective and based on what they are currently learning" (p. 3). From Lightbown and Spada's perspective then imitation is the equivalent of parroting, or in Tomasello's terms, mimicking. Imitation, regardless if it involves creation or repetition, more appropriately captures the process as a uniquely human activity. At the core of both Vygotsky's and Tomasello's understanding of imitation is its transformative potential, a feature missing from the usual interpretation of repetition. This is a crucial distinction, because, for one thing, repetition does not, in itself imply agency and intentionality, while imitation does. Many phenomena in nature repeat in the clear absence of agency and intentionality; e.g., waves breaking on a beach, the earth orbiting around the sun, the change in seasons (I owe this observation to Steve Thorne). Thus, the distinction between repetition and imitation is basic to understanding the process through which human mental capacity is formed in the transition from external to internal activity.

According to James Mark Baldwin, a North American predecessor of Vygotsky, internalization and imitation are the key processes through which social control carried out by others "gradually becomes reconstructed by the person oneself" (Valsiner 2000: 32). Baldwin distinguishes two types of imitation – *imitative suggestion* and *persistent imitation*. The former entails movement of the organism increasingly closer to a particular model from one trial to the next, and can, under given circumstances result in a "faithful replication of the model" and in fact, "going beyond the model is not possible" (Valsiner 2000: 30). The latter concept is "reconstruction of the model in new ways" (Valsiner 2000: 30).

Persistent imitation anticipates the future and as such involves "feed-forward" (instead of feedback), which enables the organism to pre-adapt to "future encounters with the world" (Valsiner & van der Veer, 2000: 153).

To be sure, "in human life, there are situations in which precise copying of the models is crucial, and others in which the models need to be creatively transcended" (Valsiner, 2000: 30). For example, in sites such as traditional educational institutions where learning is assumed to entail the exact replication of information presented by some authority, other than the learner, imitation that fails to result in something new is valued over imitation that is creative. In such cases, imitation no longer emerges as a creative way to "express oneself" (ibid.).[3]

6   Zone of Proximal Development

The site where social forms of mediation develop is the 'zone of proximal development.' This metaphor, originally proposed by Vygotsky as a way of capturing the process through which institutionalized schooling impacts on intelligence, as measured by IQ tests, has become perhaps the most well-known and widely-adopted construct of the theory. According to Vygotsky, all higher mental abilities appear twice in the life of the individual: first on the intermental plane in which the process is distributed between the individual, some other person(s) and/or cultural artifacts, and later on the intramental plane in which the capacity is carried out by the individual acting via psychological mediation. It must be emphasized again that the ZPD is not a physical place situated in time and space; rather it is a metaphor for observing and understanding how mediational means are appropriated and internalized.

Vygotsky's definition states that ZPD is the difference between what a person can achieve when acting alone and what the same person can accomplish when acting with support from someone else and/or cultural artifacts. In light of our earlier discussion of internalization and appropriation, the reader should be able to appreciate the controversies that have arisen in conjunction with how the ZPD is to be construed. Some researchers have assumed that the ZPD necessarily involves interaction between an expert and a novice in which the expert eventually transmits an ability to the novice through social interaction. This view of the ZPD, in my opinion, has received substantial support from the work of Wertsch and his colleagues on parent and child joint puzzle-solving interactions. This is not to say that on theoretical grounds that Wertsch himself sanctions such a perspective; however, because of the nature of his empirical research, it is not too difficult to understand how the expert/novice interpretation became the

---

[3] Shor (1996, p. 11) discusses the imposition of the traditional syllabus in schools and universities as the carrying out of an "epistemic illusion" in which "what has been socially and historically constructed by a specific culture becomes presented to students as undebatable and unchangeable, always there, timeless" as if it were a natural rather than a cultural creation. As such, it is to be repeated, not transformed.

accepted interpretation. In fact, L2 research that I have participated in underpins this belief as well (see Aljaafreh & Lantolf 1994). Be that as it may, several scholars are now calling for a broader understanding of the scope of the ZPD to include more than just expert/novice interaction (see Wells 1999, Kuutti 1996; Engestrom & Middleton 1996, Swain & Lapkin 1998).

If we do not lose sight of the key ingredient -- mediation -- I believe that a more robust and useful way of thinking about the ZPD can be sustained. It seems clear that people working jointly are able to co-construct contexts in which expertise emerges as a feature of the group. This is important, since without such a possibility it is difficult to imagine how expertise of any kind could ever arise; unless of course we were to assume an a priori biological endowment that specified the precise properties of the ability in question. But are we willing to accept that biology alone is responsible for the rise of literacy, numeracy, the invention of computers, legal systems, etc. ? The ZPD then is more appropriately conceived of as the collaborative construction of opportunities (in his chapter van Lier (2000) discusses these as *affordances*; Swain and Lapkin (1998) call them "occasions for learning") for individuals to develop their mental abilities.

7 Unit of Analysis

Sociocultural theory clearly rejects the notion that thinking and speaking are one and the same thing. It also rejects the communicative view of language, which dominates modern linguistic thought, at least in North America (see Carruthers & Boucher 1998). The communicative stance holds that thinking and speaking are completely independent phenomena, with speaking serving only as a means of transmitting already formed thoughts. Sociocultural theory, as we have seen, argues that while separate, thinking and speaking are tightly interrelated in a dialectic unity in which publicly derived speech completes privately initiated thought. Thus, thought cannot be explained without taking account of how it is made manifest to others through linguistic means and linguistic activities, which in turn, cannot be understood fully without "seeing them as manifestations of thought" (Bakhurst 1991, p. 60). For Vygotsky, to break the dialectic unity between speech and thought foregoes any possibility of understanding human conscious process, much in the same way, as Vygotsky frequently noted, that breaking the bond between hydrogen and oxygen foregoes any possibility of explaining the properties of water that endow it with the capacity to put out fire.

Vygotsky proposed the linguistic sign, specifically the *word* as the unit of analysis for observing the formation of functioning of higher forms of thinking, because, in the word, meaning, the central component of thought, and linguistic form are united. In making his argument, Vygotsky distinguishes between the stable, or conventional, meaning of a word and its *sense,* or personal, and contextualized, meaning that emerges from particular ways people deploy words in mediating their mental activity. It is in a word's sense that the microcosm of consciousness is to be uncovered. Not all scholars working within sociocultural theory have agreed with Vygotsky's designation of the word as the appropriate unit of analysis for the study of mediated mind. Wertsch (1985: 197), for instance, suggests that it is difficult to perceive mediated processes such as memory or attention in the sense of a word. Zinchenko (1985) argues that the appropriate unit is *tool-mediated goal-directed action*. This unit, according to Wertsch (1985: 207-208), preserves the dynamic nature of intermental and intramental organization and functioning, while at the same time it encompasses those precise functional systems that for Vygotsky defined human mental ability -- memory, problem solving, attention, intention, planning, orientation, evaluation. More recently, Prawat (1999) has proposed that sign is indeed an appropriate unit and that Vygotksy toward the end of his short life, modified his interpretation of sign from the stable Saussurean unit to something more akin to Bakhtin/Vološinov's meaning of sign as a flexible and dynamic unit whose meaning emerges from the concrete dialogic activity which it mediates (see Vološinov 1973).

8   Activity Theory

Activity theory is an outgrowth of, and for some a necessary correction, to Vygotsky's claim that higher forms of human thinking arise from symbolically mediated concrete practical behavior in the material world. The human mind, according to A. R. Luria (1973, 1979), is not properly speaking the activity of the biologically given brain, but is a *functional system* formed when the brain's electro-chemical processes come under the control of humans through as we master our culturally created symbolic artifacts. Vygotsky argued that if psychology was to explain these functional systems it had to study their formation (i.e., their history) and activity and not their structure. Vygotsky's ideas were eventually crystallized by A. N. Leontiev in his theory of activity.

Activity in Leontiev's (1978) theory is not merely doing something, it is doing something that is motivated either by a biological need, such as hunger, or a culturally constructed need, such as the need to be literate in certain cultures. Needs become motives once they become directed at a specific object. Thus, hunger does not become a motive until people decide to seek food; similarly, literacy does not become a motive for activity until people decide to learn to read and write. Motives are only realized in specific *actions* that are goal directed (hence, intentional) and carried out under particular spatial and temporal *conditions* (or what are also referred to as *operations*) and through appropriate *mediational means*. Thus, an activity comprises three levels: the level of motivation, the level of action, and the level of conditions. Activities then can only be directly observed, by others, at the level of conditions. However, the motives and goals of particular activities cannot be determined solely from the level of concrete doing, since the same observable activity can be linked to different goals and motives and different concrete activities can be linked to the same motives and goals. The illustrations given below should make these important points clear. Recently D. A. Leontiev (in press) has made a convincing argument that humans, unlike any other living species, act because something matters to them; that is, because something has meaning in their lives.

Activities are differentiated from each other by their objects and motives and not necessarily by their concrete realization as actions. Thus, the same activity can be realized through different actions and with different forms of mediation. For example, some cultures engage in collaborative hunting in which various teams take on specific responsibilities in order to bring the hunt to a successful conclusion. Thus, for instance, some teams beat drums or other instruments to scare the prey in the direction of other teams, who are armed with weapons and whose goal is to slay the animal; yet others are responsible for slaughtering the dead game, etc. Other cultures do not rely on such a division of labor when hunt; thus, all aspects of the hunt are carried out by the same individuals, say through stealthily stalking and killing the prey with a bow and arrow, spear, or rifle. In yet other cultures, the need to consume food is realized in the action of purchasing groceries at a supermarket. At the level of motive, these actions are all part of the same activity, even though they appear different in their overt manifestation. On the other hand, what appear to be the same actions can be linked to a different motive and thus constitute different activities. In the case of the drum beaters in societies that hunt collectively, it might turn out that they discover that their rhythmic is fun and so they continue to engage in this action even when the community has no need for food. Thus, what was originally part of the activity of hunting now becomes an activity in its own right, because it is linked to a different motive -- the motive of fun. Beating drums now takes on new meaning in the drummers lives. One might suspect that sport hunting arose under similar circumstances.

Wertsch, Minick and Arns (1984) provide another example of how activity theory can inform our understanding of human mental and social behavior. In their study, the researchers compared the interactions between rural Brazilian mothers and their children and urban school teachers and their students in a puzzle-copying task. The object of the task was for the adult-child dyads to copy a barnyard scene depicted in a model. The researchers hypothesized that given the contrasts between rural and urban cultures in Brazil there would be differences in the way the dyads carried out the copying activity. Briefly, the researchers found that indeed clear differences emerged between the rural and urban dyads with regard to how the children were mediated by their respective caregivers. In the case of the urban dyads, the adults preferred to offer the children strategic clues by first orienting them to the model and telling the child to construct a similar scene. Along the way, the teachers suggested that the children look at the model before selecting the appropriate animal, fence, or what have you, to place in their own scene. In no case did the teacher pick up any pieces for the child, nor did they offer direct commands such as "Pick up the duck and put it in this spot." Instead they created a linguistic scaffold which allowed the child to figure out for him- or herself what to do at each point along the way. Thus, they would produce utterances such as "Now look at the model" "Are you sure this is the correct place ?" "What comes next ?" According to the researchers, there are three important features of this activity that need to be highlighted: the children made mistakes along the way, because they were offered strategic rather than directive help; the children carried out all of the actions themselves; by directing the children's attention to the model, the teachers were not just helping the children to copy the specific scene but they were instructing them in how to work with models.

The rural dyads behaved in a markedly different way. The mothers maintained responsibility for most of the moves throughout the task. They only rarely directed the children's attention to the model, opting instead to look at the model themselves. They used much more directive rather than strategic language. Thus, they tended to say things like "Now pick up the duck and put it here." In a sense, the rural mothers used their children as tools to construct an accurate copy of the model, without imparting to their children an understanding of what the task was about. Under such direct adult regulation, however, the rural children made significantly fewer errors in copying the model than their urban counterparts. Nevertheless, because most of the task remained under adult control, the children failed to learn much about how to orient themselves toward and copy models.

Comparing the relative performance of the rural and urban dyads from the perspective of activity theory, we note that the teachers made every effort to ensure that the goal of the activity (copying a model) became shared by their students. This did not happen in the rural dyads, where the mothers preferred not to share the goal. With regard to the actual conditions under which the children selected and placed pieces in their scene, the teachers consistently tried to shift responsibility for the decisions underlying this behavior to their students, while the mothers by and large determined which pieces to select and where to place them, directing their children's behavior through linguistic means.

In attempting to explain these differences, the researchers suggest that the rural and urban dyads operated from different underlying motives, which gave rise to very different objects of activity. They reasoned that in the particular rural communities under study economic considerations are the driving motive. That is, these communities rely on the production and sale of artifacts such as pottery, clothing, and the like. In the production process, errors in performance often result in the loss of money either because materials have to be discarded when an error is made, or time is lost because a process must be undone and begun anew from the point where the error was made. Hence, the leading activity for the rural dyads, was error free performance and the way to ensure this was for the mothers to control as much of the activity as possible and share as little as possible with their children. The goal was not simply to copy the model but to produce an *error free* copy of the model. In the urban dyads, the motive underlying the activity was educational -- i.e., that children need to learn to think independently. To realize this, the teachers had to share responsibility for decision making with their students. This of course meant that in some cases, children would make inappropriate decisions, thus leading to erroneous performance. But in this case, errors were not seen as costly but as necessary conditions for the taking on of responsibility for one's actions. The point is that while the rural and urban dyads engaged in the same task -- copy the model -- they were not engaged in the same activities, because even though pieces were selected and placed, the motives and goals underlying this behavior differed.

Activities, whether in the workplace, classrooms, or other settings, do not always unfold smoothly. What begins as one activity can reshape itself into another activity in the course of its unfolding. Cobb (1998), for example, in his studies of children learning arithmetic reports a case in which the children began a project on measuring by playing shoe store, which required that they learn how to measure feet with the appropriate template. After a time, the children shifted their attention to measuring other kinds of objects and quickly lost interest in the shoe store activity. However, in order to measure objects such as chairs, tables, blackboards, and the like, they were not able to use the foot templates and had to discover a new set of measuring tools. Hence, a shift in activity gave rise to the need to discover different mediational tools for carrying out what now had become the activity of measuring objects in the world.

Thorne (1999) considers the impact of internet mediation on foreign language learner communicative activity. Using log file records and participant reports, Thorne provides evidence that learner communicative interaction is reconfigured when it is synchronously mediated through the internet. Students report feeling "less culpable" for their on-line utterances; moreover, they express feelings of a lack of supervision, even though they are aware that their instructor is on-line. Thus, the internet environment creates among the students a certain sense of freedom which allows them to say things they would probably not say in face-to-face interaction. At one point, in their interactions, some students begin to use what some people take to be obscene language -- a clear violation of the rules of the educational setting, but apparently not a violation of the chat world, at least not according to some students, who had experience with digitized culture. The teacher then steps out of the role of electronic eavesdropper and back into the role of teacher and confronts the students producing the illegal language face-to-face. This move clearly changes the nature of the activity because for one thing the rules mediating chat discussions are different from the rules mediating discussion in the educational setting. Thorne argues that the shift in the mediational means from verbal face-to-face interaction that might occur in the normal language classroom to electronically mediated interaction, in which the students were no longer facing each other physically, changed the activity of communicating and thus opened up a set of options not available in the other venue. To be sure, it occasionally gave rise to negative speech behavior, but by and large, this different form of mediation enhanced creative language use in which fun and wit were valued and which fostered dynamic engagement with others instead of comprehensible input and information exchange (see van Lier 2000).

All of this means that in any given classroom setting (or any setting for that matter), not only can activities change from one moment to the next, at any given time different activities might be underway at any given time, despite the fact that all of the participants display the same or similar overt behaviors in a task. A student might not care if he or she learned the language, as long as she passed tests and received an acceptable grade for the course, which, in turn, could enhance her chances of obtaining a good job or gaining admission to a choice graduate school. While other students engaging in the same task, might well be oriented to the goal of learning the language because, for example, they find it intrinsically interesting. Gillette (1994) reports that some of the students in her university French class had personal histories in which anything foreign, in this case, non-American, was devalued and therefore not worthy of knowing. Thus, the so-called learning strategies they deployed were not directed at learning the language, but at coping with the "imposition" of having to study a foreign language. Others of Gillette's students reported histories in which the family was intently interested in different cultures and their languages. These students showed strong evidence of strategies specifically directed at learning the language. Even if students in the same class engage in the same task they may not be engaged in the same activity. Students with different motives often have different goals as the object of their actions, despite the intentions of the teacher. A person who devalues foreignness may carry through on a pedagogical task with the sole aim of complying with the immediate demand of the teacher. Again, as Gillette's (1994) work shows, under such circumstances language learning is not likely to occur. Students then play a major role in shaping the goal and ultimate outcomes of tasks set for them by their teachers. Thus, from the perspective of activity theory, while task-based instruction could yield positive learning outcomes, there can be no guarantees, because what ultimately matters is how individual learners decided to engage with the task as an activity.

9   Conclusion

To briefly conclude this overview of sociocultural theory, it is essential to stress that despite the label "sociocultural" the theory is not a theory either of the social or of the cultural aspects of human existence, in the usual understanding of these terms. It is, rather, as I hope to have shown in the preceding discussion, a theory of mind – but a theory of mind that recognizes the central role that social relationships and culturally constructed artifacts play in organizing uniquely human forms of thinking. The theory is grounded in historical, dialectic materialism and as such it maintains that humans not only produce the conditions of their own social life, but as they produce these they are at the same time producing the conditions of their own mental life as well. Hence, for sociocultural theory there is a seamless and dialectic relationship between the concrete practical activity in the material world and the mental activity, which emerges as a consequence of and condition for this activity. With respect to second language research, those that categorize sociocultural theory as a theory of language use clearly misinterpret what the theory is all about. As I stated, it is a cognitive theory, but unlike those theories that assume that thinking is something that only occurs *in* our heads, sociocultural theory argues that we think *with* and with socially and culturally constructed concrete (e.g., computers) and symbolic (e.g., language) artifacts.

10 References

Aljaafreh, A. & Lantolf, J. P. (1994). Negative feedback as regulation and second language learning in the zone of proximal development. *The Modern Language Journal*, 78, 465-483.

Ball, A. . (2000). Teachers' developing philosophies on literacy and their use in urban schools: A Vygotskian perspective on internal activity and teacher change. In C. D. Lee & P. Smagorinsky (Eds.), *Vygotskian perspectives on literacy research. Constructing meaning through collaborative inquiry,* (pp. 226-255).

Bakhurst, D. (1991). *Consciousness and revolution in Soviet philosophy. From the Bolsheviks toEvald Ilyenkov.* Cambridge: Cambridge University Press.

Carruthers, P. & Boucher, J. (1998). Introduction: Opening up options. In P. Carruthers & J. Boucher (Eds.), *Language and thought. Interdisciplinary themes*, (pp. 1-18). Cambridge: Cambridge University Press.

Cobb, P. (1998). Learning from distributed theories of intelligence. Mind, Culture and Activity: An International Journal 5: 187-204

Cole, M. (1996). *Cultural psychology. A once and future discipline.* Cambridge, MA: BelknapPress.

Diaz, R. M. & Berk, L. E. (Eds.). (1992). *Private speech. From social interaction to self-regulation.* Hillsdale, NJ: Lawrence Erlbaum.

Dance, F. E. X. (1994). Hearing voices. In D. Vocate (Ed.)., *Intrapersonal communication.Different voices, different minds*, (pp. 195-212). Hillsdale, NJ: Erlbaum.

Elhammoumi, M. (1997). *Socio-historical psychology. Lev Semenovich Vygotsky (1896-1934). Bibliographical notes.* Lanham, MD: University Press of America.

Engestrom, Y. & Middleton, D. (Eds.). (1996). *Cognition and communication at work.* Cambridge: Cambridge University Press.
Flavell, J. (1966). La langage privé. *Bulletin de psychologie*, 19, 698-710.
Frawley, W. (1997). *Vygotsky and cognitive science. Language and the unification of the socialand computational mind.* Cambridge, MA: Harvard University Press.
Frawley, W. & Lantolf, J. P. (1985). Second language discourse: A Vygotskyan perspective. *Applied Linguistics*, 6, 19-44.
Gal'perin, P. Ya. (1967). On the notion of internalization. *Soviet Psychology*, 5, 28-33.
Gillette, B. (1994). The role of learner goals in L2 success. In J. P. Lantolf & G. Appel (Eds.), *Vygotskian approaches to second language research*, (pp. 195-214). Norwood, NJ: Ablex Press.
Homskaya, E. D. (2001). *Alexander Romanovich Luria. A scientific biography.* New York: Kluwer.
Ilyenkov. E. (1977). *Dialectic logic.* Moscow: Progress Press.
Jones, P. (1999). The ideal in cultural-historical activity theory: Issues and perspectives. In S. Chaiklin (Ed.), *Theory and practicie of cultural-historical psychology*, (pp. 281-315). Aarhus: Aarhus University Press.
Jones, P. unpublished manuscript. "The word becoming a deed": The dialectic of "free action" in Vygotsky's *tool and sign* in the development of the child.
Kozulin, A. (1990). *Vygotsky's psychology. A biography of ideas.* Cambridge, MA: Harvard *Psychological tools. A sociocultural approach to education.* Cambridge, MA: Harvard University Press.
Kuutti, K. (1996). Activity theory as a potential framework for human-computer interactionresearch. In B. Nardi, (Ed.), *Context and consciousness: Activity theory and human-computer interaction,* (pp. 17-44). Cambridge, MA: MIT Press.
Lantolf, J. P. & Appel, G. (Eds.). (1994). Theoretical framework: An introduction to Vygotskian approaches to second language research. In J. P. Lantolf & G. Appel, (Eds.), *Vygotskian approaches to second language research,* (pp. 1-32). Norwood, NJ: Ablex Press.
Leontiev, A. N. (1978). *Activity, consciousness and personality.* Englewood Cliffs, NJ: Prentice Hall.
Leontiev, D. A. in press. *The phenomenon of meaning: How psychology can make sense of it.*
Lightbown, P. & Spada, N. (1993). *How languages are learned.* Oxford: Oxford University Press.
Lucy, J. A. (1992). *Language diversity and thought. A reformulation of the linguistic relativity hypothesis.* Cambridge: Cambridge University Press.
Luria, A. R. (1973). *The working brain.* New York: Basic Books.

Luria, A. R. (1976). *Cognitive development. Its cultural and social foundations.* Cambridge, MA: Harvard University Press.

Luria, A. R. (1979). *The making of mind. A personal account of Soviet psychology.* Cambridge, MA: Harvard University Press.

Luria, A. R. (1982). *Language and cognition.* New York: John Wiley & Sons.

Newman, F. & Holzman, L. (1993). *Lev Vygotsky. A revolutionary scientist.* London: Routledge.

Prawat, R. S. (1999). Social constructivism and the process-content distinction as viewed by Vygotsky and the pragmatists. *Mind, Cultural and Activity: An International Journal,* 6, 255-273.

Prawat, R. S. (2000). Dewey meets the "Mozart of psychology" in Moscow: The untold story. *American Education Research Journal,* 37, 663-696.

Ratner, C. (1991). *Vygotsky's sociohistorical psychology and its contemporary applications.* New York: Plenum

Scribner, S. & Cole, M. (1981). *The psychology of literacy.* Cambridge, MA: Harvard University Press.

Shore, B. (1996). Culture in Mind. Cognition, Culture and the Problem of Meaning. New York: Oxford University Press.

Stetsenko, A. P. (1999). Social interaction, cultural tools and the zone of proximal development. In search of a synthesis. In S. Chaiklin, M. Hedegaard & U. J. Jensen (Eds.), *Activity theory and social practice* (pp. 235-254). Aarhus: Aarhus University Press.

Swain, M. & Lapkin, S. (1998). Interaction and second language learning: Two adolescent French immersion students working together. *The Modern Language Journal,* 83, 320-338.

Thorne, S. L. (1999). *An activity theoretic analysis of foreign language electronic discourse.* Unpublished Ph.D. dissertation. University of California, Berkeley, CA.

Tomasello, M. (1999). *The cultural origins of human cognition.* Cambridge, MA: Harvard University Press.

Valsiner, J. (2000). *Culture and human development.* London: Sage.

Valsiner, J. & van der Veer, R. (2000). *The social mind. Construction of the idea.* Cambridge: Cambridge University Press.

van der Veer, R. & Valsiner, J. 1991. *Understanding Vygotsky. A quest for synthesis.* Oxford: Blackwell.

van Lier, L. (2000). From input to affordances: Social-interactive learning from an ecological perspective. In J. P. Lantolf (Ed.), *Sociocultural theory and second language learning,* (pp. 245-259). Oxford: Oxford University Press.

Vocate, D. R. (1994). Self-talk and inner speech: Understanding the uniquely human aspects of intrapersonal communication. In D. R. Vocate (Ed.), *Intrapersonal communication. Different voices, different minds,* (pp. 3-32). Hillsdale, NJ: Lawrence Erlbaum.

Vološinov, V. N. (1973). *Marxism and the philosophy of language.* Cambridge, MA: Harvard University Press.

Vygotsky, L. S. (1978). *Mind in society. The development of higher psychological processes.* Cambridge, MA: Harvard University Press.

Vygotsky, L. S. (1987). The collected works of L. S. Vygotsky. Volume 1. Problems of general psychology. Including the volume *Thinking and Speech*, edited by R. W. Rieber & A. S. Carton. New York: Plenum Press.

Vygotsky, L. S. (1997a). The historical meaning of the crisis in psychology: A methodological investigation. *The collected works of L. S. Vygotsky, volume 3. Problems of the theory and history of psychology*, ed. by R. W. Rieber and J. Wollock, pp. 233-343. Plenum Press.

Vygotsky, L. S. (1997b). Mastering attention. In *The collected works of L. S. Vygotsky, volume 4. The history of the development of higher mental functions* (ed. by R. W. Rieber), pp. 153-177. New York: Plenum Press.

Wells, G. (1999). *Dialogic inquiry. Toward a sociocultural practice and theory of education* Cambridge: Cambridge University Press.

Wertsch, J. V. (1985). *Vygotsky and the social formation of mind.* Cambridge, MA: HarvardUniversity Press.

Wertsch, J. V. (1998). *Mind as action.* Oxford: Oxford University Press.

Wertsch, J. V., Minick, N. & Arns, F. J. (1984). The creation of context in joint problem solving.In B. Rogoff & J. Lave (Eds.), *Everyday cognition: Its development in social context*, (pp. 151-171). Cambridge, MA: Harvard University Press.

Yaroshevsky, M. (1989). *Lev Vygotsky.* Moscow: Progress Press.

Zinchenko, V. P. (1985). Vygotsky's ideas about units for the analysis of mind. In J. V. Wertsch (Ed.), *Culture, communication and cognition. Vygotskian perspectives*, (pp. 94-118). Cambridge: Cambridge University Press.

What Does SCT Research Reveal about Second Language Learning?
Howard Grabois, Purdue University, USA

1 Introduction

While the title of this chapter asks what research that is informed by sociocultural theory tell us about second language learning, perhaps an equally significant (and certainly complimentary question) would be: how do these studies help inform our knowledge of second language research methodology? From an epistemological point of view, the model of cognition which frames SCT (or any other research paradigm) will not only inform what questions are asked, but will also inform issues concerning what constitutes data, and how results are to be interpreted. Within the Vygotskyan tradition there are two areas that are of particular interest to this discussion: the notion of tools-and-result, and the historical discussion of Vygotsky's dual role of psychologist and methodologist.

The notion of tool use is central to an understanding of the sociocultural enterprise. Borrowing from Marx, who saw tool use as crucial for an understanding of social activity, Vygotsky extended the notion to encompass psychological activity as well (1978). For Vygotsky, language in particular is considered to be the most important psychological tool. On the one hand, it is the primary means for the transmission of culture, and on the other hand it is the most significant tool for the mediation of higher level cognitive processes (thinking, memory, directed attention, etc.). Newman and Holzman (1993) in their analysis of Vygotsky's notion of tool use make an interesting distinction between tools-for-result and tools-and-result. The most important difference between the two is that while tools-for-result can be ontologically understood independently of the artifacts they are used to construct or manipulate, in the case of tools-and-result there is an inherent inseparability of the two. Following the analogy of physical tools, we might think of typical hardware bought tools (hammers or screw drivers), as compared to more sophisticated machine tools (tools which are used for the production of other tools). In the case of the latter only, the tool and the results that are derived from its use are for the most part inseparable in relation to goal directed activity. For Newman and Holzman only tools-and-result constitute truly revolutionary activity; revolutionary not in the purely political sense, but in the broader sense of being transformational, in this case in relation to psychological processes.

The notion of tools-and-result proves useful for analysis of SCT informed studies of L2 learning. In the best of these studies Vygotskyan or activity theoretical concepts are not simply extracted from the theory, but rather the research question is more holistically related to a sociocultural conception of mind. In fact, Vygotsky himself went to great lengths to detail his objections to analytic reductionism (1978), using the example of water. A functional understanding of water (as something for example that can extinguish fire) cannot be had by breaking it down to hydrogen and oxygen, the former of which is combustible, and the latter of which facilitates combustion. While some researchers may extract SCT concepts from the broader theory (the zone of proximal development is one salient example of this, see Dunn and Lantolf, 1998) by doing so they effectively transform those concepts. The interconnectedness between a broad understanding of the theory and the development of research programs both informed by and embedded in that framework is one example of the notion of tools-and-result as related to L2 learning studies.

The notion of tools-and-result is also useful within the context of an historical discussion of Vygotsky's dual roles of psychologist (his determination to develop a model of mind that would resolve some of the inherent dualities in western models: objectivity/subjectivity for example), and methodologist (in relation to the practices that are used for theory building and research). This distinction also proves useful for an analysis of L2 research. In relation to psychology we can see how concepts like the zone of proximal development, private speech, or internalization become crucial for constructing the research questions that are posed in relation to L2 learning. Perhaps of equal significance, however, are the methodological practices that emerge in SCT studies, and are inherent to the theory itself. Some of these methodological issues have to do with the role of the research participants (allowing them agency as opposed to treating "subjects" as mere objects of study (Roebuck, 2000), or looking at learning in context as opposed to constructing decontextualized laboratory experiments (Coughlan and Duff, 1994). In addition, the centrality of the notion of the zone of proximal development encourages studies that observe the actual process of learning in order to be able to foresee future development.

2 The Basic Unit of Analysis

For Vygotsky the methodologist, the question of what is the basic unit of analysis for consciousness was central. The criteria he set for such a unit included the idea that it should be a part of the whole that represents a microcosm of that whole (Vygotsky 1978). For example, Vygotsky saw word meaning as an element of consciousness that encompasses all of its essential features, and thus took it to be a basic unit of analysis. While word meaning has subsequently been called into question in favor of cultural artifacts within an activity theoretical framework (Leont'ev 1978, Wertsch 1998, Cole 1996, Thorne this volume) the methodological premise has not. Applying this methodological construct to SCT-L2 research, the individual study may provide the best means of attaining a broader understanding of the field. The seminal research of Frawley and Lantolf (1985) provides an appropriate starting point not only temporally, but also in relation to theory and method for SCT-L2 research.

In this study participants were shown a sequence of drawings that formed a narrative. They were then asked to tell the story. The different groups that participated in the study included adult native speakers of English, child L1 speakers, and adult L2 learners with different levels of proficiency. An analysis of what participants produced led the researchers to the conclusions that less proficient speakers (both non-natives and children), had a lower capacity for self-regulation in relation to the task[1]. An analysis of the linguistic forms they used were then interpreted as examples of object-regulation that allowed the participants to accomplish the task. The researchers looked at issues such as pronominalisation, use of tense and aspect, and the metalinguistic organization of discourse, and described their roles in relation to cognitive issues, with particular emphasis on issues regarding the locus of regulation.

While some of the specific conclusions of this study were subsequently called into question (McCafferty 1994a) the theoretical and methodological orientation of this study provide a background that frames much of the subsequent SCT-L2 research. On the theoretical side, it presents a series of concepts that allow for analysis of L2 learning from an SCT perspective. Some of these concepts include the zone of proximal development, private speech, self-/other-/object- regulation, and internalization. Perhaps of greatest significance is the fact that these concepts are presented in such a way as to provide a coherent framework for the elaboration of a research program from a Vygotskian perspective.

On the methodological side this study establishes many of the principles and practices that will guide much subsequent SCT-L2 research. In particular they emphasize micro-analysis and functional analysis. Drawing on Vygotsky's ideas of different genetic levels of analysis (phylogenesis, sociocultural genesis, ontogenesis, microgenesis) Frawley and Lantolf (1985) emphasize the importance of microgenetic analysis for the interpretation of data. In describing micro-analysis they say that "analysis must be done of the *actual instances* of discourse *by the individual.* We make no attempt to quantify the results, since Western statistical rhetoric is based on the concept of the mean, which by definition excludes the individual." (Frawley and Lantolf 1985: 24) As regards functional analysis, they state that their concern is with "linguistic forms of discourse in terms of the roles they play in the *activity of relating a discourse*, not in terms of the forms *as pure forms.*" (Frawley and Lantolf 1985: 24) Together these ideas point towards a methodological orientation that varies greatly from research practices based on laboratory experimentation by emphasizing both context and the agency of the individual.

---

[1] Frawley (1987) defines **object-regulation** as the regulation of objects in the environment (for example by naming), **other-regulation** as the regulation of others (for example speech acts), and **self-regulation** as the highest of the three, allowing the individual to control himself and his own mind. As object- and other- control can be seen as prior to self-regulatory private speech they represent forms of regulation with lower level of intentional control.

3   The Methodologist

Coughlan and Duff (1994) directly confront some significant methodological issues by making the distinction between "task" and "activity" in second language research. They point to the fact that in many experimental designs tasks are considered to be "controllable and measurable", giving them the status of constants. This is a significant concern within a research tradition that attempts to control and isolate the number of intervening variables in any given experiment. Coughlan and Duff, however, point to the fact that there is an important distinction between task and activity. They describe the former as a "behavioral blueprint" motivated by research objectives, and the latter as the behavior that is actually produced. While tasks may have their own goal structure (either explicit or implicit), the objectives for an activity emerge from a negotiation between participants. Their central point is that while researchers may be able to control the task, they can't control what participants actually do. Hence the same task can result in different activities for different participants, or for the same participant at different times. This analysis is highly consistent with Leonte'v's (1978) analysis of activity as comprised of actions, which in turn are comprised of operations. It is only at the level of activity that the issue of motivation is crucial, while actions are concerned with more specific and immediate goals. Thus, the same action can be performed in relation to very different activities. In the same way an experimental task may be carried out in relation to very different activities once we take into account the agency of the individual. Coughlan and Duff (1994) demonstrate this through their analysis of the discourse of participants who are given the same task (description of a picture) yet due to differences in how they interact with the researcher can be seen to engage in different activities. This motivates them to call into question conventional understanding of the terms "subject" and "researcher" pointing out that expertise may be distributed rather than residing uniquely in the researcher.

Many researchers within the SCT tradition display similar methodological concerns. Roebuck (1998, 2000), elaborating on the ideas of Coughlan and Duff, states that "subjects involved in the same *task* are necessarily involved in different *activity*." This is largely due to the positioning or orientation of the participant in relation to the task, such that we need to take into account their "unique histories, goals, and capacities". Beyond this Roebuck makes the important point that while much psychological (and linguistic) research tends to focus on quantifiable results, this shifts the focus of study from the individual human mind to the aggregate. "This equation severs the crucial link between an individual and her actions and thus eliminates the agency, or the subjecthood, of individual subjects" (2000:82). She goes on to say that while quantifiable research may at times be useful, we need to remember that individual learners are not merely part of an homogenous collective. These concerns are illustrated in her own research through descriptions of the different orientations of participants in relation to tasks in which they are asked to recall reading passages (1998). These include the participant's initial orientation to the task, their orientation as readers, and even their orientation toward the self.

While not all SCT researchers display such explicit concern with methodology in their research, it is important to consider that as members of a research community they are to a certain extent involved in a set of shared practices. Research on apprenticeship (Rogoff, 1995, Lave and Wenger 1991) emphasizes learning as related to initiation into a community of practice. Lave and Wenger describe this as a process of moving from the periphery toward the center of such a community. Furthermore, contemporary activity theorists (Cole and Engeström 1993, Cole 1996) place a great deal of emphasis on the role of communities in relation to cognition. Beyond this, as we shall see, many of the methodological issues within SCT research are directly related to broader theoretical issues. It would simply be inconsistent for research within a framework which emphasizes the distributed nature of mind to adopt research techniques developed in relation to a mentalist model of individual competencies. A model of mind which is largely constructed around the mediation of cultural artifacts must necessarily employ different research techniques than a model of acquisition based on an input processing metaphor. The fact that learning and development within an SCT framework are conceptualized in relation to dialogic processes (Wells 1999) will necessarily have important methodological implications. This is not to say that the methodological practices that are prevalent within SCT research are unique to that theory, but simply that they are closely related to and in some instances derive from broader theoretical concerns.

4 The Psychologist
SCT and other models of L2 learning

Many of the differences between the theoretical assumptions within the SCT framework and other approaches to second language research are so fundamental that even agreement on the naming of the field can prove difficult. It is important to note that while second language acquisition (SLA) has come to be the predominant conventionalized term for the field, the use of the word "acquisition" points to both a mentalist model of cognition and the Krashenian heritage of second language theories.

For Vygotsky, issues concerning learning and development are central to his model of mind, and are of obvious importance to second language research. First, an SCT model of mind is one that is primarily concerned with conscious processes, and not unconsciousness. Vygotsky's concern with higher level mental functions, and the importance given to the mediation of language and cultural artifacts in both Vygotsky and activity theory are clear indications that questions of consciousness are of primary concern (see Searle, 1994 for a discussion of the centrality of consciousness for an understanding of mind). Second, a primary premise of Vygotsky's is that development follows learning as part of a dynamic process. Hence, development is not biologically predetermined (though perhaps constrained), and is more appropriately understood in terms of the social construction of mind. Finally, cognition and its development are conceptualized as distributed. This is central to Vygotsky's discussion of word meaning as a basic unit of analysis, and comes to the forefront in activity theory (see Salomon 1993 for a series of essays on distributed cognition).

Prioritizing the notion of acquisition, on the other hand, is an indication of a very different theoretical orientation. This tradition emphasizes the modularity of cognition and its biological underpinnings (Chomsky 1980). Furthermore, with its emphasis on competence it isolates cognition within the individual, and constructs it in terms of a possession metaphor: something you have as opposed to something you do. Input processing models in particular, (Krashen 1982, van Patten 2000) are predicated on a mind-as-computer metaphor (with emphasis on intermediate levels of symbolic representation) whereby issues concerning how to best provide comprehensible input often dominate, and the individual learners cognitive processes are relegated to a black box called the language acquisition device.

There are several studies that directly or indirectly address issues concerning input processing assumptions about second language learning (see Dunn and Lantolf (1998) for a theoretical discussion of the conceptual incommensurability of Krashen's i+1 and Vygotsky's zone of proximal development). Platt and Brooks (1994) challenge the usefulness of the notion "acquisition rich environment", which is predicated on an input processing model of mind and the centrality of comprehensible input. They do so by putting into question four specific assumptions: 1) that richness of environment can be determined *a priori* 2) that it doesn't take into account contemporary learning environments where learners themselves are the primary interactants 3) that it doesn't' take into account all of the functions of learner-learner interaction 4) that it fails to specify what it is that learners actually acquire. They illustrate each of these four points based on their analysis of student production in a variety of tasks: role plays in a technical language course for learners of English, and different information gap tasks.

In a study on the usefulness of recasts in the L2 classroom Ohta (2000b) challenges specific conclusions reached in previous research based on input processing assumptions. One of the primary problems with recasts suggested in these studies was that they are less effective than other means of corrective feedback as they are less likely to generate uptake. Commenting on the fact that L1 researchers in longitudinal studies found evidence for the effectiveness of recasts, Ohta collected private speech data from all students in a Japanese language class. In doing so she found that auditors not directly addressed by the teacher paid a great deal of attention to corrective feedback. Furthermore, they would engage in what Ohta terms "vicarious response", comparing their own production to that of the teacher and other students. She concludes that previous concerns about recasts were based on a teacher centered classroom model and ignored the dynamics of learner centered instruction, as well as the agency and experience of each individual learner.

In research that considers the roles of input and output for language learning, Swain (2000) challenges many of the assumptions about interaction in input processing models. Within some of these models interaction may be afforded a significant role, either as a means of generating comprehensible input, or an opportunity for learners to focus on form in relation to meaning. In relation to this discussion Swain makes two important points. First, she argues that the production of output facilitates learning in significant ways, as it requires greater mental effort and attention to the entire linguistic system than does the more strategic processing required for comprehension. Second, and perhaps most significantly, she argues that the very term "output" is predicated on a model of communication that ignores the role of language as a tool for the mediation of cognitive processes, and reduces language use to the sending and receiving of messages. Given these concerns, she questions whether the term "output" is even appropriate. In its place she forwards the concept of collaborative dialogue as being more consistent with a model of learning based on a participation metaphor rather than an acquisition metaphor.

The zone of proximal development

Issues relating to the zone of proximal development are central to Vygotskyan theory, and not surprisingly, play a central role in research on L2 learning. Vygotsky's initial formulation about the ZPD (1978) is that "it is the distance between the actual developmental level as determined by independent problem solving and the level of potential development as determined through problem solving under adult guidance or in collaboration with more capable peers". What the child can do with some form of assistance or support in the present she will be able to do autonomously in the future. While Vygotsky originally conceived of the ZPD in relation to child development, to the extent that it is a description of or metaphor for learning it also has important implications for adult L2 learners.

The related metaphor of scaffolding (Wood, Bruner, and Ross, 1976) is predicated on the idea that a framework of support can be provided for the learner by someone with greater expertise that can then contribute to the learner's development. While the notion of scaffolding is not isomorphic to the ZPD, its primary features[2] do represent concrete suggestions that could help create

---

[2] According to Wood, Bruner and Ross the major features of scaffolding are: 1) **Recruitment,** or drawing drawing the student's attention to the task, 2) **Reduction in degrees of freedom,** or

appropriate conditions for the construction of the learner's ZPD. Donato 1994) conducted a study where he looked at peer interactions among French students to determine if they would "mutually construct a scaffold out of the discursive process of negotiating contexts of shared understanding, or what Rommetveit (1985) calls intersubjectivity." (94:43). Donato found that students working in peer dyads are indeed capable of creating mutually constructed scaffolding in ways that are similar to the kind of scaffolding created in expert/novice dyads, particularly as regards questions of grammaticality. This research has important implications for classroom learning environments, particularly as regards the value of pair work/group work.

A variety of further studies explore the question of whether a zone of proximal development can be appropriately constructed among peers, rather than as part of an expert/novice dyad. This would then be seen as support for the idea that expertise may be distributed in a variety of ways, rather than residing monolithically in one individual: in the case of classroom learning, the teacher. This is similar to some of the research concerns expressed by Coughlan and Duff (1994) and their observation that for many tasks the locus of control is not uniquely situated in the researcher. Villamil and de Guerrero (1998), for example, observe the effect of peer revision on writing. They find that suggestions made during peer revision not only are often incorporated into final drafts, but also that "writers made further revisions on the basis of previous peer collaboration, suggesting a pattern of behavior conducive to self-regulation" (1998:508). Ohta (2000a) in her analysis of what she terms "assisted performance" finds further evidence for the usefulness of peer collaboration in classroom interaction. Her analysis of development from interpsychological functions to intrapsychological functions shows how a student is "able to accomplish with ease what she initially could not do without assistance." Her analysis shows awareness of the complexity of negotiation at the interpsychological level, showing the importance of teamwork and mutual sensitivity on the part of participants.

Other classroom-based research looks at the construction of the ZPD in more traditional expert/novice (teacher/student) interactions. McCormack and Donato (2000) explore the usefulness of questions during teacher-fronted activity in an ESL classroom, and ask whether these may provide appropriate scaffolding to facilitate learning. Basing their analysis on the features of scaffolding presented in Wood et al (1976), and using students private speech as their data, they found positive evidence of scaffolding in teacher questions in relation to many of the features of scaffolding, particularly as regards recruitment, reduction in degrees of freedom, and direction maintenance. In a related study, Nassaji and Wells (1998) investigate the triadic dialogue (otherwise commented on as traditional IRE or

---

simplification of the task to limit the cognitive demands, 3) **Direction Maintenance**, as related to learner motivation 4) **Marking critical features**, 5) **Frustration Control**, 6) **Demonstration**.

IRF sequences). Despite a clear preference for a more dialogic style that would encourage a more distributed and socially constructed learning environment, they do find a useful role for the triadic dialogue as a means of facilitating learning.

Private Speech and internalization

Vygotsky formulates the idea, in contrast to Piaget (Vygotsky 1978) that all speech is social in its origins. Once internalized it goes "underground" and becomes inner speech, displaying a variety of semantic peculiarities. These include a preponderance of sense over meaning, and a tendency for word meanings to combine and influence each other. Inner speech also displays syntactic abbreviation. Given these notions of social and inner speech, language has two primary functions: on the one hand it is outwardly directed as a tool for mediating our social interactions. Turned inward, it becomes a psychological tool for the mediation of mental activity. "Private speech tends to maintain its communicative features, even though it serve a different function from social speech. Private speech represents the externalization of what otherwise would remain as covert mental processes... and emerges in the face of difficult tasks" (Appel & Lantolf, 1994). Given the significance of private speech as a cognitive tool (See McCafferty 1994b for an early review of private speech research), and the fact that it represents a significant form of evidence when collected as speak aloud protocols, or when participants struggle with particularly difficult tasks, there have been a variety of studies that investigate its role for L2 learning. Issues regarding private speech are also closely related to issues of self/other/object regulation which are central to the concerns of Frawley and Lantolf (1985).

While recall protocols are an established means of collecting data for studies on reading comprehension (Bernhardt 1991), within an SCT context they are particularly useful as they allow analysis not only of the content of the recall, but of metacognitive comments as well. These comments can be seen as instances of private speech whereby the subject attempts to attain control of the task through vocalization. Given this reasoning, Appel and Lantolf (1994) conclude from analysis of recall data that the construction of meaning does not take place only while reading, but also through the mediation of private speech after the reading process has ended. Roebuck (1998) found similar evidence when comparing written recall protocols in both the L1 and the L2. As in Frawley and Lantolf (1985) these represented a variety of ways in which participants struggle to gain control of the task, and analysis includes issues of tense and aspect, epistemic stance, and means of reference. Of striking interest in this study is the observation that participants used a variety of means of gaining control over the task, including writing in the margins, and that even the position of writing on the page could provide useful information about participants' orientation.

A series of articles from an SCT perspective (McCafferty 1994a en 1994b, 1998, McCafferty & Ahmed 2000) consider gesture to be closely related to both private speech and issues of object-, other-, and self regulation. McCafferty (1998) in a study involving narrative recall and picture narration, found that "the gestures that accompany private speech are... integrated with speakers' efforts at self-expression" (232) and that use of gesture varies considerably based on a variety of factors, including proficiency, cultural origins, and task. McCafferty forwards the premise that thought, language and gesture are intertwined, such that analysis of gesture could provide insights into issues of private speech as learners struggle to attain self regulation. Furthermore, he found evidence that L2 learners may appropriate at least some gestures associated with the target language, even at relatively low levels of proficiency. McCafferty and Ahmed (2000) compare native speakers of English and Japanese to naturalistic and instructed Japanese learners of English. In this study they found some evidence for the appropriation of abstract L2 gestures on the part of naturalistic learners. Both of these studies represent preliminary evidence that inner speech, while initially formed in relation to the L1, may undergo some restructuring once the L2 becomes a significant semiotic system for the regulation of mental activity.

The notion that inner speech may be influenced by the appropriation of L2 sense and meaning is supported by two other studies within an SCT framework. Grabois (1998) in a study based on word association protocols looked at the lexical networks of L2 Spanish speakers of various levels of proficiency, as compared to L1 Spanish and English speakers. He found evidence for changes in sense and meaning of the most expert L2 speakers. While there was little effect for instructed learners, the most advanced naturalistic learners did come to approximate the networks of L1 Spanish speakers. In a study concerning the appropriation of metaphors, Pavlenko (1996) looked at the ability of L1 Russian speakers to internalize the American concept of privacy, based on their recounting short movie sequences. Once more she found that long term residents had quite commonly appropriated the L2 metaphorical concept of privacy, one that is lacking in the Russian language. Together these studies provide evidence that the appropriation of L2 inner speech, while perhaps not necessary in order to break the L2 code, may in fact be part of the learning process of advanced, naturalistic learners.

The language learner and construction of self

Within SCT research there are a variety of studies concerned with issues of identity and how the self is reflexively perceived and even constructed in relation to language. From a theoretical perspective this research draws heavily on Vygotsky's ideas of semiotic mediation, and is also informed to a large extent by concepts first elaborated by Bahktin. Hall (1995) argues that linguistic meaning is not primarily about code, but rather about the positioning of the self in relation to discourses and voices. This positioning is not only locally situated in the moment, but also in relation to sociocultural identity and the historical meanings that are embedded in linguistic resources. Bakhtin's notion of *ventriloquation*, which involves the appropriation of discursive voices and the situating (and even construction) of self in relation to those voices proves to be a particularly useful concept for an understanding of identity in relation to language and participation in discourse communities. As Kramsch (2000: 139) points out, Bahktin's notion of *dialogism* "offered a way of thinking about oneself and the world not as two separate entities in interaction with each other, but as two sides of the same coin, relative to and constitutive of each other." As regards language research Hall (1995) indicates four specific areas where this orientation proves useful: in relation to studies on language variation, in relation to issues of language assessment and communicative development, as regards the study of interaction so as to move beyond formal and even sociocultural concerns, and as a way to move beyond the constraints of established concepts such as interlanguage that may be insufficient for a full understanding of the complexity of language learning.

Gillette (1994) begins to address some issues relating to the agency of the individual learner in her study of the significance of learner goals. Her analysis is based on data relating to language learning histories, student's class notes, and language learning diaries. She argues that "examining the whole person in a rich neutral setting" proves more useful than conventional attitudinal or quantitative studies. Her findings indicate that while successful learners participation in language learning is positively influenced by personal history and life goals, ineffective learners often position themselves in relation to more local goals which are conceptualized uniquely in relation to the institutional setting; i.e. doing the minimum necessary to pass the course.

On a microgenetic level Thorne's (1999) study provides insights into the construction of self in relation to the situatedness of activity and the means of its mediation. Looking at the discourse produced by language learners in chat rooms he finds distinct differences between the rules that regulate interaction in the digital world and in the classroom. The differences in mediational means effectively changes the activity of interaction, and how students orient themselves towards that activity.

Formulating her research in relation to Vygotsky's semiotic theory, as well as the ideas of Pierce and Bahktin, Kramsch (2000) emphasizes that language learning involves intense interaction with a semiotic system, requiring the learner to make choices about the use of symbols as social psychological tools, and the positioning of the self in relation to those tools in such a way that is significant for the construction of identity. In her study ESL students are asked to summarize a story in writing, followed by class interpretation and discussion of the texts. Recognizing that the language learner receives an already constructed semiotic system, she reminds us that through the manipulation of those signs the language learner creates new meanings, and in so doing is also engaged in the discursive construction of self.

In a study that looks at the personal narratives of authors of eastern European origin who have come to produce literary works in a language learned as adults, Pavlenko and Lantolf (2000) are able to make observations about the (re)construction of self in relation to language. They frame their study to a large extent on the notion, proposed by Sfard (?), of emphasizing a metaphor of learning as participation over the more conventional metaphor of acquisition. In doing so they question what happens as an individual moves from participation in one set of discourse communities into another. They propose two phases for understanding this sort of radical transition. The first involves loss of linguistic identity, loss of the inner voice, and first language attrition. The second phase involves a (re)construction of self through the appropriation of others' voices, the emergence of one's new voice, and the reconstruction of one's personal history. They point out that, as in Vygotsky's description of child development there are significant changes in mental organization brought about through the mediation of language and social interaction.

5   Conclusions

When considering the question of what SCT Research reveals about second language learning it is important to keep in mind that SCT is not a theory of second language learning *per se*, but rather a broader theory of cognition and mind. Unlike modular theories of mind (Chomsky1983), which allow cognitive processes to be studied independently of one another, an SCT approach is by its very nature a holistic orientation towards the study of mind. We cannot separate questions of second language learning from broader issues of learning and development, and how the mind is socially constructed in a way that is situated both culturally and historically. For this reason SCT-L2 research tends to be highly reflective about its own research methods, and to position its research questions in relation to broader theoretical issues. On the methodological side it emphasizes the agency of the individual learner, and the collection of data in a way that focuses on the process of learning. On the theoretical side SCT-L2 research provides us with insights into how learning takes place through a focus on cognitive processes as distributed and mediated by cultural artifacts, with language itself as the primary means of intersubjectivity and the regulation of cognition.

6   References

Appel, G. & Lantolf, J.P. (1994). Speaking as Mediation: A Study of L1 and L2 Recall Tasks. *The Modern Language Journal* 78/4: 437-452.

Bernhardt, E. B. (1991). *Reading development in a second language: Theoretical, empirical and classroom perspectives*. Norwood NJ, Ablex Publiching Corporation.
Chomsky, N. (1980). *Rules and representations*. New York, Columbia University Press.
Cole, M. & Engeström, Y. (1993). A cultural-historical approach to distributed cognition". Edited by G. Salomon, *Distributed Cognitions: Psychological and Educational Considerations*. Cambridge UK and New York, Cambridge University Press.
Cole, M. (1996). *Cultural Psychology: A Once and Future Discipline*, Cambridge MA: Harvard University Press
Coughlan, P. & Duff, P. (1994). Same Task, Different Activities: Analysis of SLA Task from an Activity Theory Perspective. Edited by J. P. Lantolf & G. Appel, *Vygotskian approaches to second language research*, Norwood, N.J., Ablex Publishing Corporation.
Dunn, B. & Lantolf, J. P. (1998). Vygotsky's zone of proximal development and Krashen's i + 1: Incommensurable Constructs; Incommensurable Theories. *Language Learning*, 48: 411-442.
Frawley, W. & Lantolf, J.P. (1985). Second Language Discourse: A Vygotskyan Perspective. *Applied Linguistics* 6/1: 19-44.
Frawley, W. (1987). *Text and epistemology*. Norwood NJ.: Ablex Publishing Corporation.
Gillette, B. (1994). "The Role of Learner Goals in L2 Success." Edited by J.P. Lantolf & G. Appel *Vygotskian approaches to second language research*, Norwood, N.J., Ablex Publishing Corporation.
Grabois, H. (1999). The convergence of sociocultural theory and cognitive linguistics: lexical semantics and the L2 acquisition of Love, Fear, and Happiness. Edited by G. Palmer & D. Occhi, *Languages of Sentiment: Cultural constructions of emotional substrates*. Amsterdam and Philadelphia, John Benjamins Publishing.
Hall, J. K. (1995). (Re)creating Our Worlds with Words: A Sociohistorical Perspective of Face-to-Face. *Applied Linguistics* 16/2: 206-32.
Kramsch, C. (2000). Social discursive constructions of self in L2 learning. Edited by J. P. Lantolf, *Sociocultural Theory and Second Language Learning*. Oxford and New York, Oxford University Press.
Krashen, S. D. (1982). *Principles and practice in second language acquisition*. Oxford UK, Paragon Press.
Lave, J. & Wenger, E. (1991). *Situated Learning; Legitimate Peripheral Participation*. Cambridge UK and New York, Cambridge University Press.
Leont'ev, A. N. (1978). *Activity, Consciousness, and Personality*. Translated from Russian by Marie J. Hall. Englewood Cliffs, N.J. Prentice-Hall.

McCafferty, S. G. (1994a). The Use of Private Speech by Adult EST Learners at Different Levels of Proficiency. Edited by J. P. Lantolf and G. Appel, *Vygotskian approaches to second language research*, Norwood, N.J., Ablex Publishing Corporation.

McCafferty, S. G. (1994b). Adult second language learners' use of private speech: a review of studies. *Modern Language Journal* 78/4: 421-436.

McCafferty, S. G. (1998). Nonverbal Expression and L2 Private Speech. *Applied Linguistics* 19/1: 73-96. Oxford University Press.

McCafferty, S. G. & Ahmed., M. K. (2000). The appropriation of gestures of the abstract by L2 learners. Edited by J. P. Lantolf, *Sociocultural Theory and Second Language Learning.* Oxford and New York: Oxford University Press.

McCormack, D. & Donato, R. (2000). Teacher Questions as Scaffolded Assistance in an ESL classroom". Edited by J. K. Hall and L. Stoops Verplaetse, *Second and Foreign Language Learning Through Classroom Interaction.* New Jersey and London: Lawrence Earlbaum Publishers.

Nassaji, H. & Wells, G. (2000). What's the use of 'triadic dialogue'?: An investigation of teacher-student interaction. *Applied Linguistics* 21/3: 376-406.

Newman, F. & Holzman, L. (1993). *Lev Vygotsky: Revolutionary Scientist.* London and New York: Routledge publishing.

Ohta, A. S. (2000a). Rethinking interaction in SLA: Developmentally appropriate assistance in the zone of proximal development and the acquisition of L2 grammar. Edited by J. P. Lantolf, *Sociocultural Theory and Second Language Learning.* Oxford and New York: Oxford University Press.

Ohta, A. S. (2000b). Rethinking Recasts: A learner-Centered Examination of Corrective Feedback in the Japanese Language Classroom. Edited by J. K. Hall & L. Stoops Verplaetse, *Second and Foreign Language Learning Through Classroom Interaction.* New Jersey and London, Lawrence Earlbaum Publishers.

Pavlenko, A. (1997). *Bilingualism and cognition.* Unpublished Ph.D. dissertation, Cornell University, Ithaca NY.

Pavlenko, A. & Lantolf. J. P. (2000). Second language learning as participation and the (re)construction of selves. Edited by J. P. Lantolf, *Sociocultural Theory and Second Language Learning.* Oxford and New York: Oxford University Press.

Platt, E. & Brooks, P. (1994). The acquisition rich environment revisited. *The modern language journal* 78/4: 497-511m

Roebuck, R. (1998) *Reading and recall: A sociocultural approach.* Stamford CT and London: Ablex Publishing.

Roebuck, R. (2000). Subjects speak out: How learners position themselves in a psycholinguistic task. Edited by J. P. Lantolf, *Sociocultural Theory and Second Language Learning.* Oxford and New York, Oxford University Press.

Rogoff, B. (1995). Observing sociocultural activity on three planes: Participatory appropriation, guided participation, and apprenticeship. Edited by J. V. Wertsch, P. del Río & A.Alvarez, *Sociocultural studies of mind.* Cambridge UK and New York:, Cambridge University Press.

Rommetveit, R. (1985). Language acquisition as increasing linguistic structuring of experience and symbolic behavior. Edited by J. V. Wertsch *Culture communication, and cognition: Vygotskian perspectives.* Cambridge UK and New York: Cambridge University Press.

Salomon, G. (ed) (1993). *Distributed Cognitions: psychological and educational considerations.* Cambridge UK and New York: Cambridge University Press.

Searle, J. (1994). *The rediscovery of the mind.* Cambridge MA and London: The MIT press.

Swain, M. (2000). The output hypothesis and beyond: Mediating acquisition through collaborative discourse. Edited by J. P. Lantolf, *Sociocultural Theory and Second Language Learning.* Oxford and New York:Oxford University Press.

Thorne, S. (1999) *An activity theoretical analysis of foreign language electronic discourse.* Unpublished Ph.D. dissertation. University of California, Berkeley.

VanPatten, B. (2000) Thirty Years of Input (or Intake, the Neglected Sibling). Edited by B. Swierzbin, F. Morris, M. Anderson, C. Klee & E. Tarone, *Social and Cognitive Factors in Second Language Acquisition: Selected Proceedings of the 1999 Second Language Research Forum.* Somerville, MA: Casacadilla Press (pp. 287 – 311).

Villamil, O. S. & Guerrero, M. C. M. de (1998). Assessing the Impact of Peer Revision on L2 Writing. *Applied Linguistics* 19/4: 491-514.

Vygotsky, L. (1978). *Mind In Society.* Edited by M. Cole, V. John-Stiener, S. Scribner & E. Souberman. Cambridge MA: Harvard University Press.

Vygotsky, L. (1986). *Thought and Language.* edited by Alex Kozulin. Cambridge MA: MIT Press.

Wells, G. (1999). *Dialogic Inquiry: Toward a sociocultural practice and theory of education.* Cambridge UK and New York: Cambridge University Press

Wertsch, J. V. (1985). *Vygotsky And The Social Formation Of Mind.* Cambridge MA: Harvard University Press.

Wertsch, J. V. (1998). *Mind as action.* Oxford: Oxford University Press.

Wood, D., Bruner, J.S. & Ross, G. (1976). The role of tutoring in problem solving. *The journal of child psychology and psychiatry* 17: 89-100.

Cultural historical activity theory and the object of innovation
Steven L. Thorne, Pennsylvania State University, USA

"What would 'something better' look like?" Pavel Curtis, 1998

1 Introduction

This is a tremendously exciting time to be a language educator if also one that poses numerous challenges. At the fore in applied linguistics are such issues as globalization and its effects on language teaching (Cameron & Block, 2001; Kramsch & Thorne, 2001), colonial histories and the politics of language (Canagarajah, 1999; Pennycook, 1998), and the broad focus of this chapter, cultural-historical approaches to language education that make explicit the linkages between an individual's development and the social-material conditions of their everyday practice (e.g., Engeström, 1999; Chaiklin, 2001; in second language research, Lantolf, 2000; Swain, 2000; Thorne, 2000). To borrow a phrase from Ron Scollon (2001:5), and especially relevant in this tumultuous time of political volatility and conceptual change in the field, language educators are located in a "nexus of practice", a site of engagement inextricably linked to multiple other participants, practices, and histories.

Numa Markee, well known for his creative pedagogical efforts in second language education and book length treatment on curricular innovation (1997), emphasizes that "the study of how to effect educational change should be part of the basic intellectual preparation of all language teaching professionals" (1997:4). Effecting educational change, however, can be difficult on a number of levels. Institutional inertia, the need to align with other courses being taught, and standard expectations within the curriculum, are all factors that may either mitigate or make possible pedagogical innovation. Additionally, teaching approaches come into and out of vogue. Educational goals are transformed to meet the evolving needs of an increasingly diverse student population. New technologies emerge and are incorporated into everyday practices of teaching and learning. Historically, language educators have witnessed radical pedagogical shifts such as the wide-spread move from the grammar-translation to the audio-lingual method in the 1950s and 60s and the overwhelming trend toward "communicative language teaching" in the 1980s and 90s (Breen & Candlin, 1980; Savignon, 1983).

From the classroom instructor's perspective, 'change' as such can seem to lack an identifiable agency, or can even preclude an individual instructor's creativity and voice. A few questions are relevant here, and they are only partially rhetorical -- where does educational innovation come from? Does it filtered down through second language acquisition (SLA) research? Or from pedagogical texts? Perhaps change is imposed by a departmental authority? With many traditional educational approaches being challenged within applied linguistics (e.g.,

Pennycook, 2001) and elsewhere (e.g., Bourdieu & Passeron, 1977), how can language educators positively transform their everyday activity as instructors and facilitators?

In response to these aforementioned questions, I will suggest a version of cultural-historical activity theory based on the work of Yrjö Engeström. Engeström's model of activity theory has been used equally as a research framework and a heuristic supporting innovation in wide array contexts including education (Bellamy, 1996; Engeström, 1987; Thorne, 1999), healthcare (Engeström, 1993; Engeström, Engeström, Vähäaho, 1999), the postal service (Engeström & Escalante, 1996), and human-computer interaction (Kaptelinin, 1996). Activity theory does not separate understanding (research) from transformation (concrete action). That is, it encourages engaged critical inquiry wherein an investigation should afford an analysis that would lead to the development of material and symbolic-conceptual tools necessary to enact positive interventions. In fact, if we adhere to the Marxist principle on which the theory is based, as Vygotsky notes, we don't really understand something unless we are able to transform it (see Bakhurst, 1991).

A potential challenge to the use of activity theory is that it requires practitioners to conceptually move away from student or teacher or technology-centered conceptions of educational practice, and to rather consider the goings on in a classroom or school as an activity system. The problem in general with 'centering' approaches is that human activity is mediated in complex ways that typically involve other people and artifacts. A student-centered or technology-centered analysis may put into shadow the important roles that the "non-centered" actors play in educational settings, such as the instructor, curricular orientation, and low-tech artifacts (pen and paper, books, chalk board/white board, the spatial configuration of the classroom), all of which may be critical to first understanding, and subsequently improving, educational practice. Nardi notes that it is not possible to fully understand how people learn and work if the unit of analysis is "the unaided individual with no access to other people or to artifacts for accomplishing the task at hand" (Nardi, 1996:69). Yet because of the privileging of the individual as an autonomous being, some have assumed that real learning must be *a-social* and therefore unassisted. This is part of the doxa, if not orthodoxa[1], of SLA research, and certainly of assessment efforts, which typically ask what individuals can accomplish *alone* and not what can be accomplished under more typical conditions of collaboration and interaction with other people and artifacts.

Through an activity theoretical lens, one can look at orientations toward the activity at hand, and the varying roles that participants and artifacts play, without the blind spots that teacher, student, and technology-centered approaches

---

[1] Thanks to Jim Lantolf this instructive play on words.

tend to produce. Activity theory understands individuals and their goal directed activity as the focus of analysis and the key to transformation and innovation. Activity theory provides a framework that stresses human agency, but a human agency mediated by the mediational means at hand (technologies like computers and books, and also semiotic tools such as literacies, pedagogical frameworks, and conceptions of learning), the communities relevant to the situation, the implicit and explicit rules and divisions of labor in these communities, and the object, or orientation, of the activity system under consideration. A strength of activity theory is its inherent dialectical sensitivity to the inventiveness of human activity *and* the normalizing pressures of expected forms of behavior.

I will briefly discuss how activity theory might be of particular use to language educators, and will do so by first describing the evolution of activity theory (culminating in the model developed by Yrjö Engeström, 1987, 1999) and how this approach can act as a defamiliarizing technology (Tschili, 1994), as a way to for educators and students to view the language education process in a new light, and subsequently to enact innovations in the teaching and learning local to a given context. This chapter focuses specifically on the agency of teachers in their efforts to develop, implement, and assess educational innovation as illustrated by a case study of activity theory at work in second language education.

2 A brief introduction to Vygotsky and cultural historical activity theory

As Lantolf points out in his chapter (this volume), Vygotsky came to understand that higher order cognitive functions are culturally mediated by the signs and artifacts emergent of practical activity (1978, 1986; Cole, 1996). Higher order cognitive functions, including intentional memory, planning, voluntary attention, interpretive strategies, and forms of logic and rationality, develop in a way that correlates to social practices such as schooling, interaction with primary care givers, the learning and use of semiotic systems such as spoken languages, textual and digital literacies, mathematics, music, exposure to folk and "scientific" concepts, context-contingent behavioral norms, and spatial fields such as the social and functional divisions of built structures and visual artistic expression. All of these (and more, this is obviously a partial list) are uniquely human social-semiotic systems (e.g., Halliday, 1978) that evolved over time and continue to transform from generation to generation. They comprise our cultural inheritance, so to speak. Emphasizing that development moves, as it were, from the outside in, a primary Vygotskian argument is that development first occurs on an interactional and inter-mental plane (between individuals and between individuals and artifacts) and subsequently is available to individuals on an intra-mental plane. This links thought structures of individuals and communities to the social and material conditions of their everyday practice. To put this into modern parlance, Vygotsky argued that situated social interaction connected to concrete practical activity in the material world is at the source of both individual and cultural development, and in turn, cultural-societal structures provide affordances and constraints that result in the development of specific forms of consciousness (see Lantolf, this volume, for an extended discussion of mediation and internalization). This dialectical approach to the relation between subject and structure continues today to be at the core of sociological and psychological inquiry (e.g., theories of structuration, c.f., Bourdieu, 1977; Giddens, 1984; Archer, 1995) and is the corner stone of cultural historical activity theory.

Activity theory picks up Vygotsky's main ideas and attempts to operationalize and extend his brilliant, if also arguably nascent, work. Kuutti (1996:25) describes activity theory as "a philosophical and cross-disciplinary framework for studying different kinds of human practices as development processes, with both individual and social levels interlinked at the same time." First mentioned by Marx in his Theses on Feuerbach as "practical-critical activity" (1968:659, also Engeström, 1999:3), the notion of *activity* is central to this approach and is defined as goal directed action that is often habitual in nature.[2]

The intellectual roots of cultural historical psychology (which, according to Chaiklin, 2001, subsumes sociocultural theory and activity theory) extend back to 18th and 19th century German philosophy (particularly Kant to Hegel), the sociological and economic writings of Marx and Engels (specifically *Theses on Feuerbach* and *The German Ideology*) and most directly to the research of Vygotsky and his colleagues Luria and Leontiev. In contrast to the engineering-computational metaphor used in varieties of SLA, which have defined themselves and the processes they look at through terminology such as input, output, uptake, etc. (and the use and learning of language understood as 'information processing'), cultural historical psychology, though inclusive of a few lineages that variably emphasize divergent (but generally commensurate) intellectual traditions, seeks relational, historical, and non-dualist ways of reconceptualizing 'learning' and 'behavior' as 'development' and 'practice'. Within education broadly, cultural historical psychology has stimulated a shift from a focus on brain-local cognitive function to an appreciation of human developmental processes as interrelated with and contingent upon historical, cultural, institutional, and discursive contexts.

Though individual and collective development emerges through life-long interaction with types and qualities of activities, settings, and artifacts, Vygotsky stressed that individuals dynamically use symbolic and material resources in new and innovative ways and notes evidence for this creative force by the frequency

---

[2] Activity theory distinguishes three hierarchical levels of human behavior. These are activity (contextualizing framework), action (goal directed behavior), and operation (automatized actions). These levels can also be understood as different perspectives on the same event (Wells, 1999). This tristratal distinction is not exploited in this paper but interested readers are encouraged to look at Wells, 1999, and Keptelinin, 1996, for extensive discussion of this topic.

with which humans alter and transform their social and material environments and themselves (1978). This gets us to the point of this paper – to consider ways to improve language education through innovation and reasoned transformation. Creativity and innovation are at the core of the activity theory enterprise. Though activity theory is also used descriptively and analytically as a diagnostic framework, its essence is to then take a situation or condition and transform it in an effort to create something better. To borrow an often quoted line from Marx, "philosophers have only *interpreted* the world, in various ways; the point, however, is to change it." (*Theses on Feuerbach*, XI, in Tucker (Ed.), 1972:145).

3   Terms of Engagement: activity system, practice, and mediation

An *activity system* is defined by Engeström as "not only a persistent formation; it is also a creative, novelty-producing formation ..." (Engeström, 1993: 68). A particular educational context, for example, is itself a part of a number of activity systems relevant to participating individuals (for example their prior experiences with computer technology and on-line communities or their prior experience with foreign language learning), as well as the activity system of the semester-long class, the activity system of the practice of being a student at a university, the goals of this effort, and so on. Importantly, a single activity system is influenced by multiple other activity systems. In this way, an activity system such as a second language classroom may be influenced by other educational contexts as well as activity systems not directly related to education (for example, students' experiences using foreign language for work or travel, perceptions and valuations of foreign cultures as they are represented in popular culture and media, the goals and aspirations of a student and the relevance (or perceived irrelevance) of their educational experience).

Practice, sometimes with a modifier as in "educational practice" or "social practice", is a concept developed by social scientists (Bourdieu, 1990; de Certeau, 1984; Ortner, 1984) and linguists (Hanks, 1996; Scollon, 2001) to describe social action in the world. In this text, "practice" is used in the sense associated with Bourdieu (1977; 1990) to mean everyday, often habitual action that is informed by socially structured resources and competencies.

Mediation is a primary feature of activity theory and cultural historical psychology more generally and is the assertion that humans do not act directly on the world. Rather, their actions are mediated by social-semiotic tools (language, numeracy, concepts, etc) and material artifacts and technologies. Language and other semiotic systems mediate thinking and communicative interaction among people as well intra-mentally within an individual (for example subvocalization and private speech). The cultural historical perspective marks a radical epistemological shift from Cartesian derived theories of cognition and development that separate forms of knowledge from social practice. The key to this shift away from Cartesian dualism is the notion of mediation and internalization in which the mediational means are themselves cultural tools and artifacts (Cole & Engeström, 1993; Engeström, 1999; Wertsch, 1998; for a discussion of mediation within SLA, see Lantolf, 2000, and Lantolf, this volume). What might be termed habits of mind are emergent of social-material conditions in which concrete activities are carried out. This is not a deterministic relationship that can be precisely predicted; rather, the suggestion is that historical, institutional, and discursive forces (e.g., culture at given point in time and for specific communities) largely mediate individual's practical and symbolic activity.

4 The development of Activity Theory

Vygotsky initially advanced a model that included a subject and his or her object of activity. The subject cannot act directly on the object but rather employs tool mediation to carry out cognitive functions. The diagram often used to illustrate this relationship is the basic triangle. In Vygotsky's work, tool mediation, located at the vertex of the triangle, affords and constrains cognition. The common reformulation of Vygotsky's model of mediated action is depicted in Figure 1 (see also Engeström, 1999).

Artifact

Subject   **Object**

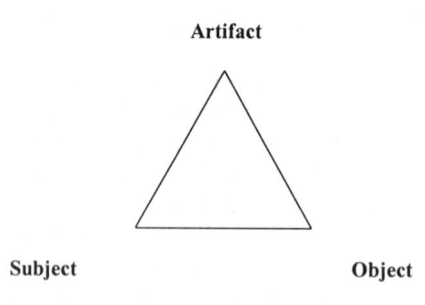

Figure 1 Vygotsky's model of mediated action.

Though useful as a model of individual cognitive functioning that observes the critical role of cultural mediation, this schematic fails to include critical societal dynamics such as communities, the rules that structure them, and "the continuously negotiated distribution of tasks, powers, and responsibilities among the participants of an activity system." (Cole & Engeström, 1993:7). Building on this critique, initially voiced by Leontiev (e.g., 1981), Engeström (1987) increased the scope of Vygotsky's model to incorporate these societal and contextual dimensions. Engeström begins this broadening process by linking the idea of activity systems to concept of context, stating that "[c]ontexts are activity systems. An activity system integrates the subject, the object, and the instruments (material tools as well as signs and symbols) into a unified whole" (Engeström, 1993:67).

The modern incarnation of activity theory provides a productive framework for mapping the complexities of social practice in educational settings. The central concern of this approach is that the actions of individuals occur at the nexus of three factors; the tools and artifacts available (e.g., languages, computers), the community and the understood rules of the community (historical and institutional rules as well as rules that are emergent of a local set of social-material conditions), and the division of labor in these community-settings (e.g., identity and social role, expected interactional dynamics). Engeström identifies the participants and processes of an activity system as *subject, object* and *outcomes, community, division of labor,* and *rules*. To schematize these relationships, Engeström developed the following diagram (1987, 1993, 1999).

**Mediational means:
Symbolic and Material artifacts**

Subject,
Subject
collective

Object ⇒ Outcome

Community   Rules   Division of Labor

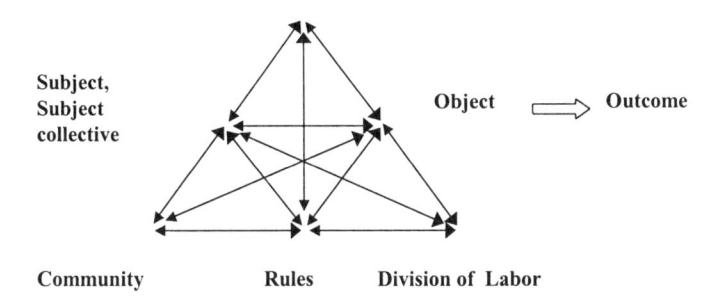

Figure 2 A complex model of an activity system

This diagram depicts the core features of an activity system. A strength of an activity theoretical approach is the conception of human activity as indivisible from functional activity systems. The areas at the base of Engeström's diagram--the community, rules, and division of labor--provide a conceptual framework that brings together local human activity and larger social-cultural-historical structures. In the upper part of the diagram the subject and his or her goal directed activity is shown to be mediated (made possible) by certain tools and artifacts. In more detail, a *subject* is an individual or subgroup whose agency is, in the emic sense, the perspective or point of view of the analysis. The *object* describes the orientation of the activity. Engeström explains that the "object refers to the 'raw material' or 'problem space' at which the activity is directed and which is molded or transformed into *outcomes* with the help of physical and symbolic, external and internal tools", which mediate the activity (1993:67). The *community* is the participants who share the same *object* that shapes and lends direction to the individual and shared activity at hand. Of particular value to this study is Engeström's inclusion of *division of labor* to the activity theory approach. With a clear link to activity theory's outgrowth of Marx and Engels' work, *division of labor* refers to the horizontal actions and interactions among the members of the community and "to the vertical division of power and status" (Engeström, 1993:67), for example the differing status of more and less popular students or between teachers and students. The *division of labor* within a *community* involves *rules* and regulational norms, each of which afford and constrain the goings on within a functional activity system. Synoptically, here are a few key points about activity theory that stand out as especially pertinent to the process of educational innovation:

- Activity theory is not a static or purely descriptive approach, rather, the use of activity theory implies transformation and innovation.
- All activity systems are heterogeneous and multi-voiced and may include conflict and resistance as readily as cooperation and collaboration.
- Activity is central. There is no 'student' or 'teacher' or 'technology' centered pedagogy from an activity theory perspective. Rather, agents play various roles and share an orientation to the activity.
- Activity systems don't work alone. Multiple activity systems are always at work and will have varying influences on the local or focus activity system at hand.

5   The Case of Peer-Revision in a Spanish Foreign language program

Antonio Jiménez and Gabriela Zapata, graduate student instructors of Spanish at Pennsylvania State University, created and implemented an intervention that they hoped would be developmentally productive for participating foreign language students of Spanish (unpublished manuscript). They reviewed the research literature on the use of peer revision in second language education between expert and novice writers (e.g., Aljaafreh & Lantolf, 1994) and between novices themselves (e.g., de Guerrero & Villamil, 1994, 2000) and were inspired by the forms of interaction reported in these studies. Within foreign language education in particular, Zapata and Jiménez found no existing research that discussed the use of peer revision in which more and less capable students, in disparate level language courses, were paired up. As one of them was teaching an advanced Spanish composition course and the other a lower-intermediate Spanish course, they designed and implemented a peer revision activity where the novice students would write essays and the more expert students would assume the role of reviewers. I wish to underscore the fact that this is a teacher project, conceptualized by language instructors (Zapata and Jiménez) and which includes an integrated pedagogical intervention and research component. Hence, this is an example of 'action research', the theoretically informed development, implementation, and analysis of an educational innovation conceptualized and carried out by teachers themselves. Additionally, as a model of innovative pedagogy, this project is modest in scope, an attribute that may be attractive (and necessary) for teachers who have limited time and material resources.

Introduction to the study-intervention

I will describe this project as it was conceptualized and carried out by Zapata and Jiménez and then will use activity theory to address its outcomes and to suggest possible improvements to the intervention itself with an eye toward future practice. Zapata and Jiménez designed a peer review process to encourage collaboration between advanced and lower-intermediate students. Working within a Vygotskian framework, their particular focus (and hope) was to create conditions that would enable a zone of proximal development to emerge through the peer review process. The zone of proximal development (ZPD) is defined by Vygotsky as "the distance between actual developmental level as determined by independent problem solving and the level of potential development as determined through problem solving under adult guidance or in collaboration with more capable peers." (1978:86; for a sophisticated discussion of the ZPD in second language education, see Kinginger, 2002, and Dunn & Lantolf, 1998). For Vygotsky, the ZPD is not only a model of the developmental process, but also a conceptual tool that educators can use to understand aspects of students' emerging capacities that are in early stages of maturation. In this way, when used proactively, teachers using the ZPD concept as a diagnostic have the potential to create conditions that may give rise to specific forms of development. From their standpoint as teacher-researchers, Zapata and Jiménez asked the following questions of the peer revision activity: 1) What kinds of feedback do reviewers provide novice writers? 2) Can e-mail peer revisions activate novice writers' and more experienced reviewers' ZPDs as foreign language writers?

Here is a brief description of the peer review activity. Sixteen students from each of the two classes participated in the project. The sixteen lower-intermediate students wrote essays in Spanish which were then read and commented on by the advanced students. The task called for the lower-intermediate students to assume to the identity of a magazine editor whose column gives advice to teens about their problems. In this case, the editor (i.e., the lower-intermediate students) addresses letters related to dress code and conflicts teens have with their parents over this issue. In writing the composition, students were asked to focus on the use of the subjunctive mood and direct and indirect pronouns. The advanced students reviewing the essays were asked to focus on these features but also to provide comments on content and other grammatical forms as appropriate.

The novice students wrote the essays during a 50-minute period and subsequently the essays were distributed to the reviewers in hard copy format. The lines of the essays were numbered for ease of reference. The advanced students were asked to review the essays and to send their comments directly to the essay writers via email. The use of email to communicate revisions solved a substantial problem as the classes met at different times and negotiating face-to-face meetings would have been logistically difficult. The reviewers were encouraged to use English in their responses. Though the use of the L1 in foreign language education is controversial, some research has suggested that L1 use allows for collaboration and interaction that may otherwise not occur or would occur at a more remedial level, and thus circumscribed L1 use may contribute to L2 development, particularly when the L1 is used as a form of metatalk about the L2 (e.g., Ánton & DiCamilla, 1998; Swain & Lapkin, 2000; see also Lantolf, 2000, for a comprehensive review of research on L1 mediation in foreign language contexts).

When the reviewers had completed their task, they sent their comments to the essay writers and were asked to respond to questions focusing on their experience (e.g., Describe your experience revising the Spanish 002 students' compositions? Do you think this activity helped you to think about the grammar of your own compositions? Would you willingly participate in such an activity again?). The lower-intermediate students were asked to re-write their essays taking account of the reviewers' comments. Like the advanced students, they were also asked to answer a number of questions about the activity (e.g., Did you understand all the reviewers comments? Did you include all the suggested changes? If you did not adopt some suggestions, why? Was this a useful activity? Would you want to do it again?). Zapata and Jiménez's rationale for the reflection survey was two fold, to provide them with a participant relative understanding of the intervention from the writers' and reviewers' perspectives, and to promote reflection on the part of participants that could help to focus their attention to the interpersonal experience that this intervention provoked.

Outcome

Due to space constraints, I will provide a synoptic overview of the outcome of this project. For the lower-intermediate students, from a total of 194 suggestions made by reviewers, 185 were incorporated into the rewrites. The percentage of incorporated suggestions, then, is very high as experienced second language teachers will recognize. Qualitatively reflecting on the experience of writing and receiving feedback on their essays, the lower-intermediate students had these responses to the revision process. I have selected only a few excerpts that reflect the general themes of their comments:

> "I didn't have any trouble understanding the suggestions or comments. Everything was clear and right to the point."
> "The advantage is that it gives the reviewers more experience and gave us the chance to get feedback from other students

"I think it's good because they have already had the class and know what kinds of mistakes to look for."

"Peer revisions are helpful because it is useful to hear the comments and criticisms of other students instead of always having them from the teacher."

A number of positive features are apparent in these excerpts (student comments in total were very positive). The use of the L1 (English) successfully mitigated potential comprehension problems, as predicted by Zapata and Jiménez (this is indirectly referenced in excerpt 1). Excerpts 2-4 illustrate the encouraging effect of feedback from what Murphey and Murakami call "near peer role models" (1998). Murphey and Murakami designed a variety of tasks that paired together students of varying levels of communicative competence (in their study, Japanese students of ESL). Based on the analysis of pedagogical interventions supporting exchanges with "near peers", Murphey and Murakami suggest that interaction with modestly advanced students can be a motivating experience for students at lesser stages of development. That is to say, for relatively novice language learners, feedback from students only a year or two in advance of their present writing ability may, in addition to the explicit focus of providing corrections on linguistic structure, provide a proximal proficiency goal that interaction with native or near native instructors may not. In essence, the reviewers may represent, to the lower-intermediate students, an obtainable level of foreign language expertise.

Evidence that near-peer role modeling may be occurring in the email revision task is seen in excerpt 3 where a student specifically aligns herself with the advanced students through reference to their shared experience of working through the lower-intermediate course. Excerpt 4 again shows a lower-intermediate student asserting solidarity with the advanced students and at the same time indicates a stance of resistance toward the authority of the course instructor. What was the experience like for the advanced student reviewers? The following are representative excerpts from advanced student-reviewers as they were written in the post-activity survey:

[The essays] made me aware of how much I've forgotten. I should look over all the expressions again and familiarize myself with vocabulary studied years ago."

"I recognize obvious mistakes but also see things I'm not sure about. This helps me know what things I should check over, look up, etc."

"Usually we do not get a chance to see where we came from. Learning new concepts is hard. We forget how we used to write, so being able to identify more basic problems is reassuring."

"I learned more about how to revise a paper and what to look for."

"I learned that I have come a long way in my writing. I also learned that it must be hard being a teacher and trying to figure out what their students are trying to say."

A first thing to note about the reviewer comments is that they reflect heterogeneous experiences of "the same task" (see Coughlan & Duff, 1994, for a discussion problematizing the conception of "one task" when multiple participants are involved). This is to be expected as activity systems often include heterogeneous voices illustrating a differential experience even when the overall orientation, or object of the activity, is shared. Excerpts 5 and 6 suggest that for some reviewers, the activity of responding to 'novice' writers' texts presented a constructive challenge to their own sense of competency. Excerpt 7 illustrates a renewed self-awareness about the difficulty of additional language learning and makes explicit reference to solidarity with the lower-intermediate students, mirroring the gist of excerpts 3 and 4 above. Excerpts 8 and 9 reflect what I expected to see when the plans for this project were first discussed—that advanced students would develop better editing and authoring skills through participation in the institutionally sanctioned role of instructor. Palincsar & Brown (1984) term a switching around of student power positions in the classroom "reciprocal teaching", where students occupy the structural role of the teacher and in turn see the educational process in a new light. Sociocultural researcher James Wertsch links reciprocal teaching to a reorganization of 'participant structures' (Phillips, 1972, in Wertsch, 1998). Participant structures are the naturalized cultural norms that generate typical interactional patterns and the identities that they create and represent, examples of which include the commonly cited Initiation, Response, Evaluation (IRE) sequence that classroom discourse researchers have documented extensively across a wide range of educational contexts (for such research on language classes, see Allright, 1980; van Lier, 1988 and 1996; for non-language research, see Erickson, 1986; Mehan, 1982). The appropriation and appreciation for students of what might be called 'teacherly practices' marks a distinct alteration in the usual division of labor of educational setting. Being put in the position of expert may increase the sense of knowledge and authority for participants who typically inhabit the discursive and institutional confines of a 'student' subject position, the entailments of which are to receive and demonstrate knowledge but rarely to act as an authority or expert.

Addressing this point from another perspective, Firth and Wagner decry a "general preoccupation with the learner, at the expense of other potentially relevant social identities" (1997:288). Liddicoat builds on this theme and states that in a number of communicative contexts in language education and language its related research (he particularly addresses those used in SLA experimental research), the communicative activity "can be typified as institutional forms of talk in which the roles of the participants in the interaction are defined by, and constrained by, the task and the context" (1997:314). In evidence in the voices of these student participants, the practice of reciprocal teaching shifts the division of labor in an activity setting and affords opportunities for constructing a new perspective on the writing process and their progress as developing language experts.

Problems and Solutions to Problems

Overall, from both the perspective of participating students and Zapata and Jiménez as the analysts, the peer review intervention was largely a success. As evidenced in their responses to the reflection survey, students in both classes indicated that the activity was productive. From a cultural historical perspective, there is also ample indication that a zone of proximal development was constructed/open up that provided insight and relatively long term reflection into their collective and individual language development. A primary outcome of the peer review activity, perhaps not necessarily a problem, is that though the reviewers' instructions encouraged both content and grammatical revisions, of the 185 revisions suggested by the advanced students, 160 were grammatical in nature. The grammatical suggestions focused on subject-verb agreement (21 revisions), pronouns (17 revisions), articles and verb forms (13 revisions of each), spelling and subjunctive mood (12 revisions of each), verb tense (10 revisions), and so on down to word order (only 1 revision). Of the 25 content revisions, 11 addressed rephrasing, 7 vocabulary use, and 4 revisions each concerned the deletion or addition of information. Based on a few of the reviewers' post-activity comments, some of the Spanish essays were difficult for them to understand. Decreased comprehension may have contributed to the overwhelming focus on syntactic and morphological revisions, as these features can be addressed somewhat independently of semantics. Excerpts from the reviewers' reflection survey corroborate the comprehension problems:

> "Some sentence structures were difficult to understand."
> "The only difficult thing was trying to figure out what the writer wanted to say. It was hard when the sentences made no sense."

With two clear problems outlined, an over emphasis on linguistic form at the expense of content and comprehension difficulties for the advanced student reviewers, we will consider what an activity theoretical analysis of this situation might suggest in terms of altering the rules, division of labor, and mediating artifacts of the system to potentially improve outcomes.

With two clear problems outlined, an over emphasis on linguistic form at the expense of content and comprehension difficulties for the advanced student reviewers, we will consider what an activity theoretical analysis of this situation might suggest in terms of altering the rules, division of labor, and mediating artifacts of the system to potentially improve outcomes.

*Possible face-to-face meetings?
Peer revision tasks and guides
Email
L1 & L2
Mediating Artifacts

Subjects: Spanish FL Ss

Essay writing and reviewing
Inter-class collaboration
Student solidarity

Object ⟹ **Outcome**

Rules
Dialogic interaction over email

Community
Lower intermediate students
Advanced students

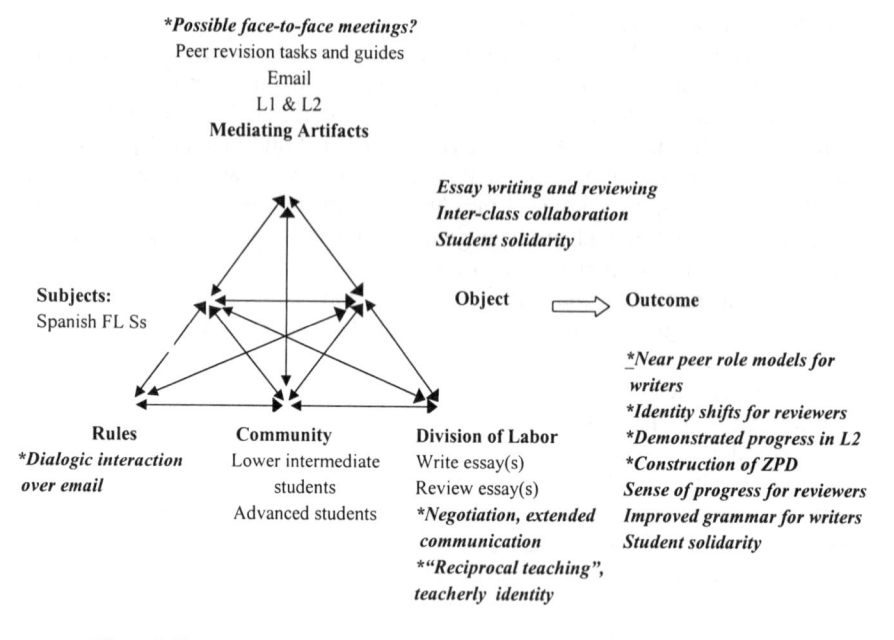

Division of Labor
Write essay(s)
Review essay(s)
*Negotiation, extended communication
*"Reciprocal teaching",
teacherly identity

*Near peer role models for writers
*Identity shifts for reviewers
*Demonstrated progress in L2
*Construction of ZPD
Sense of progress for reviewers
Improved grammar for writers
Student solidarity

Figure 3 The current peer review system and future innovations

There is evidence that the object of the peer review activity as it was initially conceived, to facilitate cross-ability interaction that would be developmentally productive for students in both classes, was largely successful. The indications for some of the predicted outcomes are robust, notably a sense of progress as language learners and insight into their own near-past as novices for the advanced group, and grammatical assistance for the lower intermediates. Both groups noted a new-found solidarity with one another. As only one class period was used in each of the two Spanish classes, this is quite a reasonable outcome for such a brief exercise. A number of possible outcomes, however, would require a longer time commitment and certain changes in the rules, division of labor, and mediating artifacts of the activity system to see their complete fruition. In figure 3 I have noted in italics areas that are likely to improve with changes to the system. Alteration in the rules, division of labor, and mediating artifacts are additionally marked by asterisks (*). Outcomes that would be furthered through changes in the system are marked in italics, and new or more robustly documentable outcomes that were only hinted at in the initial peer revision activity are marked by an asterisk (*).

The innovations to this system are the following. The rules were initially to exchange only one draft and revision; this was expanded to incorporate regular and dialogic interaction so that reviewers could ask questions of writers when comprehension was difficult, and writers could request follow-up assistance from reviewers, perhaps in the process of writing multiple drafts of an essay; the division of labor has also been augmented to include negotiation and the commitment to an extended set of interactions. As the majority or all of the predicted interactions would take place via email, the promise of extended collaboration is especially important. In a number of studies examining internet mediated tasks, communication researchers have discovered that the expectation of longer term commitment directly correlates to the building of stronger relationships and higher levels of interpersonal engagement (e.g., Walther, 1996). Strengthened interpersonal relationships, in relation to the peer revision activity, are predicted to enhance the near-peer role model effect for the lower-intermediate students (e.g., Murphey & Murakami, 1998) and for the advanced students, their construction of language expert identities through practices of "reciprocal teaching" (Palincsar & Brown, 1984). At the top of the triangle, a last possible change is suggested—to consider the possibility of face-to-face encounters if the logistical arrangements could be arranged. This may not be necessary or even be desirable for all students, but some may wish to pursue this option should the near-peer and mentoring relationships continue to develop.

The goal of activity theory is to define and analyze a given activity system, to diagnose possible problems, and to provide a framework for implementing innovations. This modest example of an already well-conceived classroom activity, peer revision linking disparate levels of foreign language students, is now revisioned in such a way that its benefits can be more fully realized.

6. Discussion

Activity theory posits an ecology that unifies social practice and human consciousness. This is, social practice and cognition are interdependent aspects of activity. Taking such a point of view seriously has potentially tremendous effects when applied to pedagogical work. Within language education particularly, activity theoretical goals of instruction and the desired outcomes of classroom activity are forced beyond a focus on what students know and rather extend to who participants are becoming (Lave & Wenger, 1991). Taking activity theory seriously also presents challenges to assessment and would encourage taking what emerges during joint activity as the 'product' or evidence of development (Swain, 2000). For language education professionals, this creates a more complex scenario of classroom goals and expectations which now can be seen to include issues such as social identity (Norton, 1997, 2000) the discursive construction self (Kramsch, 2000; Pavlenko & Lantolf, 2000), and the distributed nature of what has been historically mis-recognized as individual cognitive activity (Salomon, 1993). Using their own experience of the email mediated production of a co-authored academic article that I have made frequent reference to in this chapter, Cole and Engeström note that "it may be in no small measure owing to such new forms of joint-activity-at-a-distance that we have made the current rediscovery that thinking occurs as much among as within individuals." (1993:43)

7   Doxa in the house: A final note on Perspective

There are many ways in which the doxa, the accepted, uncontested, and naturalized arena of habitual activity, of epistemology and disciplinary particularity, of pedagogical conviction even, are difficult to challenge and see beyond. In a recent book examining technologies as they are used in everyday human activity, Bonnie Nardi and Vicky O'Day address the elusiveness of perception. The example they discuss references research on "inattentional blindness" (Mack & Rock, 1998), a claim made by visual perception researchers which suggests that processing visual information is a conscious act that requires focused attention to the visual field. Routine and repeated activities are susceptible to inattentional blindness, and inattentional blindness may also occur when or if one is unready to pay attention to certain objects in the visual field (Nardi & O'Day, 1999:15). What is the typical division of labor in your classroom? How often are students placed in expert roles? What is the object of activity and is it the one you want it to be (or even think it is)? There are no correct answers to these questions, of course, but inattentional blindness is an occupational hazard in the field of education that can be combated, if not entirely defeated, through attention to the community, rules, division of labor, and mediational means that facilitate progress toward the object of activity. It is hoped that this discussion of activity theory and its subsequent application to a small-scale pedagogical intervention will itself become a mediational affordance to educators interested in the transformation of educational practice.

NOTES

I wish to thanks Antonio Jiménez and Gabriela Zapata for first, conceiving of and implementing the creative and valuable peer editing project, and second, for their generosity in allowing me to discuss their work and build upon the data that they gathered. I also wish to voice my appreciation to Jim Lantolf for his careful review of this manuscript.

8   References

Aljaafreh, A. & Lantolf, J. (1994). Negative feedback as regulation and second language learning in the zone of proximal development. *The Modern Language Journal* 78:465-483.

Allright, D. (1980). Turns, topics, and tasks: Patterns of participation in language learning and teaching. In Diane Larsen-Freeman (Ed.), *Discourse analysis in second language research.* Rowley, MA: Newbury House Publishers.

Ánton, M. & DiCamilla, F. (1998). Socio-cognitive functions of L1 collaborative interaction in the L2 classroom. *The Canadian Modern Language Journal* 54:314-342.

Archer, M. S. (1995). *Realist social theory: A morphogenetic approach.* Cambridge: Cambridge University Press.

Bakhurst, D. (1991). *Consciousness and revolution in Soviet philosophy: From the Bolsheviks to Evald Ilyenkov.* Cambridge: Cambridge University Press.

Bellamy, R. K. E. (1996). Designing educational technology: Computer-mediated change. In B. A. Nardi (Ed.), *Context and consciousness: Activity theory and human-computer interaction.* Cambridge, MA: MIT Press, 123-146.

Bourdieu, P. (1977). *Outline of a theory of practice.* Cambridge: Cambridge University Press.

Bourdieu, P. (1990*). In Other Words: Essays towards a reflexive sociology.* Stanford: Stanford University Press.

Bourdieu, P., & Passeron, J.C. (1977). *Reproduction in education, society, and culture.* London: Sage Publications.

Breen, M., & Candlin, C. (1980). The essentials of a communicative curriculum in language teaching. *Applied Linguistics* 1:89-112.

Cameron, D. & Block, D. (1991). *Globalization and language teaching.* London: Routledge.

Canagarajah, S. (1999). *Resisting linguistic imperialism in English teaching.* Oxford: Oxford University Press.

Chaiklin, S. (2001). The institutionalization of cultural-historical psychology as a multnational practice. In S. Chaiklin (Ed.), *The theory and practice of cultural-historical psychology.* Aarhus: Aarhus University Press, 15-34.

Cole, M. (1996). *Cultural psychology: A once and future discipline.* London: The Belknap Press of Harvard University Press.

Cole, M. & Engeström, Y. (1993). A cultural-historical approach to distributed cognition. In G. Salomon (Ed.), *Distributed Cognitions: Psychological and Educational Considerations.* Cambridge: Cambridge University Press, 1-46.

Coughlan, P. & Duff, P. (1994). Same task, different activities: Analysis of a SLA task from an activity theory perspective. In J. Lantolf & G. Appel (Eds.), *Vygotskian approaches to second language research.* Norwood, NJ: Ablex Publishing company, 173-191.

de Certeau, M. (1984). *The practice of everyday life.* Berkeley: University of California Press.

de Guerrero, M. & Villamil, O. (1994). Social-cognitive dimensions of interaction in L2 peer revisions. *The Modern Language Journal* 78:484-496.

de Guerrero, M. & Villamil, O. (2000). Activating the ZPD: Mutual scaffolding in L2 peer revision. *The Modern Language Journal* 84:51-68.

Dunn, B & Lantolf, J. (1998). Vygotsky's zone of proximal development and Krashen's i + 1: Incommensurable Constructs; Incommensurable Theories. *Language Learning*, 48: 411-442.

Engeström, Y. (1987). *Learning by expanding: An activity theoretical approach to developmental research.* Helsinki: Orienta-Konsultit.

Engeström, Y. (1993). Developmental studies of work as a test bench of activity theory: The case of primary care medical practice. In J. Lave & S. Chaiklin, (Eds.), Understanding practice: Perspectives on activity and context. Cambridge: Cambridge University Press, 64-103.

Engeström, Y. (1999). *Perspectives on activity theory.* Cambridge: Cambridge University Press.

Engeström, Y., Engeström, R., & Vähäaho, T. (1999). When the center does not hold: The importance of knotworking. In S. Chaiklin, M. Hedegaard, & U. J. Jensen (Eds.), *Activity Theory and Social Practice: Cultural-Historical Approaches.* Aarhus University Press, 345-374.

Engeström, Y.& Escalante, V. (1996). Mundane tool or object of affection? The rise and fall of the postal buddy. In B. A. Nardi (Ed.), *Context and consciousness: Activity theory and human-computer interaction.* Cambridge, Mass.: MIT Press, 325-374.

Erickson, F. (1996). Qualitative methods in research on teaching. In M. C. Wittrock (Ed.), *Handbook of research on teaching.* New York: Macmillan, 119-161.

Firth, A., & Wagner, J. (1997). On discourse, communication, and (some) fundamental concepts in SLA research. *Modern Language Journal*, 82/1:91-94.

Giddens, A. (1984). *The constitution of society.* Cambridge: Polity.

Halliday, M.A.K. (1978). *Language as social semiotic: The social interpretation of language and meaning.* London: Arnold.

Hanks, W. (1996). *Language and communicative practice.* Boulder, Co.: Westview Press.

Kapetlinin, V. (1996). Activity theory: Implications for human-computer interaction. In B. A. Nardi (Ed.), *Context and consciousness: Activity theory and human-computer interaction.* Cambridge, Mass. MIT Press, 45-68.

Kinginger, C. (2002*). Defining the zone of proximal development in US foreign language education.* Applied Linguistics 23/2:240-261.

Kramsch, C. (2000). Social discursive constructions of self in L2 learning. In J. Lantolf, (Ed.), *Sociocultural perspectives on second language learning.* Oxford: Oxford University Press, 133-154.

Kramsch, C., & Thorne, S. (2001). Foreign language learning as global communicative practice. In D.Block and D. Cameron (Eds.) *Globalization and language teaching*. London: Routledge.

Kuutti, K. (1996). Activity theory as a potential framework for human-computer interaction research. In B.Nardi (Ed.), Context and consciousness: Activity theory and human computer interaction. Cambridge, MA: MIT Press.

Lantolf, J. (2000). Second language learning as a mediated process. *Language Learning*, 33/2:79-96.

Lave, J. & Wenger, E. (1991) *Situated Learning: Legitimate peripheral participation*. Cambridge: Cambridge University Press.

Leontiev, A.R. (1981). *Language and cognition*. Washington, D.C.: Winston.

Liddicoat, T. (1997). Interaction, social structure, and second language use. *Modern Language Journal*, 81/3:313-317.

Mack, A.., & Rock, I. (1998). *Inattentional blindness*. Cambridge, MA: MIT Press.

Markee, N. (1997). *Managing curricular innovation*. Cambridge: Cambridge University Press.

Marx, K. (1945). Theses on Feuerbach. In R. Tucker (Ed.), *The Marx and Engels Reader*. New York, W. W. Norton & Company, 143-145.

Murphey, T., & Murakami, K. (1998). Teacher facilitated near peer role modeling for awareness raising within the zone of proximal development. *Academia Literature and Language*. Nanzan University, Nagoya: Japan, 1-29.

Nardi, B. A. (1996). Studying context: A comparison of activity theory, situated action models, and distributed cognition. In B. A. Nardi (Ed.), *Context and consciousness: Activity theory and human-computer interaction*. Cambridge, Mass.: MIT Press, 69-101.

Nardi, B., & O'Day, V. (1999). *Information ecologies: Using technology with heart*. Cambridge, MA: MIT Press.

Norton, B. (1997). Language, identity, and the ownership of English. *TESOL Quarterly* 31:409-29.

Norton, B. (2000*). Identity and language learning: Gender, ethnicity, and educational change*. Essex: Longman.

Ortner, S. (1984). Theory in anthropology since the sixties. *Comparative Studies in Society and History*, Vol 26, No. 1.: 126-166.

Palincsar, A. S., & Brown, A. L. (1984). Reciprocal teaching of comprehension-fostering and comprehension-monitoring activities. *Cognition and Instruction* 1:117-175.

Pavenko, A., & Lantolf, J. (2000). Second language learning as participation in the (re)construction of selves. In J. Lantolf (Ed.), *Sociocultural theory and second language learning*. Oxford: Oxford University Press, 155-178.

Pennycook, A. (2001). *Critical applied linguistics: A critical introduction*. Mahwah, NJ: Lawrence Erlbaum.

Pennycook, A. (1998). *English and the discourses of colonialism.* London: Routledge.
Phillips. S. (1972). Participant structures and communicative competence: Warm Spring children in community and classroom. In C. Cazden, V. John, and D. Hymes (Eds.), *Functions of Language in the Classroom.* New York: Teachers College Press, 370-394.
Salomon, G. (1993). *Situated cognitions: Psychological and educational considerations.* Cambridge: Cambridge University Press.
Savignon, S. (1983). *Communicative competence: Theory and classroom practice.* Reading, MA: Addison-Wesley.
Scollon, R. (2001). *Mediated discourse: The nexus of practice.* London: Routledge.
Swain, M. (2000). The output hypothesis and beyond: Mediating acquisition through collaborative dialogue. In J. Lantolf (Ed.), *Sociocultural theory and second language acquisition.* Oxford: Oxford University Press, 97-114.
Swain, M. & Lapkin, S. (2000). Task-based second language learning: The uses of the first language. *Language Teaching Research* 4:251-274.
Thorne, S. (1999). *An activity theoretical analysis of electronic foreign language discourse.* Ph.D. dissertation, University of California, Berkeley, CA.
Thorne, S. (2000). Second language acquisition and the truth(s) about relativity. In J. Lantolf (Ed.), *Sociocultural theory and second language acquisition.* Oxford: Oxford University Press, 219-244.
Tschili, B. (1994). *Architecture and disjunction.* Cambridge, MA: MIT Press.
van Lier, L. (1988). *The classroom and the language learner.* New York: Longman.
van Lier, L. (1996). *Interaction in the language curriculum: Awareness, Autonomy, & Authenticity.* New York: Longman.
Vygotsky, L. (1978). *Mind in society.* Cambridge, MA: Harvard University Press.
Vygotsky, L. (1986). *Thought and Language.* Cambridge, MA: The M.I.T. Press.
Walther, J. (1996). Computer-mediated Communication: Impersonal, Interpersonal, and Hyperpersonal Interaction. *Communication Research* 23/1:3-43.
Wells, G. (1999). *Dialogic inquiry: Toward a sociocultural practice and theory of education.* Cambridge: Cambridge University Press.
Wertsch, J. V. (1998). *Mind as Action.* Oxford: Oxford University Press.

Part II
Communicative Language Teaching

Language, Identity, and Curriculum Design: Communicative Language Teaching in the 21st Century
Sandra J. Savignon, The Pennsylvania State University, USA

1   Introduction

Some thirty years ago when I had settled on a dissertation topic and was making plans for my experimental sections of French as a foreign language at the University of Illinois, a senior colleague quipped, "Communicative competence. That will be a good topic for a few years. Then what will you do?" To his surprise, no doubt, as well as my own, that concern has never come up. Communicative competence and what is known now as communicative language teaching (CLT) remain today as fresh and provocative a topic as one could find.

What *has* changed in the intervening years is the language of my research focus. In the 1960s I not only taught basic French language courses at the University of Illinois, for three consecutive summers I taught secondary school teachers of French at a Level IV Institute at Coe College, funded by the National Defense Education Act (NDEA). This was during the Cold War, and the United States had budgeted funds to improve the preparation of secondary school teachers in the areas of mathematics, science, and foreign languages. Our teaching methodology was dubbed the "New Key". Audiolingualism was likened to a bright shiny key that would "unlock" the door to language learning. Dialogue memorization, patterned structure drill, and "backward buildup," the repetition of incremental segments starting from the end of an utterance, constituted the core of our activities. There was also a required course in the "linguistic" foundations of audiolingualism, a course where our group of teacher participants learned to identify phonemes and morphemes and were introduced to the structural patterns of spoken French. My French native speaker husband also taught at these summer institutes. In two summers we had saved enough money to buy our first car, a Ford Falcon. "The gravy train!" my colleague quipped.

Some of my earliest work as an applied linguist was in the bilingual context of Canada. I recall one particular visit to consult with the Ministry of Education regarding assessment of communicative competence for civil service employees. At the Ottawa airport I explained the purpose of my entry to the passport control officer . "Oh!" she exclaimed, they're trying to get all us old hens to learn French. And now they're bringing in the Americans to help them!"

In the years to follow, my research increasingly came to focus on the acquisition and assessment not of French, but of English. An invitation to serve on the TOEFL Committee of Examiners marked my official entry into EFL/ESL circles. Before long I found myself a speaker on the topic of communicative language teaching at the Educational Testing Service (ETS) headquarters in Princeton, NJ and universities and language centers throughout the United States and abroad.

2 Focus on the Learner

Communicative language teaching (CLT) refers to both processes *and* goals in classroom learning. The central theoretical concept in communicative language teaching is of course *communicative competence*, a term that was introduced into discussions of language use and second or foreign language learning in the early 1970s (Jakobovits, 1970; Savignon, 1971). Competence was defined in terms of the *expression, interpretation*, and *negotiation* of meaning and looked to both psycholinguistic and sociocultural perspectives in second language acquisition research to account for its development (Savignon 1983; 1997). Identification of *learner communicative needs* provided a basis for curriculum design in Europe, Jan Van Ek (1975, 1976) is one of first and best known advocates of CLT. Already in 1971 the Council for Cultural Cooperation had constituted a small multinational group of experts to examine the feasibility of a unit / credit system for foreign language learning by adults. The work of this group resulted in a number of exploratory studies and practical applications, first for English and followed by other European languages. The end result was the elaboration of curriculum for modern language learning in schools (Van Ek, 1976).

By definition, CLT puts the focus on the learner. Learner communicative needs serve as a framework for elaborating program goals in terms of functional competence. This implies global, qualitative evaluation of learner achievement as opposed to quantitative assessment of discrete linguistic features. Considerable controversy over appropriate language testing persists, and many a curricular innovation has been undone by failure to make corresponding changes in evaluation. The assessment of learning outcomes remains a central focus in meeting educational challenges worldwide (see Shohamy, 2001; Stansfield, 1993).

Depending on their own preparation and experiences, teachers differ in their reactions to CLT. Some welcome the opportunity to select or develop their own materials, providing learners with a range of communicative tasks. And they are comfortable relying on more global, integrative judgements of learner progress. Others feel understandable frustration at the seeming ambiguity in discussions of communicative ability. Negotiation of meaning may be a lofty goal, but this view of language behavior lacks precision and does not provide a universal scale for assessment of individual learners. Ability is viewed, rather, as variable and highly dependent upon context and purpose as well as upon the roles and attitudes of all involved. An additional source of frustration for some teachers is second language acquisition research that shows the route of language acquisition to be largely unaffected by classroom instruction (Ellis 1985, 1997).

Although they support the informal observations of teachers, namely that textbook presentation and drill do not insure use of these same structures in spontaneous self-expression, the findings are nonetheless disconcerting. They contradict both grammar-translation and audiolingual precepts that place the burden of acquisition on teacher explanation of grammar and controlled learner practice of syntactic and phonological patterns. They are further at odds with textbooks that promise "mastery" of "basic" language forms. Teacher rejection of research findings, renewed insistence on tests of discrete grammatical structures, and even exclusive reliance in the classroom on the learners' mother tongue, when possible, to be sure they "get the grammar," have been in some cases reactions to the frustration of teaching language as communication.

Moreover, with its emphasis on sentence-level grammatical features, the dominant second language acquisition research paradigm itself has served to bolster a structural focus, obscuring discoursal and generic dimensions of language acquisition. Documentation of cross-varietal differences of English, for example, focuses most often on sentence-level lexical and syntactic features. In language testing, attempts to represent norms for a standard English for international communication, for example, the ETS Test of English for International Communication (TOEIC), reflects this emphasis (Lowenberg, 1993). The hegemony of essentially Western conventions at the levels of discourse and genre is less easily represented or challenged. Pressures for a "democratization" of discursive practices (Fairclough, 1992) have in some settings resulted in genre mixing and the creation of new genres. In professional communities, however, conformity to the practices of an established membership continues to serve an important gate-keeping function (Foucault, 1981). The privilege of exploiting generic conventions becomes available only to those who enjoy a certain stature or visibility. With particular reference to the academic community, Bhatia (1997) summarizes the situation as follows:

> Much of the academic discourse still fails to acknowledge the sources of variations, especially those of marginality and exclusion, giving the impression that there is, or should be, no variation in the way genres are constructed, interpreted and used (369).

The challenge for language teaching is to reflect this variety and at the same time encourage learners to develop the skills they need to participate in the negotiation of sociolinguistic conventions. In addition, the selection of a teaching approach appropriate to the attainment of communicative competence requires an understanding of sociocultural differences in styles of learning. Curricular innovation is best advanced by the development of local materials and methods which, in turn, rests on the involvement of classroom teachers. Berns (1990:104) summarizes the principles of CLT:

1. Language teaching is based on a view of language as communication. That is, language is seen as a social tool which speakers use to make meaning; speakers communicate about something to someone for some purpose, either orally or in writing.

2. Diversity is recognized and accepted as part of language development and use in second language learners and users as it is with first language users.

3. A learner's competence is considered in relative, not absolute, terms of correctness.

4. More than one variety of a language is recognized as a model for learning and teaching.

5. Culture is seen to play an instrumental role in shaping speakers' communicative competence, both in their first and subsequent languages.

6. No single methodology or fixed set of techniques is prescribed.

7. Language use is recognized as serving the ideational, the interpersonal, and the textual functions and is related to the development of learners' competence in each.

8. It is essential that learners be engaged in doing things with language, that is, that they use language for a variety of purposes in all phases of learning. Learner expectations and attitudes have increasingly come to be recognized for their role in advancing or impeding curricular change.

3   Shaping a Communicative Curriculum

In attempting to convey the meaning of CLT to both preservice and inservice teachers, I have found it helpful to think of a communicative curriculum as consisting potentially of five components (Savignon, 1983, 1997). These components may be regarded as thematic clusters of activities or experiences related to language use. They provide a way to represent teaching strategies that promote communicative language use. The term *component* to categorize these activities seems particularly appropriate in that it avoids any suggestion of sequence or level. Organization of learning activities into these components is intended *not* to sequence an instructional program, but, rather, to highlight the *range of options* available in curriculum planning and to suggest ways in which their very interrelatedness can benefit the learner.

Language Arts, or language analysis, is the first component on the list. Language arts include those things that language teachers often do best. In fact, it may be *all* they have been taught to do. Language arts include many of the exercises used in mother tongue programs to focus attention on formal accuracy. In an FL/SL program they are concerned with the forms of language, including syntax, morphology, and phonology.

Language for a Purpose, or language experience, is the second component. In those classrooms where the language being learned is of necessity the language of instruction, there is an immediate and natural need for learners to use it. When this happens, language use is a built-in feature of the learning environment. In those far more common settings where the teacher shares with learners a mother tongue, special attention needs to be given to providing learners with opportunities for experience in their new language. Learners who are accustomed to being taught exclusively in their mother tongue are often uncomfortable if the teacher speaks to them in the language they are presumably learning, expecting them not only to understand but perhaps to respond. They need to be shown that making an effort to get the gist, using strategies to interpret, express, and negotiate meaning, are important to the development of communicative competence.

My Language is Me: Personal Language Use relates to the learner's emerging identity in their new language. The most successful teaching programs are those that take into account the affective as well as the cognitive aspects of language learning. They seek to involve learners psychologically as well as intellectually. Personal language use implies, above all, respect for learners as they use their new language for self-expression. Personal language use includes recognition that the norms followed by those in the "inner circle" of the users of a language (Kachru, 1992) may not be an appropriate goal for learners. To return once more to the example of English, in today's post-colonial, multicultural world those in the "outer" and "expanding circles" outnumber those in the inner circle by a ratio of more than 2 to 1 (Crystal, 1997). Given the current reality of English language use, then, reference to the terms "native" or "native-like" in the evaluation of communicative competence is clearly inappropriate. Even the decision as to what is or is not one's "native" language is arbitrary and is best left to the individual concerned.

Learners may welcome apprenticeship in a new language as an opportunity. When asked what it was like to write in English, Korean novelist Mia Yun (1998), replied that it was "like putting on a new dress." Writing in English makes her feel fresh, lets her see herself in a new way, offers her freedom to experiment. At the same time, the struggle to find new ways of self-expression can be accompanied by feelings of alienation and estrangement:

Give me a name, America, make of me a Buzz or Chip or Spike.....No longer a historian but a man without histories let me be. I'll rip my lying mother tongue out of my throat and speak your broken English instead (Rushdie, 2001: 75).

Language teachers in the 21st century should be prepared to address these sometimes conflictual feelings, helping learners to experience bilingualism as both a useful and attainable goal.

You Be...., I'll Be...: Theater Arts is the fourth component of a communicative curriculum. The world is indeed a stage, and on this stage we play many roles, roles for which we improvise scripts from the models we observe around us. Sociocultural rules of appropriateness have to do with these expected ways. Familiar roles may be played with little conscious attention to style. On the other hand, new and unfamiliar roles require practice, with an awareness of how the meanings we intend are being interpreted by others. Sometimes there are no models. Women of my generation who found themselves in roles assigned primarily to men, whether as firefighters, professors, or CEOs, had to adapt existing models to ones with which they could be comfortable. Although our numbers have increased, our choices remain constrained. Within the international community of applied linguists we are well aware that participation depends upon the adoption of not only Western but male and predominantly monolingual perspectives on the construction and dissemination of knowledge (Cameron, 1998; Lakoff, 1975).

If the world can be thought of as a stage, with actors and actresses who play their parts as best they can, theater may be seen as an opportunity to experiment with roles, to try things out. As occasions for language use, role-playing and the many related activities that constitute theater arts are likewise a natural component of language learning. The role of the teacher in theater arts is not unlike that of a coach, to provide support, strategies, and encouragement for learners as they explore new ways of being.

Beyond the Classroom is the fifth and final component of a communicative curriculum. Regardless of the variety of communicative activities in the classroom, their purpose remains that of preparing learners to use their new language in the world beyond. The inclusion of experiences beyond those provided in the classroom itself often begins with an identification of learners' interests and goals. Pen pals and exchange stays have long been an integral part of language learning, along with magazine and newspaper subscriptions to provide insights into current L2 culture. The rapid expansion of the Internet and of computer-mediated communication (CMC) in recent years has of course increased the opportunities for beyond-the-classroom L2 communication, English language communication, in particular. Kinginger (this volume) documents a telecollaboration project between EFL learners in France and FFL in the U. S., an admittedly high-tech example of L2 learning opportunities beyond the classroom walls. In addition, many classroom learners may engage in a variety of L2 communicative exchanges with which the teacher is unfamiliar. These experiences can enhance the L2 classroom learning experience if learners are encouraged to develop the strategies needed to participate successfully in such exchanges and to view such experience as an opportunity to increase their overall communicative competence.

4 Sociolinguistic Issues
Natives and foreigners

Numerous sociolinguistic issues await attention. As a starting point, teachers should begin by asking themselves whose language they teach and for what purpose. What is their own relationship to the English language? Do they consider it to be *foreign, second, native* or *target*? The *Webster's New International Dictionary*, 2nd edition, published in 1950, a time when language teaching in the United States was on the threshold of a period of unprecedented scrutiny, experimentation, and growth, provides the following definitions of the terms used so often in reference to language. *Foreign* derives from Middle English *foraine, forene*, Old French *forain* and Latin *foras*, meaning *out of doors*. Modern definitions include "situated outside one's own country; born in, belonging to, derived from, or characteristic of some place other than the one under consideration.....alien in character; not connected; not pertinent; not appropriate"(p. 988).

Those who are identified as teaching English as a foreign language, perhaps in a department of foreign languages should ask themselves why? What does the label "foreign" signal to colleagues, learners, and the community at large? In the U.S., to arouse national pride and assail their opponents, politicians are fond of evoking the dreaded F word, for example, *foreign* influences, *foreign* money, and *foreign* oil. On the other hand, the foreign students who used to walk American university campuses and whose numbers have become increasingly important for balancing budgets in higher education have been replaced by *international* students. What may be a problem is the teacher's communicative competence. Is she a native speaker of the language she teaches? If not, does she consider herself to be bilingual? If not, why not? Is it a lack of communicative *competence*? Or, rather, a lack of communicative *confidence*? Is she intimidated by native speakers?

For an interpretation of the term "native speaker" *Webster's International Dictionary*, 2nd edition, is not very helpful. Native is defined as "one that is born in a place or country referred to; a denizen by birth; an animal, a fruit or vegetable produced in a certain region; as, a native of France." Several expressions that use native as a modifier follow: native bear, native bread, native cabbage, native dog, native sparrow, most of them referring to Australian species, such as koala bear and dingo. There is no mention of native speaker. To understand the meaning of native speaker in language teaching today, we must look to American structural linguistics. There we find the use of native speaker "informants" to provide data for previously undescribed, unwritten languages and Chomsky's evocation of the "ideal" native speaker in his elaboration of transformational-generative grammar. In both cases the native speaker, real or imagined, is the authority on language use. In audiolingual language teaching, the native speaker became not only the model to be followed but judge. The widely adopted ACTFL Oral Proficiency Guidelines, for example, included a level descriptor that tolerates grammatical "errors" that "do not disturb the native speaker" (American Council on the Teaching of Foreign Languages, 1986). That phrase has always conjured up for me images of people sitting around with big signs that say "NATIVE SPEAKER. DO NOT DISTURB." Having lived most of my adult life with a native speaker of French, I suppose I am no longer intimidated, or even impressed. Nor, I should add, is he intimidated or impressed by my American English. Native speakers of French, American English, or whatever language are fine. But they do not *own* the language they use. Nor are they by definition alone competent to teach and evaluate learners. (For perspective on the role of 19th century colonization and 20th century popular culture in the social construction of English and its native speakers as modern, civilized, and thus superior (see Pennycook, 1998, 2001).

There remains the term *target*, used frequently by methodologists and language acquisition researchers alike. *Target language* is laden with both behaviorist and militaristic associations. A *target* is not unlike the "terminal behavior" in behaviorist learning theory. And *target language* evokes the Army Specialized Training Programs (ASTP) that provided an experimental setting for the audiolingual methods and materials developed in the 1960s for teaching languages in U. S. schools. Evoking as it does a monolithic, fixed goal for all, reference to language as a target misrepresents both process and goal in language learning.

The classroom as social context

Along with other sociolinguistic issues in language acquisition, the classroom itself as a social context has been neglected. Classroom language learning was the focus of a number of research studies in the 1960s and early 1970s, for example Smith and Berger (1968), Smith (1970), Savignon (1971). However, language classrooms were not a major interest of the second language acquisition research that rapidly gathered momentum in the years that followed. The multi-faceted nature of educational settings was an obvious deterrent. Other difficulties included the lack of well-defined classroom processes to serve as variables and lack of agreement as to what constituted learning success. Not surprisingly, researchers eager to establish second language acquisition as a field worthy of inquiry turned their attention to more narrow, quantitative studies of the acquisition of selected morphosyntactic features.

Increasingly, however, research attention is being directed to the social dynamics and discourse of the classroom. What does teacher-learner interaction look like? What happens during pair or group work? If language use is essential for the development of communicative competence, the nature and amount of language use in classroom settings needs to be examined closely. Is the focus truly communicative, that is, on the negotiation of meaning, rather than on practice of grammatical forms? Who participates? Who initiates the discourse? Questions related to patterns of communication and opportunities for learner negotiation of meaning become all the more compelling as technological advances dramatically increase and alter the nature of these opportunities. Email, chat rooms, on-line teaching materials, and video-conferencing are, in effect, redefining the concept of "classroom" and, with it, the roles of teachers and learners (see Savignon, 1997).

5   Communicative Language Teaching and Teacher Education

Considerable resources, both human and monetary, are being deployed around the world to respond to the need for language teaching that is appropriate for the communicative needs of learners. In the literature on CLT, teacher education has not received adequate attention. What happens when teachers try to make changes in their teaching in accordance with various types of reform initiatives, whether top-down ministry of education policy directives or teacher generated responses to social and technological change. A number of recent reports of reform efforts in different nations provide a thought-provoking look at English language teaching today as the collaborative and context-specific human activity that it is. Themes appear and reappear, voices are heard in one setting to be echoed in yet another. Such first-hand observation provides valuable insights for researchers, program administrators, and prospective or practicing teachers who work or expect to work in these and other international settings.

Curricular reform in Japan

Several recent studies have focused on curricular reform in Japan. Redirection of English language education by *Mombusho*, the Japan Ministry of Education, includes the introduction of a communicative syllabus, the Japan Exchange and Teaching (JET) Program, and overseas inservice training for teachers. Previous encouragement to make classrooms more "communicative" through the addition of "communicative activities" led to the realization by Mombusho that teachers felt constrained by a structural syllabus that continued to control the introduction and sequence of grammatical features. With the introduction of a new national syllabus, structural controls were relaxed and teachers found more freedom in the introduction of syntactic features. The theoretical rationale underlying the curriculum change in Japan includes both the well known Canale and Swain (1980) model of communicative competence and the hypothetical classroom model of communicative competence, or "inverted pyramid," proposed by Savignon (1983).

Minoru Wada (1994:1), a university professor and senior advisor to Mombusho in promoting English language teaching reform in Japan, explains the significance of these efforts :

> The Mombusho Guidelines, or course of study, is one of the most important legal precepts in the Japanese educational system. It establishes national standards for elementary and secondary schools. It also regulates content, the standard number of annual teaching hours at lower level secondary (junior high) schools, subject areas, subjects, and the standard number of required credits at upper level secondary (senior high) schools. The course of study for the teaching of English as a foreign language announced by the Ministry of Education, Science, and Culture in 1989 stands as a landmark in the history of English education in Japan. For the first time it introduced into English education at both secondary school levels the concept of *communicative competence*. [.....] The basic goal of the revision was to prepare students to cope with the rapidly occurring changes toward a more global society. The report urged Japanese teachers to place much more emphasis on the development of communicative competence in English.

Following the educational research model for classroom language teaching adapted by Kleinsasser (1993) in considering language teachers beliefs and practices Sato (2000) reports on a year-long study of teachers of English in a private Japanese senior high school. Multiple data sources, including interviews, observations, surveys, and documents, offer insight into how EFL teachers learn to teach in this particular context. Among the major findings was the context-specific nature of teacher beliefs which placed an emphasis on *managing* students, often to the exclusion of opportunities for English language learning.

High stakes public examinations in Hong Kong and Costa Rica

Using both qualitative and quantitative methods, Cheng (1997) has documented the influence of a new, more communicative English language test on the classroom teaching of English in Hong Kong, a region that boasts a strong contingent of applied linguists and language teaching methodologists and has known considerable political and social transformation in recent years. In keeping with curricular redesign to reflect a more task-based model of learning, alternative public examinations were developed to measure learners' ability to make use of what they have learned, to solve problems and complete tasks. At the time curricular changes were introduced, English language teaching was characterized as "test-centered, teacher-centered, and textbook-centered" (Morris et al., 1996). Cheng's ambitious multi-year study found the effect of washback of the new examination on classroom teaching to be limited. There was a change in classroom teaching at the content level but not at the methodological level.

The role of washback in Costa Rica, a small nation with a long democratic tradition of public education, contrasts with the findings of the Hong Kong Study. Quesada-Inces (2001), a teacher educator of many years experience reports the findings of a multi-case study to explore the relationship between teaching practice and the *Bachillerato* test of English, a national standardized reading comprehension test administered at the end of secondary school. Although teachers expressed a strong interest in developing learner communicative ability in speaking and writing English, the reading comprehension test was seen to dominate classroom emphasis, particularly in the last two years of secondary school. The findings match what Messick (1996) has called "negative washback," produced by construct under-representation and construct irrelevance. The Bachillerato test of English does not cover all the content of the curriculum; ultimately it assesses skills less relevant than those skills that go unmeasured. The English testing situation in Costa Rica is not unlike that described by Shohamy (1998) in Israel where two parallel systems can be seen to exist, one the official national educational policy and syllabus, the other reflected in the national tests of learner achievement. Quesada-Inces concludes his report on a personal note:

> I cannot understand that so much effort is lost in pretending to have quality education when all we care about is a percentage that tells us that things are right on the surface...[ ]..the Ministry of Education division that is concerned with national tests is the Quality Control Division, a denomination which suggest mass production of merchandise in a factory. I hope this project can help so that my children, my children's children, and all Costa Rican children are treated more like human beings in schools than as mere production merchandise (249-250).

English in Taiwan

In another Asian setting, Wang (2000, 2002) has looked at the use and teaching of English in Taiwan. Adopting a sociocultural perspective on language use and language learning prerequisite to pedagogical innovation, Wang considers attitude, function, pedagogy (Berns, 1990), and learner beliefs with respect to classroom teaching practice. A national initiative to promote CLT in schools has led to the introduction of English at the 5th grade level. On a visit in the spring of 2001 to address an island-wide meeting of university professors of English, I had occasion to hear the newly-elected mayor of Taipei affirm (in English) his ambitious goals for the city. He wants to make Taipei a bilingual environment, with all signs in English as well as in Chinese. He emphasized the need for English if Taiwan is to remain economically competitive and made specific reference to the TOEFL scores of students in mainland China, Hong Kong and Singapore. The very presence of the mayor at a professional meeting of English teachers signals a recognition of the need for cooperation in attaining goals of communicative competence.

> Much has been done to meet the demand for competent English users and effective teaching in Taiwan. Current improvements, according to the teacher experts, include the change in entrance examinations, the new curriculum with a goal of teaching for communicative competence, and the island-wide implementation in 2001 of English education in the elementary schools. However, more has to be done to ensure quality teaching and learning in the classrooms. Based on the teacher experts' accounts, further improvements can be stratified into three interrelated levels related to teachers, school authorities, and the government. Each is essential to the success of the other efforts (Wang, 2002, :145).

The European Union

Learner autonomy and intercultural communication are essential to language education in continental Europe where communicative competence in two or more languages is often the norm. The free flow of people and knowledge within the European Union and the recent adoption of a European currency signal both the need and the opportunity for language learning accompanied by sociocultural awareness. Experimentation is now underway with an array of programs that place new demands upon both learners and teachers. The implications for language teacher education are far reaching.

A statewide curriculum for foreign language learning in Russia (includes goals in sociocultural competence as part of an overall communicative competence (Saphonova, 1991)). Language and culture are seen as both inextricably entwined and changing. This interrelationship is best understood through engagement in a dialogue of cultures (Bahktin, 1981) Attainment of sociocultural competence is seen to rest on the incorporation of strategies designed to help learners recognize this interrelationship and to cope with a range of potential sources of intercultural misunderstanding and conflict they are likely to encounter. Sociocultural strategies designed on the model of the coping strategies for language learners described in Savignon (1972) will prepare learners for participation in a dialogue of cultures, both present and future (Savignon & Sysoyev, in press).

Uses of network-based computer-mediated communication (CMC) for language teaching have focused primarily on creating discourse communities. Brammerts (1996), for example, describes the creation of the International E-Mail Tandem Network, a project funded by the European Union that involves universities from more than 10 countries. Developed to promote "autonomous, cooperative, and intercultural learning" (121), it constitutes an extension of the tandem learning initiated in the 1970s in an effort to unite many states in a multicultural, multilingual Europe. Pairs of learners from different language backgrounds create a "learning partnership" in the pursuit of the mutual development of both communicative and intercultural competence. The network has expanded to include a number of bilingual subnets, for example, Danish-German, French-English, German-Arabic, each with a bilingual forum to provide an opportunity for questions and discussion (see also Wolff, 1994). Autonomous learning influences teaching methodology and dramatically changes the roles of the language teacher and the language learner. To cope with these changes, future teachers have to be prepared both practically and academically. The multilingual European context in which these teacher educators work serves to underscore the importance of innovation in teacher development. An example of an innovation in this area is the Socrates Lingua A project on learner autonomy in communicative foreign language teaching (Van Esch & St. John , 2003).

Curricular Standards in the U. S. A.
There is renewed concern for sociocultural awareness in U. S. foreign language education as well. Goals 2000 marked the first time in U. S. history that the federal government addressed issues of curriculum and assessment. The National Curricular Standards for the Foreign Languages that resulted from this effort reflect the emphasis on intercultural communication that was integral to their guiding philosophy:

> Language and communication are at the heart of human experience. The United States must educate students who are linguistically and culturally equipped to communicate successfully in a pluralistic American society and abroad. This imperative envisions a future in which ALL students will develop and maintain proficiency in English and at least one other language, modern or classical. Children who come to school from non-English backgrounds should also have opportunities to develop further proficiencies in their first language (ACTFL, 1999, p.7).

A total of 11 standards are organized into five different goal areas, known as "The Five C's" (Communication, Cultures, Connections, Comparisons, and Communities). Each area consists of 2-3 standards and sample progress indicators for grades 4, 8 and 12.

In each of the studies reported in this brief overview, the research was both initiated and conducted by local educators in response to local issues. While each is significant in its own right, they are by no means comprehensive and can only suggest the dynamic and contextualized nature of language teaching in the world today. Nonetheless, the settings that have been documented constitute a valuable resource for understanding the current global status of CLT. Viewed in kaleidoscopic fashion, they appear as brilliant multi-layered bits of glass, tumbling about to form different yet always intriguing configurations. From these data-rich records of language teaching reform on the threshold of the 21st century four major themes emerge, suggestive of the road ahead:

1) The highly contextualized nature of CLT is underscored again and again. It would be inappropriate to speak of CLT as a teaching 'method' in any sense of that term as it was used in the 20th century. Rather, CLT is an approach that understands language to be inseparable from individual identity and social behavior. Not only does language define a community; a community, in turn, defines the forms and uses of language. The norms and goals appropriate for learners in a given setting, and the means for attaining these goals, are the concern of those directly involved. The challenge for teacher education is considerable. From the perspective of postmodern critical theory, Kinginger (2000) provides a potentially useful overarching discussion of both theoretical and practical issues in meeting the challenge. Using the notion of "error" in language learning/teaching, Kinginger illustrates how teachers can be helped to develop interpretive skills for evaluating and using competing expert discourses in making decisions concerning their own teaching practice. The development of interpretive and reflective skills offers a very practical and fruitful alternative for language teacher education that currently seems compelled to choose between a single methodological stance or a bewildering smorgasbord of options from which teachers are invited to make their selection.

2) Directly related both to the concept of language as culture in motion and to the multilingual reality in which most of the world population finds itself is the futility of any definition of a native speaker. The term came to prominence in descriptive structural linguistics in the mid 20th century and was adopted by language teaching methodologists to define an ideal for language learners. Currently, sales by British and American presses of profitable publications for learners and teachers of English as a global language are aided by lingering notions that "authentic" use of English somehow requires the involvement of a "native" speaker.

3) One cannot help but be struck by the richness of the data found in many of the texts, including surveys and interviews with teachers. As is true within the social sciences more generally, we are increasingly aware that in our attempts to discern system or rationality, we have been led to focus on certain observable patterns while at the same time disregarding all that defies classification. Just as the implementation of CLT is itself highly contextualized, so, too, are the means of gathering and interpreting data on these implementations. When I shared these and other reports with a group of graduate students in applied linguistics, I was pleased by their response to one text in particular. They liked the account by a Japanese teacher of how she relates the communicative teaching of English to precepts of Zen Buddhism (Kusano Hubbell, 2002). Many found her narrative to be "novel," and "refreshing," For an Argentinean woman it "represented CLT not

only as a theoretical ideal but also as something highly adaptable to the realities of many different settings." She found it annoying that "CLT has primarily been depicted from a Eurocentric or North American point of view" (Savignon, 2002: 210).

4) The influence of language tests on language teaching is overwhelming. Time and again, assessment appears to be the driving force behind curricular innovations. In many settings, demands for accountability along with a positivistic stance that one cannot teach that which cannot be described and measured by a common yardstick continue to influence program content and goals. Irrespective of their own needs or interests, learners prepare for the tests they will be required to pass. High stakes language tests often determine future access to education and opportunity. They may also serve to gauge teaching effectiveness. And yet, tests are seldom able to adequately capture the context embedded collaboration that is the stuff of human communicative activity. A critical reflexive analysis of the impact of tests on language teaching practice, then, would seem a good place to enter into a consideration of how language teaching practices in a given context might be adapted to better meet the communicative needs of the next generation of learners.

6 References

American Council on the Teaching of Foreign Languages (1986). ACTFL proficiency guidelines. Hastings-on Hudson, NY: ACTFL.
American Council on the Teaching of Foreign Languages (1999). *Standards for foreign language learning in the 21st century*. Lawrence, KS: Allen Press.
Bakhtin, M. (1981). *The dialogic imagination*. In Holquist, M. (Ed.). (C. Emerson & M. Holquist, trans.). Austin, Texas: University of Texas Press.
Berns, M. (1990). *Contexts of competence: English language teaching in non-native contexts*. New York: Plenum.
Bhatia, V. (1997). The power and politics of genre. *World Englishes* 16, 369-371.
Brammerts, H. (1996). Language learning in tandem using the Internet. In Warschauer, Mark (Ed.), *Telecollaboration in foreign language learning*. Manoa: Second Language Teaching and Curriculum Center, University of Hawai.
Cameron, D. (1998). Why is language a feminist issue?" In Cameron, D. (Ed.). *The feminist critique of language*. London: Routledge.
Canale, M. & Swain, M. (1980). Theoretical bases of communicative approaches to second language teaching and testing. *Applied Linguistics* 1:1-47.

Cheng. L. (1997). The washback effect of public examination change on classroom teaching: An impact study of the 1996 Hong Kong Certificate of Education in English on the classroom teaching of English in Hong Kong secondary schools. Ph. D. dissertation. The University of Hong Kong.

Crystal, D. (1997). *English as a global language.* Cambridge: Cambridge University Press.

Ellis, R. (1985). *Understanding second language acquisition.* Oxord: Oxford University Press.

Ellis, R. (1997). *SLA research and language teaching.* Oxford: Oxford University Press.

Fairclough, N. (1992). *Discourse and social change.* Cambridge: Polity Press.

Foucault, M. (1981). *The archeology of knowledge.* New York: Pantheon.

Jakobovits, Leon (1970). *Foreign Language Learning: A psycholinguistic analysis of the issues.* Rowley, MA: Newbury House.

Kachru, B. B. (1992). World Englishes: Approaches, issues, and resources. *Language Teaching* 25: 1-14.

Kinginger, C. (2000). Genres of power in language teacher education: Interpreting the 'experts.' In Savignon, S. J. (Ed). *Interpreting communicative language teaching: Contexts and concerns in teacher education.* New Haven: Yale University Press, 193-208.

Kleinsasser, R. C. (1993). A tale of two technical cultures: Foreign language teaching. *Teaching and Teacher Education, 9*: 373-383.

Kusano Hubbell, K. (2002). Zen and the art of English language teaching. In Savignon, S. J. (Ed). *Interpreting communicative language teaching: Contexts and concerns in teacher education.* New Haven: Yale University Press, 82-89.

Lakoff, R. (1975). *Language and woman's place.* New York: Harper & Row

Lowenberg, P. (1992). Testing English as a world language: Issues in Assessing non-native proficiency. In Kachru, Braj. B. (Ed.). *The other tongue: English across cultures*, 2nd edition. Urbana: University of Illinois Press.

Messick, S. (1996). Validity and washback in language testing. *Language Testing* 13: (3).

Morris, P. et al. (1996). Target oriented curriculum evaluation project: Interim report. INSTEP. Hong Kong: The University of Hong Kong Faculty of Education.

Pennycook, A. (1998). *English and the discourses of colonialism.* London: Routledge.

Ellis, R. (2001) *Critical applied linguistics.* New York: Erlbaum.

Quesada-Inces, R. (2001). Washback overrides the curriculum: An exploratory study on the washback effect of a high-stakes standardized test in the Costa Rican EFL High School Context. Ph. D. dissertation. The Pennsylvania State University.

Rushdie, S. (2001) Summer of Solanka. *The New Yorker Magazine*, July 16.

Saphonova, V. (1991). *A sociocultural approach to teaching modern languages.* Moscow: Vysshaya Shkola.

Sato, K. (2000). EFL Teachers in context: Beliefs, practices, and interactions. Ph. D. dissertation. The University of Queensland, Australia.

Savignon, S. J. (1971). A Study of the effect of training in communicative skills as part of a beginning college French course on student attitude and achievement in linguistic and communicative competence. Ph. D. dissertation. University of Illinois, Urbana-Champaign.

Savignon, S. J. (1972). *Communicative Competence: An experiment in foreign language teaching.* Philadelphia: Center for Curriculum Development.

Savignon, S. J. (1983). *Communicative competence: Theory and classroom practice.* Reading, MA: Addison-Wesley.

Savignon, S. J. (1997). *Communicative competence: Theory and classroom practice.* 2nd edition. New York: McGraw Hill.

Savignon, S. J. (Ed.). (2002). *Interpreting communicative language teaching: Contexts and concerns in teacher education.* New Haven: Yale University Press.

Savignon, S. & Sysoyev, P. (In press.) Sociocultural strategies for a dialogue of cultures. *Modern Language Journal.*

Shohamy, E. (1998). Testing methods, testing consequences: Are they ethical? Are they fair? *Language Testing*, 14-15.

Shohamy, E. (2001). *The power of tests: A critical perspective on the uses of language tests.* Harlow, England: Longman.

Smith, P. (1970). *A comparison of the cognitive and audiolingual approaches to foreign language instruction: The Pennsylvania foreign language project.* Philadelphia: Center for Curriculum Development.

Smith, P. & Berger, E. (1968). *An assessment of three foreign language teaching strategies using three language laboratory systems.* Washington, D. C.: U. S. Office of Education.

Stansfield, C. W. (1993). Ethics, standards, and professionalism in language testing. *Issues in Applied Linguistic*s 4 (2) 189-206.

Van Ek, J. (1975). *Systems development in adult language learning: The Threshold level in a European unit credit system for modern language learning by adults.* Strasbourg: Council of Europe.

Van Ek, J. (1976). *The threshold level for modern language learning in schools.* Groningen: Wolters-Noordhoff-Longman.

Van Esch, K. & St. John, O. (2003) *A Framework for Freedom. Learner autonomy in foreign language learning and teaching.* Frankfurt am Main: Peter Lang Verlag.

Wada, M. (Ed.) (1994). *The Course of study for senior high school: Foreign languages* (English version). Tokyo: Kairyudo

Wang, C. (2000). A Sociolinguistic profile of English in Taiwan: Social context and learner needs. Ph. D. dissertation. The Pennsylvania State University.

Wang, C. (2002). Innovative teaching in EFL contexts: The case of Taiwan. In Savignon, S. J. (Ed.) *Interpreting communicative language teaching: Contexts and concerns in teacher education.* New Haven: Yale University Press, 131-154.

Wolff, J. (1994). Ein TANDEM für jede Gelegenheit? Sprachlernen in verschiedenen Begegnungssitutationen. *Die Neueren Sprache, 93*, 374-385.

Yun, M. (1998). *House of the winds.* New York: Interlink Books. Interview on NPR Weekend Edition, Sunday, Nov. 15, 1998

Research Insights and Communicative Language Teaching
Diane Musumeci, University of Illinois at Urbana-Champaign, USA

1 Introduction

Communicative language teaching (CLT) is an instructional approach that developed in response to a perceived need for second language instruction to produce learners with the ability to use the second language in actual communication. It reflects an understanding of language as a means of communication, that is, as primarily social behavior. Because, by definition, CLT recognizes different subcomponents of competencies (Canale and Swain, 1980; Bachman, 1990) that contribute to the whole that is communicative competence, it also entails language acquisition in its broadest sense, as a complex system to which social, psychological, emotional and cultural factors all contribute. As such, this view of language is in contrast to, for example, a more restricted view of language as primarily cognitive behavior, a system composed of a mental lexicon and set of linguistic rules. As Savignon states (this volume), CLT views learners' ability "to interpret, express and negotiate meaning" in the second language as both the process and the product of instruction. In this chapter, I will present some of the empirical evidence that supports tenets of CLT. The discussion will concentrate on second language acquisition research that addresses these three abilities: the interpretation (in section 3), as well as the expression and negotiation (in section 4) of meaning. In doing so, I will present research findings within both psycholinguistic and sociolinguistic paradigms. Finally, in section 5, I will outline new directions in second language acquisition research and their implications for CLT.

2 The Relationship between Language Learning and Language Teaching

Language teaching does not always have as its aim the development of communicative competence. When it does, however, and then fails to meet those expectations, what happens? Learners can be convinced that they are incapable of learning another language (For research on affective factors in second language learning, see Horwitz et al, 1986; Young, 1991; McIntyre & Gardner, 1989; McIntyre &Gardner, 1994; Young, 1999); teachers can blame the book, the method, or themselves (For a discussion of instructional roles and the Atlas Complex, see Lee & VanPatten, 1995); or everyone can simply throw their hands in the air and lament second language teaching in general,

> Camp followers and military attendants, engaged in the kitchen and in other menial occupations, learn a tongue that differs from their own, sometimes two or three, quicker than the children in schools learn Latin only, though children have an abundance of time, and devote all their energies to it. And with what unequal

progress! The former gabble their languages after a few months, while the latter, after fifteen or twenty years, can only put a few sentences into Latin with the aid of grammars and of dictionaries, and cannot do even this without mistakes and hesitation. Such a disgraceful waste of time and of labour must assuredly arise from a faulty method. (Comenius, 1657)

As the date on the quote indicates (and as you may have guessed from the reference to Latin), frustration with the results of conventional language instruction is not a new phenomenon. Language teachers and learners have faced the challenge of acquiring communicative competence in the classroom context for centuries. Some administrators have given up, as evidenced by the recent decision at a well-respected, private U.S. university to eliminate foreign language instruction from its campus curriculum altogether and relegate it to study abroad (Schneider, 2001) or in less dramatic, more subtle ways as institutions rely more and more heavily on private language schools to deliver language instruction, divesting themselves of the responsibility and expense. The majority, however, continue to struggle to meet learners' needs to acquire functional language ability within the academic setting. In light of decades of empirical studies on second language acquisition, perhaps the greatest impetus for communicative language teaching comes from teachers' own experiences in classrooms where, despite their and their students' sustained efforts, little useful language ability ever develops. (For an historical perspective on the relationship between theory and practice in second language teaching, see Musumeci, 1997.)

What *is* the relationship between language learning and CLT? How is it possible that students can spend years in language classes and never attain enough proficiency to meet their communicative needs? What has over thirty years' of research in second language acquisition contributed to our knowledge of what teaching toward communicative competence looks like? Importantly, much of the research that provides insights into the mechanisms of language acquisition itself also supports principles of CLT.

3   The Interpretation of Meaning

A primary source of empirical evidence that sustains the importance of engaging learners in meaningful activity in the second language in order to promote communicative competence comes from the Canadian French immersion context. In early and often-cited studies (Harley & Swain, 1984; Lapkin, 1984; Swain, 1985) researchers reported that students who learned subject matter through the medium of the second language--from teachers who also provided the necessary linguistic and non-linguistic support to make such language accessible--outperformed on every measure students who were taught language in the conventional model. Because the predominantely cognitive focus in early second language acquisition research favored a psycholinguistic perspective--it focused on what was going on in the learner's head as she or he attempted to make meaning from language data—the success of immersion education was viewed in light of learners' exposure to the second language for the purpose of extracting meaning. The notion of 'input,' or more exactly 'comprehensible input' was paramount (Krashen, 1982 and 1985), and many studies and much theory-building were devoted to the examination of the nature of input: its quantity and quality, what makes it comprehensible, how input becomes intake (what the learner extracts from the input to create her internal grammar), etc. Part of the legacy of this research is a full and rich description of teacher talk and the conventions that native speakers use to make their language comprehensible to even the most novice learners (Hatch, 1983; Long, 1983; Wesche & Ready, 1985; Larsen-Freeman & Long, 1991). The focus of attention was the teacher/native speaker and what she or he provided; the learner was the recipient. However, closer investigation of students' language skills, even after years of meaningful exposure to the second language, indicated that comprehensible input is a necessary, but insufficient condition for language acquisition (Long, 1990).

It turns out that, although the students in the Canadian French immersion classrooms were indistinguishable from native speakers on tests of interpretive skills, they were clearly far from native-like on some of the expressive measures, particularly with regard to verb morphology and use of the formal 'you' (Swain, 1985). Lest one conclude that learners' failure to achieve native-like performance on these measures indicate a failure of immersion education, per se, it is important to keep in mind the immersion students' overall fluency, interpretive skills, and significantly superior performance on all measures compared to students who had been taught in the conventional way. The overall picture from immersion education demonstrates convincingly its advantages over conventional instructional practices in producing communicative competence. Indeed, the continued success of immersion education and the research evidence that continues to eschew from it has provided the impetus for numerous content-based language teaching initiatives throughout the world (Krueger & Ryan, 1993; Johnson & Swain, 1997; Snow & Brinton, 1997).

The findings of immersion education research stimulated investigations into the possible sources of learners' gaps in performance, as researchers attempted to discern whether they were attributable to deficiencies in the input (Swain, 1988 & 1993) or a failure to provide a focus on form in communicative classrooms (Lightbown & Spada, 1990). With regard to the former, research demonstrated how impoverished classroom language could be in terms of both the variety of structures (Swain, 1988) and sociolinguistic features (Kasper, 1997) it presents.

With regard to error correction and feedback, researchers made a discovery that has tremendous consequences for language teaching, at least in terms of the acquisition of grammatical forms; namely, that explicit instruction, including error correction, appears to have very limited benefits. Instead, grammatical structures appear to be acquired according to an immutable developmental sequence which route is unaffected by instruction (Ellis, 1985, 1997). These findings explain what reflective teachers have puzzled over for years: namely, that although structures have been taught and perhaps even tested with some success, learners seem to 'forget' them once the focus changes from explicit attention to the structure to spontaneous language use.

4   The Expression and Negotiation of Meaning

Swain (1985), in a seminal discussion of the results of Canadian French immersion education and their consequences for second language acquisition theory, posited that, in addition to comprehensible input, successful language acquisition required also 'comprehensible output' on the part of the learners. Such output, or pushed performance, would force learners to refine their output to make it more closely match native-like models. Accordingly, output lets learners "test hypotheses about the L2, experiment with new structures and forms, and expand and exploit their interlanguage resources" (Pica et al 1989: 64). Although the function of output is couched within a psycholinguistic framework rather than on the role of language use in the acquisition process, the research does highlight the negotiated interaction in the process of learning another language. It shifted the focus of attention from what the teacher/native speaker does with the language to what the learner does with it. Researchers may not all agree on the exact nature of this role—that is, whether negotiation serves simply to provide the learner with additional input or whether engagement in the social interaction itself is the contributing factor--however, even within the psycholinguistic framework, most would confirm that negotiated interaction is fundamental to the process. Meaningful interaction in the second language provides learners with opportunities to test their hypotheses about how the language works. It may also serve to move learners from a system of purely semantic processing into one that demands syntactic processing of the input (Kowal & Swain, 1997). Because much of the data comes from the experimental setting, the amount of negotiation that actually takes place in ordinary classroom interaction is an area for continued investigation (Musumeci, 1996).

Not all of the early research approached the development of communicative competence from a purely psycholinguistic perspective. From the beginning, researchers working within a sociolinguistic framework were concerned with language as social behavior. They looked at learners' use of language as an essential factor in the acquisition process, focusing their attention on the discourse level, rather than on the word or sentence level (Hatch, 1978, 1992). In a landmark study, Savignon (1972) reported that university students learning French as a foreign language who spent just one of five class sessions per week engaged in meaningful, communicative acts outperformed students in the conventional French classes on a test of communicative ability. The result is perhaps not surprising, since one can argue that the conventionally taught group, which studied and practiced grammar, did not participate in real communication. In hindsight, it may even seem logical that students learned what they had practiced. On the contrary, the results of Savignon's study were far from banal; they contradicted the logic of the time; namely, that the study and practice of grammar leads to functional language ability. Instead, the research provided clear evidence for an essential and overlooked component of the curriculum. CLT holds that language is as "a social tool that speakers use to make meaning; speakers communicate about something to someone for some purpose" (Berns, 1990), hence for learners to become competent communicators in the language they must spend time using the language to communicate with others. The study of grammar, even accompanied by extensive practice, in and of itself does not lead to learners being able to use the language for real communicative purposes.

Ultimately, Savignon's study remains foundational in CLT because it illustrates the necessity of including communicative tasks in the curriculum if communicative competence is the desired outcome of instruction. The nature of such tasks, whether they are teacher-fronted or learner-centered, conducted in a whole class setting, in pairs, or in small groups, whether they require one-way or two-way communication and how characteristics of individual learners may affect their performance during the tasks have been and continue to be vital areas of research (Gass & Varonis, 1985; Crookes, 1989; Pica et al, 1989; Young, 1999; Ortega, 1999). Lee (1999) offers descriptions of task-based instruction based on research findings. While the research can provide useful direction for the creation of tasks that generally tend to increase learner production and interaction in the second language, it also reveals the complex interaction of task attributes, the roles and characteristics of the participants, and the organizational structure of the task itself, all of which may affect the outcome of the task, and presumably, of learning (Zuengler, 1989; Zuengler & Bent, 1991; Foster, 1998; Dörnyei, 2002). Moreover, it points out common classroom practices that fail to result in any communicative language use at all (Kinginger, 1990).

5   New Directions in Second Language Research

Earlier, I cited the limited role that instruction plays in second language acquisition. This is not to say that instruction has no effect. Instead, it elucidates the limitations surrounding the role of explicit instruction in grammar for the acquisition of structural features. The precise nature of the contribution that instruction makes in second language acquisition continues to be a source of debate. Some researchers argue that, although the route of development in second language acquisition may be immutable, the rate of that development--that is, how quickly learners move through the developmental sequence--may be amenable to instruction. Current 'focus on form' research investigates what types of intervention may be effective and when (Long, 1991; Doughty & Brown, 1998; Mackey & Phlip, 1998, Spada & Lightbown, 1999; McCollam Wiebe, 2002).

However, the current interest in focus on form, while certainly justifiable and important, continues to address only the linguistic performance of the learners. It affords little attention to language as social behavior, especially with respect to the appropriateness of learners' performance. Furthermore, it continues to rely heavily on a native-speaker norm to measure learners' success. Wong-Fillmore (1992) points out the difficulties in identifying who is a native speaker, citing the varieties of models and relevant expertise that teachers bring to the classroom. In a lucid outline of communicative competence across a variety of contexts, Berns (1990) reminds us of the validity of maintaining diversity in both models for and measures of learners' performance in the communicative curriculum. As sociolinguists remind us, "it is not always necessarily the case that learners wish to become identified as members of the target language group. Thus, they may opt for speech varieties that symbolize such non-membership and diverge in some way from the target community" (Hartford, 1997:98). Indeed, the very notion of a "target community" is problematic, as Savignon (this volume) points out. Within the Canadian French immersion education context, Tarone and Swain (1995) posit the construction of speech communities within the classroom setting itself. From yet another perspective, Kinginger (this volume) reports recent research on varieties of language use and their impact on the learning of French by post-secondary students.

The extent to which a focus on form within a communicative framework can be used effectively with the often widely diverse population of learners that teachers encounter in second language classrooms is an open question. However, explicit instruction in other areas of communicative competence remains ripe for investigation, especially in the area of pragmatics (Billmyer, 1990; Bardovi-Harlig & Hartford (1993). Markee (2000) speaks convincingly to the necessity of including conversation analysis, in addition to experimental--and largely quantitative--studies, as a method of second language acquisition research for the insights that it can contribute to the language learning process, especially with regard to how learners acquire meaning in conversational contexts.

Finally, the recent rediscovery of Vygotsky has led researchers working within a sociocultural framework to posit the primacy of interaction between novice and expert as the initial stage of learning, a stage that prefigures restructuring of the individual's cognitive system (Aljaafreh & Lantolf, 1994; see also Lantolf and Grabois, this volume). Within this framework, Swain and Lapkin (1998, in press) address the role that learners' engagement in socially mediated metalanguage may play in the development of communicative competence. In a follow-up study, Leeser (in progress) investigates the impact that the expertise of the learner has on the process; that is, to what extent does it matter how expert the 'expert' is? Research of this type promises to provide new insights into the role of learners as co-constructors of discourse and the contribution of negotiated interaction in second language acquisition.

6 Conclusion

I began this chapter by defining communicative language teaching in terms of language use; namely, the interpretation, expression, and negotiation of meaning. Whether communicative competence is a reasonable goal of instruction in a particular instructional context is a decision that is made in light of myriad intervening factors, including - but certainly not limited to - instructional resources - both human and material - programmatic and institutional goals and cultural considerations. Where one or more of the components of CLT is not an instructional goal, the principles of communicative language teaching may or may not apply. Likewise, both the choice to teach toward communicative competence and the particular instantiations of an appropriate methodology can only be determined by the participants in that endeavor. Research in second language acquisition, which purpose is to elucidate the mechanisms by which learning occurs, does not dictate classroom practice. In conjunction with local expertise, however, it can contribute to the decision-making process at all levels of the curriculum.

7 References

Aljaafreh, A. & Lantolf, J. P. (1994). Negative feedback as regulation and second language learning in the zone of proximal development. *The Modern Language Journal, 78,* 465-483.
Bachman, L. (1990). *Fundamental considerations in language testing.* Oxford: Oxford University Press.
Bardovi-Harlig, K. & Hartford, B. (1993). Learning the rules of academic talk: A longitudinal study of pragmatic development. *Studies in Second Language Acquisition, 15,* 279-304.
Berns, M. (1990). *Contexts of competence: English language teaching in non-native contexts.* New York: Plenum.
Billmyer, K. (1990). "I really like your lifestyle": ESL learners learning how to compliment. *Penn Working Papers in Educational Linguistics,* 6(2), 31-48.
Canale, M. & Swain, M. (1980). Theoretical bases of communicative approaches to second language teaching and testing. *Applied Linguistics,* 1, 1-47.
Comenius, J. A. (1657). *Didactica magna.* [The great didactic]. In M. W. Keatinge. (Trans., Ed.). (1907). *The great didactic of John Amos Comenius.* Vol. 2. London: Adam and Charles Black.
Crookes, G. (1989). Planning and interlanguage variation. *Studies in Second Language Acquisition, 11,* 367-383.

Dörnyei, Z. (2002) Motivational determinants of the quality and quantity of student performance in communicative language tasks. Paper presented at the Annual Conference of the American Association of Applied Linguistics. Salt Lake City, Utah. April 6.

Doughty, C. & Williams, J. (1998). *Focus on form in classroom second language acquisition.* Cambridge: Cambridge University Press.

Ellis, R. (1985). *Understanding second language acquisition.* Oxford: Oxford University Press.

Ellis, R. (1997). *SLA research and language teaching.* Oxford: Oxford University Press.

Foster, P. (1998). A classroom perspective on the negotiation of meaning. *Applied Linguistics, 19,* 1-23.

Gass, S. & Varonis, E. (1985). Task variation and non-native/non-native negotiation of meaning. In S. Gass and C. Madden. (Eds.). *Input in second language acquisition.* Rowley, MA: Newbury House.

Grabois, H. (this volume)

Harley, B. & Swain, M. (1984). The interlanguage of immersion students and its implications for second language teaching. In A. Davies, C. Criper and A.P. R. Howatt. (Eds.). *Interlanguage.* Edinburgh: Edinburgh University Press.

Hartford, B. (1997). Sociolinguistics in language teacher preparation programs. In K. Bardovi-Harlig and B. Hartford. (Eds.). *Beyond methods: Components of second language teacher education.* New York: McGraw-Hill.

Hatch, E. (1978). Discourse analysis and second language acquisition. In E. Hatch. (Ed.). *Second language acquisition: A book of readings.* Rowley, MA: Newbury House.

Hatch, E. (1992). *Discourse and language education.* Cambridge; Cambridge University Press.

Horwitz, E. K., Horwitz, M. B. & Cope, J. (1986). Foreign language classroom anxiety. *The Modern Language Journal, 70,* 125-132.

Johnson, R. K. & Swain, M. (Eds.) (1997). *Immersion education: International perspectives.* Cambridge: Cambridge University Press.

Kasper, G. (1997). The role of pragmatics in language teacher education. In K. Bardovi-Harlig and B. Hartford. (Eds.). *Beyond methods: Components of second language teacher education.* New York: McGraw-Hill.

Kinginger, C. (1990). *Task variation and classroom learner discourse.* Unpublished doctoral dissertation. University of Illinois at Urbana-Champaign.

Kinginger, C. (this volume)

Kowal, M. & Swain, M. (1997). From semantic to syntactic processing. In R. K. Johnson and M. Swain. (Eds.). *Immersion education: International perspectives.* Cambridge: Cambridge University Press.

Krashen, S. D. (1982). *Principles and practice in second language acquisition.* New York: Pergamon.

Krashen, S. D. (1985). *The Input hypothesis: Issues and implications.* New York: Longman.

Krueger, M. & Ryan, F. (Eds.). (1993). *Language and content: Discipline- and content-based approaches to language study.* Lexington, MA: DC Heath.

Lantolf, J.(this volume)

Lapkin, S. (1984). How well do immersion student speak and write French? *Canadian Modern Language Review, 40, 5,* 576-585.

Larsen-Freeman, D. & Long, M. (1991). *An introduction to second language acquisition research.* London: Longman.

Lee, J. F. (1999). *Tasks and communicating in second language classrooms.* New York: McGraw-Hill.

Lee, J. F. & VanPatten, B. (1995). *Making communicative language teaching happen.* New York: McGraw-Hill.

Leeser, M. (in progress). The relationship between L2 proficiency and metatalk during collaborative tasks in content-based classrooms.

Lightbown, P. & Spada, N. (1990). Focus on form and corrective feedback in communicative language learning. *Studies in second language acquisition, 124(4),* 429-448.

Long, M. (1983). Linguistic and conversational adjustments to non-native speakers. *Studies in second language acquisition, 5,* 177-193.

Long. M. (1990). The least a second language acquisition theory needs to explain. *TESOL Quarterly, 24, 4,* 649-665.

Mackey, A. & Phlip, J. (1998). Conversational interaction and second language development: Recasts, responses, and red herrings? *The Modern Language Journal, 82,* 338-356.

Markee, N. (2000). *Conversation analysis.* Mahwah, NJ: Lawrence Erlbaum.

McCollam Wiebe, K. (2002). Learner readiness versus instructional type in L2 Spanish stage development. Paper presented at the Annual Conference of the American Association of Applied Linguistics. Salt Lake City, Utah. April 7.

McIntyre, P. D. & Gardner, R. C. (1989). Anxiety and second-language learning: Toward a theoretical clarification. *Language Learning, 39,* 251-275.

McIntyre, P. D. & Gardner, R. C. (1994). The subtle effects of language anxiety on cognitive processing in the second language. *Language Learning, 44,* 283-305.

Musumeci, D. (1996). Teacher-learner negotiation in content-based instruction: Communication at cross-purposes? *Applied Linguistics, 17:3.* Oxford: Oxford University Press. 286-325.

Musumeci, D. (1997). *Breaking tradition: An exploration of the historical relationship between theory and practice in second language teaching.* New York: McGraw-Hill.

Ortega, L. (1999). Planning and focus on form in L2 oral performance. *Studies in Second Language Acquisition, 17,* 109-148.

Pica, T., Holliday, L., Lewis, N. & Morgenthaler, L. (1989). Comprehensible output as an outcome of linguistic demands on the learner. *Studies in Second Language Acquisition, 11,* 63-90.

Savignon, S. (1972). *Communicative competence: An experiment in foreign language teaching.* Philadelphia Center for Curriculum Development.

Savignon, S. (this volume)

Schneider, A. (2001). A university plans to promote languages by killing its languages department. *Chronicle of Higher Education.* March 9.

Snow, M. A. & Brinton, D. (Eds.). (1997). *The content-based classroom.* White Plains, NY: Longman.

Spada, N. & Lightbown, P. (1999). Instruction, first language influence, and developmental readiness in second language acquisition. *The Modern Language Journal. 83,* 1-22.

Swain, M. (1985). Communicative competence: Some roles of comprehensible in put and comprehensible output in its development. In S. Gass and C. Madden. (Eds.). *Input in second language acquisition.* Rowley, MA: Newbury House.

Swain, M. (1988). Manipulating and complementing content teaching to maximize second language learning. *TESL Canada Journal, 6,* 68-83.

Swain, M. (1993). The output hypothesis: Just speaking and writing aren't enough. *The Canadian Modern Language Review, 50, 1,* 158-164.

Swain, M. & Lapkin, S. (1998). Interaction and second language learning: Two adolescent French immersion students working together. *The Modern Language Journal, 82,* 320-337.

Swain, M. & Lapkin, S. (2002). Talking it through: Two French immersion learners' response to reformulation. *International Journal of Educational Research*, 37, 3-4, 285-304.

Tarone, E. & Swain, M. (1995). A sociolinguistic perspective on second language use in immersion classrooms. *The Modern Language Journal, 79,* 166-178.

Wesche, M. & Ready, D. (1985). Foreigner talk in the university classroom. In Gass, S. and Madden, C. (Eds.). *Input in second language acquisition.* Rowley, MA: Newbury House.

Wong Fillmore, L. (1992). Learning a language from learners. In Kramsch, C. and McConnell-Ginet, S. (1992). (Eds.) *Text and context: Cross-disciplinary perspectives on language study.* Lexington, MA: DC Heath.

Young, D. J. (1991). Creating a low-anxiety classroom environment: What does the anxiety research suggest? *The Modern Language Journal, 75,* 426-439.

Young, D. J. (1999). (Ed.). *Affect in foreign language and second language learning.* New York: McGraw-Hill.

Zuengler, J. & Bent, B. (1991). Relative knowledge of content domain: An influence on native-non-native conversations. *Applied Linguistics, 12,* 397-415.

Zuengler, J. (1989). Performance variation in NS_NNS interactions: Ethnolinguistic difference or discourse domain? In S. Gass, C. Madden, D. Preston and L. Selinker. (Eds.). *Variation in second language acquisition: Discourse and pragmatics.* Clevedon, England: Multilingual Matters.

Communicative Foreign Language Teaching Through Telecollaboration
Celeste Kinginger, Penn State University, USA

1 Introduction

This chapter explores several of Savignon's components of the communicative curriculum as they relate to foreign language learning through *telecollaboration*. The telecollaborative approach involves the application of global electronic networks to foreign language education (Kramsch and Thorne, 2001; Warschauer, 1996). Internationally dispersed learners use technical communication tools such as email, synchronous chat, threaded discussion or videoconferencing in order to support social interaction, discussion, debate and intercultural exchange. The technology provides unprecedented access to resources and to people, including representatives of the linguistic communities under study, and therefore offers a new level of dynamism and immediacy to pedagogical exchange.

However, the underlying rationale for the approach is not new, but grounded in the history of direct intercultural exchange in language teaching (e.g., Freinet, 1994). Moreover, the approach described here is an outgrowth of perennial concerns within communicative language teaching for authenticity of learning tasks and materials, variety of discourse options, the significance of learners' epistemic roles in the classroom (Nystrand, et al., 1997), and the role of the classroom in fostering language awareness (van Lier, 1996) and learner autonomy (Benson, 2001). The translation of communicative precepts and theories into classroom practice must show how to value the contingent, unpredictable outcomes of interaction between learners and resources (Savignon, 1997; Kinginger, 2002), and how to provide a variety of learning opportunities that include but also transcend the regularities of classroom discourse (Kramsch, 1985).

To appreciate the value for learners of one-time-only, unpredictable and context-specific events, the approach adopts the perspectives on language as culture described by Kramsch (1993). Kramsch encourages the profession to take seriously the models elaborated by researchers in anthropological linguistics and discourse analysis, who attend to the *particular* social contexts of language learning and use. In these models, the "deep structure" of the language is more than a set of universal, abstract grammatical rules. Rather, this "deep" structure is common knowledge informed by a shared history of experience with the same "prior texts" (Becker, 1995). Texts and contexts shared by communities are invoked in particular settings of language use as people negotiate meaning. Kramsch (1993) offers the example of an American Coca-Cola commercial that condensed the archetypal "rags-to-riches" story into a 60-second format. According to Kramsch, the meaning potential of this commercial exists not only in the raw material of word and image, but also (and more significantly) in the history of the target audience's exposure to such stories and the egalitarian values, work ethic, and myths of unlimited upward mobility associated with them. In other words, the meaning of language in use, and even of relatively mundane texts such as a television commercial, is embedded in a relationship of intertextuality linking language use to worldview and specific cultural practices voiced in a whole array of prior texts. In order to attain an integrated language ability, learners must explore both their own prior texts and those of the communities whose language they are studying, developing repertoires of contextually situated language ability via participation in a range of meaningful events.

Several writers (McCarthy and Carter, 1994; van Lier, 1995; Schäffner and Wenden, 1995) have further argued that the educational potential of language study should not be reduced to units of pragmatic language use ability. By encouraging learners to reflect upon the cultural aspects of language use --- its power to highlight certain interpretations of reality, the social organization of its forms --- language teaching becomes "useful" to the degree that it helps people to make the adjustments needed not only for engaging in verbal exchanges with others, but also for understanding them.

Expanding on these notions, Kramsch (1993) has described an experiential approach to learning language as culture, suggesting that in addition to facts about the speech communities under study, learners need access to discovery processes leading to insight about the intersections and interstices between different cultures. Learners can cultivate an understanding of their own positions as observers of another way of life. The search for a "third place" thus focuses both on the culture under study and on the learner's own identity, inviting the learner to adopt an intercultural stance.

> This approach involves dialogue. Through dialogue and the search for each other's understanding, each person tries to see the world through the other's eyes without losing sight of him or herself. The goal is not a balance of opposites, or a moderate pluralism of opinions, but a paradoxical, irreducible confrontation that may change one in the process. (Kramsch, 1993: 231)

Among numerous suggested classroom projects, Kramsch proposes examining parallel texts or translations; role-playing; and performing exercises in self-presentation via writing and selection of images.

In the remaining sections of this chapter, I will offer an account of telecollaborative language learning and its relationship to the principles of communicative language teaching. Section 2 provides general guidance on the design of telecollaborative courses. Section 3, 4, and 5 explore three components of communicative language teaching as they may be realized within telecollaborative approaches: Personal Language Use, Language With a Purpose, and Language Analysis.

2 Course Design: Within and Beyond the Classroom

In course design for telecollaborative language instruction, the most salient aspect is the inclusion of other people, very often a parallel class in a distant locale. In my own ongoing experience since 1992, documented here, the arrangement has involved English speaking classes learning intermediate or advanced level French in the United States, paired with French-speaking classes studying English in France at similar levels (e.g., Kinginger, Gourvès-Hayward, & Simpson, 1999). A key objective is to strive for the creation of "third places" through study and experience of intercultural communication. As separate classes and in inter-class conversations across the Atlantic, students engage in a variety of tasks involving parallel French and American texts.

Course design is guided by several major concerns. First, we try to ensure the presence of an overarching topical agenda within which individual communicative acts are expected to make sense. Topics may be nominated by the instructor or negotiated with the class, but they must be broad and inclusive enough to be reflected in a variety of texts. Secondly, learners are placed in "significant and serious epistemic roles" (Nystrand et al., 1997, p. 72); in addition to acting as "students," they are "authors" of their own texts (Kramsch, A'Ness, & Lam, 2000) and "partners" in exchange with the parallel class. Third, learning is to take place in large part via collaboration and discovery via juxtaposition of parallels as suggested in Kramsch (1993).

In designing telecollaborative courses, several practical issues must be resolved. The most obvious of these are the problems of syllabus synchronization and establishment of parallel levels across different institutions and educational systems. A further issue is the social organization of educational practice in different societies, where the basic descriptions, participation configurations and expected outcomes of courses may vary in unexpected ways (Belz, 2002). One tentative solution is to view appropriation of selected conceptual and communication tools—which are subsequently applied to analytic work on particular texts—as the main business of the course.

In our own case, we have taken conceptual tools from scholarly literature on intercultural communication (e.g., Scollon & Scollon, 2001) and on French/American cultural differences (e.g., Carroll, 1987; Wylie & Brière, 1995). In each course, communication tools have been selected from among the following: 1) email keypal partnerships (analogous to penpal relationships but realized through the use of email) ; 2) whole class email threaded discussions; 3) web publication of student writing and multi-media projects; 4) synchronous Internet Relay Chat; and 5) real-time videoconferencing in whole-class or small group formats.

Typical assignments for telecollaborative courses might include:
- exercises in presentation of self and of local cultural phenomena in the language under study

- analyses of parallel texts, including remakes of films, popular children's books,
- televised talk shows, advice literature, or news coverage of the same phenomenon in both countries
- written or multi-media projects exploring the cultural meaning of core constructs such "individualism," "liberty," or "privacy" (See Furstenberg et al., 2000; also Morgan & Cain, 2000 for description of a project on "law and order")
- inter-class discussion via email, chat, or videoconferencing

In carrying out all of their assignments, students are expected to divide their language use into equal parts of English and French. Every attempt is made to achieve equity in terms of language learning opportunities for the two classes in terms of exposure to their peers' language practice and practice in using the language. The students are also expected to use the conceptual and technical tools at their disposal for an initial approach to their "third place" as critical observers, and on access to the other class for verification or discussion of particular insights. In the following samples, I provide examples drawn from several different telecollaborative courses, to illustrate how the approach relates to the components of a communicative curriculum.

3 Personal Language Use

For Savignon (this volume), an emphasis on personal language use relates to the learner's emerging identity as a second language user, and implies a high level of respect for learners' self-expression in the language under study. Telecollaborative language learning offers an additional dimension to such activity, particularly for foreign language classes in remote locales, in that it directly problematizes addressivity (Morgan & Cain, 2000). In standard classroom arrangements, the range of addressees for student language production is limited to the teacher and fellow students. In a telecollaborative arrangement learners are involved in intercultural dialogue with a peer or group of peers elsewhere, and the interactants' knowledge of everyday cultural environments does not always overlap.

Of particular interest here is that when students describe themselves or their home context, many of their assumptions are truly foreign to their partner class in France or the United States, and the concepts involved do not correspond in any direct way to the vocabulary of French or American English. To further specify the example, let us take the case of an American university-level class from the fall semester of 2000. This class, in their fourth semester of French language study, was paired with a class at a graduate telecommunications school in Brittany. The class decided that their exchange with the French class would be facilitated if they constructed a webpage describing their campus and daily lives, a process involving several stages. First, the students as a whole group decided which phenomena might be of interest, and how to prioritize their selection. Then, they formed smaller working groups to write about these topics, with some students electing to work individually. The composition of the webpages was achieved through "the writing process," (Scott, 1996) a pedagogy that emphasizes continuous attention to both form and content through editing, revision and rewriting. First drafts were subjected to peer review of content and photo layout in class, the second drafts were corrected and commented upon by the instructor and the third drafts were published on the webpage.

One of the American students, Anita[1] elected to publish a page about campus nightlife, and for this she needed to describe the peculiar American campus institution of the "fraternity." Although the French students who would read her page might have some familiarity with the concept through exposure to media coverage of fraternity hazing scandals or perhaps the 1978 film, "Animal House," Anita's task was to describe this phenomenon in French, as the direct request of her email keypal (Example 1):

EXAMPLE 1
Sun, 1 Oct 2000
a propos j aimerais bien que tu m explique un peu ce que c est que les fraternités car ca n existe pas vraiement en france

[*by the way I would really like you to explain a bit about what fraternities are because that doesn't really exist in France*]

Faced with the task of explaining a concept that "doesn't really exist in France," Anita opted not to use the American English word but to offer an elaborate explanation incorporating the voice of her French interlocutor (Example 2):

EXAMPLE 2
Les Fraternités: Pour les gens qui adorent danser, les fraternités sont très populaires. Mais, qu-est-ce qu'une fraternité? Eh bien, c'est un organisme pour les garçons. Ce gens passent la plupart d'un semestre en faisant des choses bizarres avant d'être initiés au groupe (mais ça est une autre histoire, un autre sujet!)

Volià, les fraternités ont l'air de grandes maisons élégantes, mais ne vous trompez pas! Ils ont beaucoup des fêtes chaque week-end pour leurs habitants. Les fêtes sont payées par les fraternités, et quelquefois, ont des thèmes. Tu me demandes, "Comment est-ce que les gens ont des fêtes dans leurs maisons?" Eh bien, les "frères" de la fraternité habitent d'en haut, et les fêtes sont sur au rez-de-chaussée et au sous-sol.

Les fêtes aux fraternités sont un peu comme les discothèques aux grandes villes, je pense, mais plus petites. Ils est toujours nécessaire de faire la queue pour y entrer. Souvent, il est utile de connaître les frères qui gardent la porte parce que quelquefois, seulement les gens qui ont leurs noms sur une liste peuvent aller dedans (c'est vrai!).

*[**Fraternities:** For people who love to dance, the fraternities are very popular. But, what is a fraternity ? Well, it is an organization for boys. These people spend the better part of a semester doing strange things before they are initiated into the group (but that is another story, another subject !)*

Now, the fraternities look like large, elegant houses, but make no mistake ! They have a lot of parties every weekend for their members. The parties are paid for by the fraternities, and sometimes they have themes. You ask me, « How do people have parties in their houses ? » Well, the « brothers » of the fraternity live above, and the parties are on the first floor or in the basement.

Fraternity parties are a little bit like discotheques in big cities, I think, but smaller. You always have to wait in line to get in. Often it is useful to know the brothers who are guarding the door because sometimes only people whose names are on a list can go it (its true !)]

In constructing her webpage, Anita's process of revision involved much more than attending to the accuracy of the language. The construction of the page also became a process of trying on the point of view of French students, discovering cultural phenomena taken for granted, and deciding how to go about presenting a genuine, adequately explicit description of a phenomenon that is meaningful to her in her home context. This kind of personal self-expression, mediated by the presence of a real interlocutor, is a first step toward the discursive flexibility and cultural understanding that are enhanced by participation in dialogue.

4 Language for a Purpose

In commenting on the purpose of language use in the classroom, Savignon (1997) emphasizes the needs of "foreign" language learners, i.e. those who are learning a language outside a wider social context of its use. For such learners, special efforts are required to ensure that opportunities to use the language are available and that such opportunities are valued and taken up by students. In the telecollaborative classroom, the main purpose of inter-class language use is the negotiation of meaning in a broad sense, that is, the exchange of perspectives in an attempt to achieve "intersubjectivity." Here, intersubjectivity does not necessarily mean "agreement" but rather an informed outlook on the variety of positions offered in dialogue and an effort to understand the other's point of view. Such an attempt implies willingness to subject the other's position to scrutiny and to have one's own position similarly scrutinized (Habermas, 1998). In telecollaborative dialogues, students often find themselves positioned by their interlocutors as representative members of national cultures, as illustrated in the exchange below.

This interaction (Example 3) is excerpted from an email exchange in the fall of 1999 between Cathy, an American student enrolled in a fourth-year French course, and her keypal, Jean-Luc, a French student enrolled in an advanced English course at a graduate engineering school in Brittany. The event that triggered the exchange was a question about French objections to the use of hormones in American beef, posed by one of the other American students during a whole-class real-time videoconference. Jean-Luc, writing in English, takes up the position of spokesperson for the French position on this controversy in Turn 1, explaining the role attributed to government intervention in such cases. In her turn (#2), Cathy counters Jean-Luc's position citing a utilitarian argument to the effect that hormones increase production without affecting quality. In response, Jean-Luc appeals to his personal experience of noticing a real difference in quality (Turn #3). Before returning to her position as representative of "la philosophie américaine" in Turn #4, Cathy then shares with Jean-Luc her realization, though conversation with him, that her experience of the problem is different from his. The interaction on this topic closes with a restatement of each point of view:

EXAMPLE 3

1) Jean-Luc: This is really a misunderstanding... We consider that hormoned beef is dangerous for health, and that we should do something against it. Thus (French attitude) we ask the goverment to protect us i.e : to forbid it. In the U.S you would just say :" don't eat it" in France, we think it's the government's job to do this for us...And we can't understand that you block our products, since we do this to protect our health, and you respond to protect your economic interests, in France, this seems completely selfish and immorall

2) Cathy: C'est intéressant. Aux États-Unis, on ne pense pas que l'utilization des hormones dans le boeuf est dangereuse à la santé. Avec les hormones, il y a plus de la viande par vache, mais la qualité de la viande n'est pas inférior.
[*That is interesting. In the United States, we don't think that the use of hormones in beef is dangerous for our health. With hormones, there is more meat per cow, but the quality of the meat is not inferior.*]

3) Jean-Luc: I really do feel the difference between normal and hormoned beef...

4) Cathy: Peut-être je n'ai mangé que le boeuf avec les hormones, donc je ne peux pas dire d'après mon expérience.Et, oui, c'est la philosophie américain que si on n'aime pas un produit, il faut le boycotter; pour nous, si on continue à acheter et à manger ce boeuf, on le trouve acceptable.
[*Maybe I have only eaten beef with hormones, so I can't say according to my experience. And yes, it is the American philosophy that if we don't like a product, we should boycott it; for us, if we continue to buy and to eat this beef we find it acceptable.*]

5) Jean-Luc: and the French one is if it isn't good, it should be forbided, and it's the government's job to do so, with taxes etc...

Interactions of this type offer "broadened discourse options" (Kramsch, 1985) to learners at many levels: freedom to nominate and explore topics, responsibility for the qualities of their own contributions, and opportunities to try on social roles that extend beyond those normally available to "students."

5   Language Analysis

As Savignon's chapter in this volume has emphasized, a communicative language curriculum includes a Language Arts component devoted to analysis of the language and focus on its formal properties. Language analysis is greatly facilitated in telecollaborative courses through the availability of extensive interaction with highly proficient language users and through the resultant availability of corpora representing this proficient language use. An overview of archived email and synchronous chat transcripts reveals that students frequently rely on members of their partner classes for general assistance in coping with issues of grammatical accuracy in self-expression.

Furthermore, in a series of detailed studies examining these data, Kinginger (2000) and Belz and Kinginger (in press)[2] have explored the extent to which peer-to-peer interaction in telecollaboration serves to disambiguate the social meaning of grammatical forms. These studies have focused on the provision of peer assistance to students learning to use the pronouns of address ("tu" v. "vous" in French, "du" vs. "Sie" in German). Example 4, illustrating this phenomenon, is an excerpt from a synchronous chat taking place in March, 2002 via Microsoft NetMeeting. Two American students, Roger and Liz, were interacting with one French student, André. Throughout the 78 turns in the chat thus far, Roger and Liz had addressed André using the formal second-person pronoun, "vous," although André had asked them to use the informal form ("tu") at the outset and had intervened two more times to point out the reasons for this choice. That is, because he was alone and because he was not old ("je ne suis pas vieux!'). In turn #1 of the excerpt, André introduced the topic of appropriate address form for the third time, by asking the American students how *tu* and *vous* had been explained to them. One of the American students then replies with an explanation based on habitual interaction (Turn #2), which André counters with an encouragement to use the informal form and an explanation based on common age (Turns #3 and #4). When Roger and Liz finally comply with his request in Turn #5, André's reaction is clearly one of gratitude and enthusiasm. The students then proceed to discuss the parameters for appropriate pronoun use in the remaining turns.

EXAMPLE 4

1. André:12:45:22 -- que vous a-t-on dit à propos de l'utilisation de "tu" ou de "vous"?
[what did they tell you about the use of "tu" or of "vous"?]

2. Roger Liz:12:45:41 -- je pense que si nous parlons tous le temps, je voudrais utiliser "tu"
[I think that if we talk all the time, I would like to use "tu"]

3. André:12:45:50 -- alors vas-y
[so go ahead]

4. André:12:46:11 -- même des gens que tu ne connais pas, s'ils ont ton âge tutoiyez les
[even people you don't know, if they are your age call them "tu"]

5. Roger Liz:12:46:12 -- comme tu veux;)
[as you(T) wish;)]

6. André:12:46:18 -- cool! Merci
[cool! Thanks]

André:12:46:30 -- c'est d'abord une question d'âge
[first of all it's a question of age]

Roger Liz:12:46:40 -- les gens qui ont le meme age, en general je utilise "tu"
[people who are the same age in general I use "tu"]

Roger Liz:12:46:43 -- a mon avis, oui
[in my opinion, yes]

André:12:46:58 -- entre jeunes, personne ne se vouvoie même si on a 5 ans de différence
[between young people nobody uses "vous" even if there are 5 years of difference]

In tracing the history of individual learners' participation in interactions such as the one excerpted above, we find marked changes in the performance of American students, many of whom demonstrate little awareness of the social indexicality of address at the beginning of the course. These changes occur in the context of explicit assistance from French or German speaking peers provided during electronically mediated interaction, and lead in every case to more consistently appropriate use of these forms.

As demonstrated in Kinginger (1998), the language used by the partner class during telecollaborative exchanges may also serve as an object of analysis in explicit exercises designed to raise learner awareness of contextual features of linguistic variation. In this case, the American students involved were in their third year of university-level French study at a regional state university in the midwestern United States. They had had little exposure to spoken French of any kind before their participation in a whole class videoconference with a class of "educated native speakers" in France. The transcript of the videoconference was used in the first instance to clarify the meaning of the French students' contributions. In subsequent lessons, however, it was also used to explore specific morphosyntactic features of the spoken language used by the French students in order to compare these features with those of the written standard as portrayed in the grammar textbook.

Example 5 illustrates the differences between the spoken French of an educated native speaker participating in a videoconference, and a more standard-like version of the same utterance written according to the grammatical rules in a typical American French-language textbook. This utterance occurred in the context of discussion about child-rearing practices and the various sanctions that might be imposed on children as a result of unacceptable behavior.

EXAMPLE 5
Native Speaker: pas de dessert, t'as jamais eu?
    [*no dessert, did you ever get?*] (Data from Kinginger, 1998)
Standard: N'as-tu jamais été privé de dessert?
    [*Have you never been deprived of dessert?*]

Like many of the French students' contributions to the videoconferences, the utterance in Example 5 serves to illustrate several features of spoken French that deviate from the standard written French normally taught in textbooks (Joseph, 1988). These features include:
- fronting, or "left dislocation" (Barnes, 1990) of the utterance topic, "pas de dessert"
- reduction of the subject pronoun "tu"
- elimination of the negative particle "ne"

- lack of special interrogative word order, preponderance of questions posed by intonation rather than by inversion of the subject and the verb (Valdman, 1992)

According to Lippi-Green, "the inability to use or recognize the social markings of linguistic variants is one of the most significant problems of second language learners, and one that is rarely dealt with in the classroom, where the myth of standard language has a stronghold." (Lippi-Green 1997, p. 30). In the telecollaborative classroom, videoconferences and other communicative events provide rich corpora of authentic language use in a variety of media. Although it is unclear that the language forms used by partner classes should in every case be seen as targets for language acquisition, it is certain that the use of these forms provides classroom learners a glimpse of the real world of language inhabited by users of the language they are studying. One way to handle the availability of "real" language in the classroom is to focus language variety *per se* and to engage learners in active observation and analysis of the corpora at their disposition.

6 Conclusion

The language teaching profession's enthusiastic reception of global networking is fully justified: telecommunications technology offers unprecedented access both to materials and to people who are members of the linguistic communities we study. As the profession becomes increasingly engaged in the design of learning opportunities using these new tools, it is important that the technology be integrated at the service of coherent teaching approaches, and not seen as an end in itself. In the telecollaborative approach as described here, the function of technology is not to organize the classroom, but to enhance the communicative curriculum, that is, to support the activity of people who are learning to understand one another through self-representation, topical dialogue, mutual assistance and analysis of linguistic form. Through their access to each other, students in telecollaborative courses practice the creation of "third places", and learn that the adequacy of their generalizations about language or culture is always *relative*. This process may be pertinent not only to their understanding of French / American intercultural communication, but also to the increasing relevance of critical awareness in all forms of cross-cultural communication.

Note
1. All students mentioned in this chapter have been assigned pseudonyms to protect their privacy.
2. This research is funded by a United States Department of Education International Research and Studies Program Grant (CFDA No.: 84.017A) for which the author is co-principal investigator.

7 References

Barnes, B. (1990). Apports de l'analyse du discours à l'enseignement de la langue. *French Review* 64: 95 – 107.

Becker, A.L. (1995). *Beyond Translation: Essays Toward a Modern Philology.* Ann Arbor: University of Michigan Press.

Belz, J. & Kinginger, C. (In press). The cross-linguistic development of address form use in telecollaborative language learning: Two case studies. *Canadian Modern Language Review.*

Belz, J. (2002). Social dimensions of telecollaborative language study. *Language Learning and Technology* 6 (1): 60 – 81.

Benson, P. (2001). *Teaching and Researching Autonomy in Language Learning.* New York: Pearson Education.

Carroll, R. (1987). *Evidences invisibles: Américains et français au quotidien.* Paris: Editions du Seuil.

Freinet, C. (1994). *Oeuvres pédagogiques.* Paris: Editions du Seuil.

Furstenberg, G., Levet, S., English, K., & Maillet, K. (2001). Giving a virtual voice to the silent language of culture: The CULTURA project. *Language Learning and Technology* 5 (1): 55 – 102.

Habermas, J (1998). *The Inclusion of the Other: Studies in Political Theory.* Cambridge, MA: MIT Press.

Joseph, J. (1988). New French: A pedagogical crisis in the making. *Modern Language Journal* 72: 31 – 36.

Kinginger, C. (1998). Videoconferencing as access to spoken French. *The Modern Language Journal,* 82(4): 502-513.

Kinginger, C. (2000). Learning the pragmatics of solidarity in the networked foreign language classroom. In Hall, J. K and Verplaetse, L. S. (Eds.), *Second and foreign language learning through classroom interaction* (pp. 23-46). Mahwah, NJ: Erlbaum.

Kinginger, C. (2002). Defining the Zone of Proximal Development in U.S. foreign language education. *Applied Linguistics* 22(2).

Kinginger, C., Gourvès-Hayward, A., & Simpson V. (1999). A tele-collaborative course on French-American intercultural communication. *French Review,* 72(5): 853-866.

Kramsch, C. (1985). Classroom interaction and discourse options. *Studies in Second Language Acquisition,* 7(2): 169-183.

Kramsch, C. (1993). *Context and Culture in Language Teaching.* New York: Oxford University Press.

Kramsch, C., A'Ness, F., & Lam, W.S.E. (2000). Authenticity and authorship in the computer-mediated acquisition of literacy. *Language Learning and Technology* 4(2): 78 – 104.

Kramsch, C. & Thorne, S. (2001). Foreign language learning as global communicative practice. In Block, D. & Cameron, D. (Eds.), *Language learning and teaching in the age of globalization.* London: Routledge.

Lippi-Green, R. (1997). *Language with an Accent: Language Ideology and Discrimination in the United States.* New York: Routledge.

McCarthy, M. & Carter, R. (1994). *Language as Discourse: Perspectives for Language Teaching.* New York: Longman.

Morgan, C. & Cain, A. (2000). *Foreign Language and Culture Learning from a Dialogic Perspective.* Buffalo, NY: Multilingual Matters.

Nystrand, M. et al. (1997). *Opening Dialogue: Understanding the Dynamics of Language and Learning in the English Classroom.* New York : Teachers College Press.

Savignon, S. (1997). *Communicative Competence: Theory and Classroom Practice,* Second Edition. Reading, MA: Addison-Wesley.

Schäffner, C. & Wenden, A. L.(1995). *Language and Peace.* Brookfield, VT: Dartmouth Publishing Company.

Scollon, R. & Scollon, S. W. (2001). *Intercultural Communication: A Discourse Approach,* Second Edition. Oxford: Blackledge.

Scott, V. (1996). *Rethinking Foreign Language Writing.* Boston, MA: Heinle and Heinle.

van Lier, L. (1995). *Introducing Language Awareness.* London: Penguin Press.

van Lier, L. (1996). *Interaction in the Language Curriculum: Awareness, Autonomy and Authenticity.* London: Longman.

Valdman, A. (1992). Authenticity, variation, and communication in the foreign language classroom. In C. Kramsch & S. McConnell-Ginet (Eds.), *Text and context: Cross-disciplinary perspectives on language study* (pp. 79-97). Lexington, MA: D.C. Heath.

Warschauer, M. (Ed.) (1996). *Telecollaboration in foreign language learning: Proceedings of the Hawai'i Symposium.* Honolulu, HI: University of Hawai'i, Second Language Teaching and Curriculum Center.

Wylie, L. & Brière, J.-F. (1995). *Les Français,* Second Edition. Englewood Cliffs, NJ: Prentice Hall.

Part III

Intercultural Communicative Competence in Foreign Language Education

Intercultural communicative competence in foreign language education. Integrating theory and practice.
Lies Sercu, Leuven University, Belgium

1 Intercultural communicative competence as a new objective of foreign language education

In current-day foreign language teaching theory, 'communicative competence' is no longer considered as comprising linguistic, sociolinguistic and pragmatic competences only. It is now understood that, in order to communicate successfully in a foreign language in intercultural situations, language users also need intercultural competences (see e.g. Council of Europe, 2001). To make this enlarged understanding clear, the objective of foreign language teaching is now termed 'intercultural communicative competence' (ICC).

The fact that intercultural competence is increasingly considered an important aspect of communicative competence is a relatively new development. At the same time, this evolution builds on previous convictions regarding what non-linguistic knowledge, skills and attitudes language users needed if they were to achieve native speaker competence in a foreign language. For a long time now, foreign language educationists have considered it a natural pedagogical aim to encourage in learners an interest in, knowledge about and an open attitude towards foreign cultures, peoples and countries. The notion of culture was then largely based on the equivalence of one nation-one culture-one language, and on the expectation that a 'culture shock' would take place upon crossing national borders. Familiarising language learners with the society and culture(s) of the community or communities in which a language is spoken, was thought to be beneficial to learners, in the sense that this sociocultural knowledge would help them to blend into the foreign society and not stick out as non-natives to that society. The communicative situation, though in se intercultural, was not looked upon that way. Rather, it was treated as a monocultural situation in which only the culture of the target community was involved. The foreign language learner had to learn to adapt to the foreign culture and learn the foreign customs, conventions, world views, attitudes and values, as well as the sociolinguistic and pragmatic typicalities of communication in the foreign culture, so as not to make cultural mistakes.

Intercultural competence teaching, though building on the above described landeskunde teaching approaches, departs from a quite different perspective on the knowledge, skills and attitudes needed for communication in multilngual and multicultural situations. In intercultural foreign language teaching, all communicative situations are considered as being intercultural. They always involve at least two, and in many cases, more than two, cultures. As Müller puts it, one can say that the presence alone of an interlocutor from a 'foreign' culture (as a coparticipant, not a bystander) determines sufficiently a situation as being intercultural (Müller, 2000a). 'Culture' no longer rests on the equivalence of one nation-one culture-one language. The term 'intercultural' may also refer to communication between people from different ethnic, social, gendered cultures within the boundaries of the same national language. It is used to characterise communication, say, between Italian-Belgians and Turkish-Belgians, between working-class and upper-class people, between gays and heterosexuals, between men and women. What is more, the intercultural nature of the situation cannot simply be described as the sum total of the relevant cultural characteristics of all cultures involved. Rather, intercultural situations are constituted by the coparticipants themselves as they use various components of the given situation for setting common cultural grounds and situating their communicative interaction. For example, when a group of people from Sweden, Belgium, the United States and China meet in New York in order to discuss business arrangements, the various cultural systems involved in this situation may consciously or unconsciously (co)determine the interactional framework. In the given situation, the following cultures could be used as common frames of interaction: the culture of each individual interlocutor ($C1$ = Swedish male (business) culture), $C2$ = Belgian male (business) culture), $C3$ = North-American male (business) culture, $C4$ = Chinese male (business) culture), the cultural domain in which the speakers are currently interacting ($C5$ = North-American mixed (business) culture), the cultural domain of the foreign language being used ($C6$ = probably English in this case and likely to be linked to some often neutrally perceived Anglo-American (business) culture). Any second language classroom, in which students from various cultural backgrounds learn the language of the country where they reside, could be analysed in the same way as described above, though the culture of the country in which the students reside will probably function as the common frame of interaction.

Seen from this intercultural perspective, it can be said that what a foreign language learner needs to learn in order to attain communicative competence is not how to adapt to any one of the foreign cultures present, and forget about his/her own cultural identity. Rather, the task of the participants in such an intercultural situation will be to negotiate, by means of implicit or explicit cues, a situationally adequate system of (inter)cultural standards and linguistic and pragmatic rules of interaction. "In an intercultural situation, coparticipants need to apply metacognitive thinking and master specific, non-face threatening actions to index or to monitor the mutual culture-specific production and reception of linguistic actions and knowledge bases." (Müller, 2000: 295-296). In practice, the grounds of each intercultural situation can be established within the cultural frames mentioned above in the example (C1, C2, C3, C4, C5 or C6). The coparticipants may also constitute a new cultural framework which they create at hoc (C7) and which would include profitable aspects of several cultural domains for the benefit of the group and its members' communicative goals.

In a foreign language education context, Byram and Zarate (1997) have defined an interculturally competent person as someone who can cross borders and can mediate between two or more cultural identities. The 'intercultural speaker' is not a cosmopolitan being who floats over cultures, much like tourists tend to do. Rather, intercultural speakers are committed to turning intercultural encounters into intercultural relationships. They are not satisfied with a view from the outside, with marvelling at differences and at what seems exotic and intriguing about another culture. An intercultural speaker is determined to understand, to gain an inside view of the other person's culture, and at the same time to contribute to the other person's understanding of his/her own culture with an insider's point of view. The intercultural speaker is sensitive to the many respects in which communicative interaction is culture-bound or culture-specific, and knows how to deal with intercultural differences in communication.

2 The acquisition of intercultural communicative competence: What is there to learn?

Though intercultural communicative competence has been demonstrated to be a legitimate goal of foreign language education, it is as yet by no means clear how this objective can best be achieved. In the recent past, quite a number of different instructional approaches have been put forward by language teachers and researchers as approaches favouring the acquisition of ICC. (see for example, Byram & Fleming, 1998; Morgan & Cain, 2000).

These teaching approaches can be broadly classified under three headings, namely (1) approaches that focus on cultural contents and invite learners to relate the foreign culture to their own in an intercultural way (intercultural culture teaching approaches)[1]; (2) culture exploration approaches, which stimulate learners to autonomously investigate particular aspects of the foreign culture, and (3) linguistic awareness of culture approaches, which aim to integrate the teaching

---

[1] It is important to point out here that the traditional culture teaching approaches, in which a body of cultural information is passed on to learners in a monologic way, cannot be labelled 'intercultural'. The main objective of these approaches is to pass on information regarding the countries traditionally associated with the foreign language learned. In the case of English, these countries are the UK and, to a lesser extent, the USA. In the case of German, these countries are the Federal Republic of Germany and, to a far lesser extent, Austria and Switzerland. In the case of French, these countries are France, and to a far lesser extent, Canada or Wallonia (in Belgium). The dimensions of the target culture typically dealt with are, in decreasing order of presence in many foreign language courses: leisure activities in the foreign country, tourist highlights & Culture, geography, transportation and commerce (Sercu, 2000).

of language and culture and to enhance learners' metacognitive awareness of intercultural issues. In actual teaching, many approaches are found which combine aspects of these three types.

To varying degrees these approaches all aim to promote the acquisition of culture-specific, and sometimes culture-general, knowledge, positive attitudes towards cultural diversity and intercultural communication, as well as the acquisition of intercultural communicative skills. In line with developments in educational practice in general, recent approaches place the emphasis firmly on activities and tasks carried out by the learner. They consider the learner, not the teacher, as the key agent in the learning process and aim to promote learner autonomy in culture learning, as in language learning.

A number of attempts have already been made to describe systematically what learners need to acquire in order to become proficient intercultural speakers of a foreign language. Below one conceptual framework in which intercultural communicative competence is broken down into a number of constituents is presented and discussed. The framework was developed by Byram & Zarate (1994) for the Council of Europe and further expanded on by Byram (1997). Like other definitions of ICC (Allen, 1985; Krashnick, 1988, Doyé, 1991), the Council of Europe's definition also makes reference to a knowledge, a skills and an attitude dimension.

The constituents of intercultural competence in this model are referred to as *savoirs*. In French, 'savoir' can refer to both knowledge and skills. These *savoirs* are not to be considered in isolation. They are to be considered as integrated and intertwined with the various dimensions of communicative competence, namely linguistic competence, sociolinguistic competence and discourse competence, which together can be considered a sixth *savoir*, namely *savoir communiquer*. The constituent parts of intercultural competence will be briefly described below. In the next section, two constituents will be elaborated on, namely *savoirs* and *savoir-apprendre*. Consideration will also be given to what implications the new goals of foreign language teaching, namely the acquisition of intercultural communicative competence and learner autonomy, have for the selection of cultural contents *(savoirs)* and culture teaching approaches (*savoir-apprendre*).

The first *savoir*, *savoirs* with a plural 's', can be said to constitute the knowledge dimension of the conceptual framework. It can be circumscribed as 'a system of cultural references which structures the implicit and explicit knowledge of a culture' (Byram & Zarate, 1994). These *savoirs* together constitute the frame of reference of the people living (in) a particular culture. The words and gestures which people use, the behaviours they display, the values they believe in, the symbols they cherish, etc. are always culture-bound and carry meaning within a particular cultural frame of reference.

- *Savoir-apprendre* and *savoir-comprendre* together constitute the learning skills dimension of the conceptual framework. *Savoir-apprendre* refers to "the capacity to learn cultures and assign meaning to cultural phenomena in an independent way". *Savoir-apprendre* is related to *savoir-comprendre*, which refers to the capacity to interpret and relate cultures. These two *savoir*s are clearly in line with the answers that theorists of education have formulated in response to the changing and expanding nature of the world in which people need particular strategies to continue learning throughout their lives. Thus, the terms reflect constructivist theories of autonomous learning, as they have been formulated in, for example, Scardamalia and Bereiter (1991, 1994) or Wood & Wood (1996).

- *Savoir-être* and *savoir-s'engager* are best considered together since they refer to a general disposition that is characterised by "a critical engagement with the foreign culture under consideration and one's own" (*savoir-s'engager*) (Byram, 1997: 54) and "the capacity and willingness to abandon ethnocentric attitudes and perceptions and the ability to establish and maintain a relationship between one's own and the foreign culture (*savoir-être*)".

- *Savoir-faire* refers to the overall ability to integrate the different constituent *savoirs* and act in an interculturally competent way in intercultural contact situations, to take into account the specific cultural identity of one's interlocutor and to act in a respectful and co-operative way.

From the description of the different constituent parts of intercultural competence, it will be clear that the acquisition of intercultural communicative competence involves the development of interlanguage, intercultural competence, and learner autonomy. Since interlanguage development is not in focus in this chapter we will not elaborate on it here, but rather focus on ways to enhance learners chances to develop their intercultural competence as well as their capacity to take control of their culture learning.

Nevertheless, it deserves underlining that many teaching approaches that aim at the acquisition of intercultural competence in a foreign language, except perhaps the linguistic awareness approaches to culture, will need to reconsider the balance between teaching and learning time focusing on interlanguage development and teaching and learning time devoted to interculture development. It will be important to explore more balanced middle-grounds, so as to increase the chances of both interculture and interlanguage development. The approaches taken in foreign language education should in other words become more content- and less language-driven than has hitherto been the case. In language-driven approaches to content-based instruction, language learning is what matters and content is merely a, hopefully motivating, vehicle for language learning (Met, 2000). In intercultural approaches to foreign language education, the cultural contents are to be given primary emphasis at repeated stages in the learning process and teachers and students should be held accountable for content outcomes.

Apart from the need to revise the ratio between focus on language and focus on culture, a second revision urges itself upon us. It concerns the balance between teacher control and learner control over the learning process. The so-called 'information explosion' has both increased the quantity of learning that is expected of students and altered its quality. There is a growing awareness of the educational implications of the rapid obsolescence of task-specific skills and factual (cultural) knowledge leading to an emphasis on transferable learning skills. The successful learner is increasingly seen as a person who can take charge of his own culture-and-language learning and is able to construct knowledge directly from experience of the world, rather than one who responds well to instruction (Benson, 2001: 18-19). In spite of a slight swing towards autonomous learning in foreign language education, teaching tends to have remained confined to the largely teacher-centred passing on of mostly linguistic and some cultural information, and to creating opportunities for practising particular language skills and strategies. Consistent training of learner autonomy never really got off the ground. Learner autonomy was associated with lack of direction, learner laziness, loss of quality and omission of linguistic accuracy work. Learner autonomy was subject to still another misinterpretation, namely that it requires learners to work in isolation from one another (Little, 2000). More adequate conceptions of the construct of 'learner autonomy' and of how it can be achieved have taken away some of the initial distrust. The concept of autonomy has now become part of the mainstream of research and practice within the field of education. In foreign language education approaches that promote learners' autonomous engagement with more naturalistic language settings have been labelled 'task-based approaches' or 'problem-based approaches'. These approaches certainly challenge learners from a linguistic and a communicative point of view. However, from an intercultural competence point of view, the learning potential of the problems that have commonly been selected tends to have been low. The challenge for foreign language education is to develop task-based approaches that also engage learners in intercultural learning processes.

4   Integrating theory and practice

The acquisition of intercultural communicative competence and the promotion of learner autonomy have now been established as legitimate goals of foreign language education. In addition, there is a groundswell of opinion in favour of approaches that value the acquisition of cultural knowledge and culture learning skills as important and valuable outcomes of foreign language education.

In what follows, we want to elaborate on two constituents of the conceptual framework, namely *savoirs* and *savoir-apprendre*. We propose a set of criteria that can be used to select cultural contents and culture learning tasks that will help to implement an approach to the teaching of intercultural communicative competence. In addition, this approach aims at fostering learner autonomy and promoting an adequate understanding of cultures and of the way in which cultures affect our communication and our lives.

The criteria are to be considered as tools, not dogma (cf. Sercu, 2002) They can help course planners and teachers decide on the contents and tasks they select for a particular group of learners. They can also help educators account for the choices they make. In task-based course design accountability is a key term. Educators have to be able to explain why particular elements of knowledge are deemed valuable and others are not, or why particular tasks deserve learner investment of time and energy while others do not.

4.1 The cultural contents (*savoirs*) of foreign language education revisited
Culture-specific and culture-general knowledge

In the contemporary world of international and intercultural (professional) communication, the differences in cultural frameworks between the people involved in the intercultural communicative situation may be considerable. Language education that wants to provide learners with the knowledge, skills and attitudes they will need in this intercultural world should, therefore, by necessity raise learners' awareness of the ways in which culture-specific assumptions may affect communication. On the basis of a needs analysis, it should promote learners' familiarity with the specific cultural frames of reference with which they will most likely interact. Since it will in many cases be difficult to draw up a fixed list of the particular cultures with which learners will interact, foreign language education should also, in an illustrative way, promote learners' familiarity with the different dimensions in which cultures may differ. Thus, at a culture general level, it is important for learners of a foreign language to know in which domains cultural differences may exist and may therefore cause communicative disturbance, irrespective of the specific cultures involved in a particular intercultural situation. The aspects of culture which have been shown to have major influence on intercultural communication are: *(1) Ideology*: history, and world view, which includes beliefs, values, and religion; *(2) socialization*, which includes (a) education, enculturation, acculturation; (b) primary and secondary socialization and (c) theories of the person and of learning; *(3) forms of discourse*, including (a) functions of language: information and relationship; negotiation and ratification; group harmony and individual welfare; (b) non-verbal communication, including kinesics (the movement of our bodies), proxemics (the use of space) and concept of time; *(4) face systems/ social organization*, which includes: (a) kinship, (b) the concept of self; (c) ingroup-outgroup relationships; (d) *Gemeinschaft* and *Gesellschaft* (Scollon & Scollon, 1995: 127-128). Foreign language courses, aiming to promote the acquisition of culture-independent intercultural communicative competence, should include materials that direct learners' attention towards the various cultural dimensions that may cause communication breakdown in intercultural situations.

Learning chances & relevance for learners

Teaching civilisation or 'Landeskunde' has traditionally been about teaching "the truth" about the foreign culture or cultures associated with particular foreign languages. The traditional cultural curriculum covers a body of knowledge addressing a large number of cultural domains. In an attempt to present learners with a representative picture of a particular culture, these topics include: geography, politics, Culture, tourist highlights, education, food & drink, transport, the media, etc. Information is given at the institutional level as well as at the micro-level of daily life (Risager, 1991). Care is taken to present learners with an up-to-date picture.

In these traditional approaches, the point of reference has been the foreign culture(s) usually associated with the foreign language learned, not the learner. However, as Lyotard suggested as early as 1984, the legitimisation of all knowledge included in any curriculum is its performativity for the learner. Therefore, the question one should ask is whether or not this body of knowledge is of any use or interest to a particular learner group. In addition, one should consider whether these learners can relate to and understand the information presented to them. Presenting 13-year-olds, for example, with a survey of a country's political system may not make for much cultural learning since research has shown that these learners are not yet ready for this topic and will surely not be able to compare political systems in a nuanced way (Cain & Briane, 1994).

When selecting cultural contents one should also reflect upon whether these contents will not confirm already existing stereotypes which learners may have (Sercu, 2000). This may be the case when presenting learners with an image of 'strange British food', 'neonazi attacks on immigrant people in Germany' or 'examples of chauvinistic French attitudes'.

One may also ask whether knowing the names of the major rivers in a country or the titles of the main literary masterpieces will help learners acquire the skills and knowledge they need in intercultural contact situations. Cultural information that seems particularly relevant in this respect is what one should be aware of when interacting with someone originating from the foreign culture, so as not to cause feelings of irritation in one's interlocutor or be irritated by the behaviour of one's interlocutor. The cultural contents selected should have the potential of raising the learner's awareness of possible cultural differences and misunderstandings, as well as of the feelings, opinions and attitudes these differences may bring about in people whose intercultural competence is not well-developed. The cultural contents should be both culture specific and culture general. Since it is impossible to predict with which cultures learners will interact in the foreign language they are learning, a large variety of culture specific topics, originating from a variety of different cultures should be included in foreign language courses, so as to promote learners' understanding of the various cultural dimensions with respect to which cultures can differ and which may cause communication breakdown.

This kind of cultural information will typically be linked to differences in interpersonal relationships, body language, visiting conventions, ritual behaviour, etc. These topics do not merely aim at making sure that learners do not make cultural mistakes. The contents are also used to stimulate reflection in learners on their own culture, and on what they consider normal from their own cultural point of view. They will also help learners relate what they consider normal to what is considered normal in the context of another cultural frame of reference. In addition, these topics make it clear to learners that culture matters in language learning, and that using a foreign language always implies that one enters a cultural world that may be different from one's own.

Adequate representation of cultures

The received common-sense view of culture typical of foreign language education to date continues to pass on the conviction that the essence of a particular culture or people can be passed on. In foreign language teaching, cultural contents continue to be presented from a monoperspectival point of view, and culture continues to be conceived as a static, monolithic, idealised, undiversified object of study.

It is surprising that this notion of culture persists to date and has remained largely unexamined in view of developments in critical anthropology, philosophy, literature or cultural studies, which have all criticised reductive, static, monolithic and deterministic views of culture, and have come to use postmodernist concepts of culture (Clifford, 1992; Appadurai, 1996; Atkinson, 1999). These concepts lend expression to the character of current societies, which are non-deterministic, forever changing and fluid. Today's societies are composed of people who are members of many different groups and, therefore, carry many different identities. People do not envisage themselves as simply members of homogeneous, unified cultural groups, as simply the embodiments of a particular culture's rules, conventions, behaviours, norms and values. Yet and at the same time, they cannot deny that they are always members of particular social or cultural groups, and as such receive 'guidance' on how to behave and what to believe (see e.g. Bourdieu *et al.*, 1998). This membership does, however, not deprive them of the right to be different and depart from the norm, and in that way to a certain extent affect the rules of the groups to which they feel they belong.

With a view to developing intercultural competence in learners, it is essential that foreign language education uses a concept of culture that adequately reflects the character of the world in which learners are living. Therefore, it is imperative to make it clear to learners that other cultures, like their own, are anything but homogeneous, all-encompassing entities. It is important to unveil the fissures, inequalities, disagreements, cross-cutting influences, as well as the agreements and elements of stability that exist in and around all cultures. "The acknowledgement and acceptance of multiple, complex cultural identities (....) should be a first principle of ESL teaching and teacher preparation." (Atkinson, 1999: 644).

One way to ensure that learners gain an adequate view of their own and of other cultures is to complement the hitherto commonly chosen outsider approach to the presentation of foreign cultures with an insider approach. An insider approach goes beyond presenting one perspective on a particular aspect of the foreign culture. It investigates different understandings which members of that culture may have of, for example, particular political or ethical issues, or the different attitudes they may hold towards particular values, institutions, behaviours or symbols.

Presenting learners with multiple perspectives will promote a dynamic view of cultures, and help learners understand that all cultures are continuously influenced by other cultures and cannot be considered in a territorialised way, as being bound to a particular geographical part of the world or as locked within the boundaries of a particular nation state.

Presenting cultures as unbounded and as related to other cultures may also bring power relationships that exist within and between cultures more to the forefront. Pratt (1991), for example, coined the term *contact zones* to describe "the social spaces where cultures meet, clash, and grapple with each other, often in highly asymmetrical relations of power, such as colonialism, slavery, or their aftermaths as they are lived out in many parts of the world today" (Pratt, 1991: 34). Culture teaching has until now chosen not to touch upon existing power relationships. The responsibility of foreign language teachers to develop awareness in learners of the political implications of cultural relationships is a politically and ethically contested issue. An adequate presentation of cultures cannot, however, pass over such historical and present-day relationships.

4.2 Culture teaching in foreign language education revisited

Important though an adequate selection of cultural contents in foreign language education may be, it will not suffice to enhance learners' acquisition of a cultural knowledge base or their autonomous handling of constantly changing intercultural situations. In addition to acquiring a culture-specific and a culture-general knowledge base, learners also need to become autonomous learners and users of cultural *savoirs*.

Scaffolding learning while respecting the characteristics of developmental processes

Throughout the history of foreign language teaching authors have tried to design exercise typologies that could meaningfully integrate a variety of exercise types and adequately scaffold the learning process. Taking into account insights from educational psychology, developmental psychology and, in the case of foreign language learning, linguistics, exercise typologies attempt to grade language learning. They organise different exercise types into a systematic whole that holds the promise of grading the learning process in such a way that steady progress can be made towards the goals of learner autonomy and the acquisition of a high level of knowledge, skill and competence (Sercu, 2000).

The educational concepts that have been particularly important in this respect are those of 'meaningful learning' (Ausubel *et al.*, 1978) and 'levels of processing' (Craik & Lockhart, 1972), as well as taxonomies of cognitive objectives (De Corte *et al.*, 1981). Respecting the characteristics of developmental processes in intercultural course design requires that all culture practice activities are chosen in such a way that they are meaningfully related to learners' knowledge about the particular culture in focus and their general understanding of cultures, as well as to their autonomous culture learning skills and their overall level of intercultural communicative competence. Observing the hierarchical principles underlying De Corte's taxonomy of cognitive objectives demands that course developers try to encourage deep levels of involvement with the cultural savoirs offered, and strive for an increase in the complexity of cognitive operations and in the degree of independence learners show when processing information.

Despite the fact that a number of exercise typologies observing the above mentioned principles have been developed in a foreign language teaching context (e.g., Neuner *et. al.*, 1985), foreign language textbooks to date seem to include mostly culture learning tasks that can be classified as apperception and reproduction tasks, requiring only low levels of involvement with the cultural contents offered (Sercu, 2000a). It seems that what textbook writers have been doing is throw chunks of culture at learners, have them read some texts that deal with cultural topics, and hope that this cultural foot-bath will eventually have a positive effect on pupils' mind sets, and turn them into open-minded and tolerant citizens. The learning tasks in textbooks tend not to invite pupils to process, apply or reflect on any previously acquired information regarding the target culture and people. Pupils are not normally expected to compare cultures, empathise with the points of views of other people, or practise critical culture learning skills. Most tasks are individual learning tasks: learners acquire information alone. They do not work together to construct additional knowledge. Constructivist tasks in which learners construct knowledge themselves, explore cultures, take multiple perspectives on a cultural issue, are rare. The approach to culture teaching is non-recursive. Cultural contents are offered on one occasion only. The learner is not invited to reorganise or reconsider prior knowledge in the light of new information, nor to identify traces of prior texts and events as they appear in new contexts.

Promoting learner autonomy

The concept of 'learner autonomy' has now become part of the mainstream of discussions in education. Benson (2001) distinguishes three interdependent levels at which learners may exercise control over learning: the level of learning management, the level of control over cognitive processes and the level of control of learning content. Management of one's own learning, the first level of control involved in the acquisition of learner autonomy, entails efficient planning, monitoring and evaluation of one's learning path (Wenden, 1995). Control over cognitive processes is understood as a matter of the psychology of learning. It is concerned with particular mental processes associated with the idea of control. Good autonomous learners are able to direct their attention efficiently towards learning goals and learning contents, to exercise reflection on their learning in efficient ways and to apply metacognitive knowledge in ways which are beneficial to the advancement of their learning. The third level of control, the control over learning content is a question of knowing what one wants to learn, or knowing what has to be learned in order to interpret and convey meanings that are uniquely one's own. Control over the content of learning necessarily involves learners in social interactions regarding the right to determine and achieve their own learning goals. These interactions may take place with other learners in the collective negotiation of learning goals and tasks, or with teachers and higher authorities in the negotiation of the curriculum.

Implementing this three-tier framework in foreign language education implies that learners are confronted with tasks and activities that help them acquire the learning skills they need to become increasingly autonomous and competent intercultural speakers of the foreign language. Learners may already have acquired particular managerial skills and cognitive and meta-cognitive strategies in the context of learning one or more foreign languages, or in the course of their learning careers. Nevertheless, course developers should try to design tasks that make explicit to learners what culture learning and the acquisition of intercultural competence involve.

In the context of the acquisition of intercultural competence, exercising control over the contents of one's learning implies that learners know in which respects cultures may differ and can affect intercultural communication. The tasks set in foreign language classrooms should familiarise learners with these cultural dimensions, and also urge them to reflect on and make explicit what cultural information they think they will need to acquire, as well as how they are going to go about acquiring that cultural background knowledge. Tasks should refrain from setting cultural topics to be explored. Rather they should invite learners to reflect on their existing beliefs, make them explicit, and help them consider whether these beliefs are justified or need adjustment. If adjustment is needed, teachers and tasks should help learners decide on the topics they want to explore and on how to go about exploring them. Teachers may ask students to write a reflective diary in which students enter comments regarding the cultural information they have encountered, their interpretation of that information, the strategies they have used to acquire additional information regarding a particular aspect of a foreign culture, etc. Thus, teachers assist learners to transcend the perimeters of the textbook and the classroom in order to investigate cultural manifestations in a real-life environment. They may confront learners with alternative views and reflect together with learners on the appropriateness of revising and expanding existing knowledge or current culture learning strategies.

The tasks set should also make it clear to learners what planning, monitoring and evaluating one's progress in the area of intercultural communicative competence involves. It should be clear to learners what knowing a culture involves and how one can go about acquiring cultural knowledge. Tasks should help learners discover what demands are inherent in culture learning tasks, what steps can be taken to perform a cultural task, what criteria can be used to assess the outcomes of one's culture learning activities.

Teachers who want to help their learners develop independent self-regulated strategies should be able to choose from a range of scaffolding approaches. These may take the form of modelling and explaining approaches to solving intercultural problems or answering intercultural questions. They may discuss with students which sources they will need to arrive at a balanced and multiperspectival picture of a particular cultural phenomenon, and how they can critically evaluate the information provided by these different sources. They may prompt students to evaluate different culture learning strategies or to brainstorm different solutions to cultural problems.

In summary, in order to promote autonomy in the acquisition of intercultural competence it will be important to encourage reflection on culture, beliefs about culture and about the culture learning process at repeated times. Reflection should be directed both towards the contents of learning as towards the culture learning process itself. Conscious reflection on learning experiences and the sharing of such reflections with other learners in cooperative groups makes it possible to increase one's awareness of culture learning as well as one's autonomy as a learner.

5. Conclusion

The intercultural turn in foreign language education is about more than simply continuing to teach communicative competence and, in addition, passing on an extensive body of information about the foreign culture(s) which tend(s) to be associated with the foreign language one is teaching. The acquisition of intercultural communicative competence, of course, requires that one increases one's familiarity with foreign cultures, with one's own culture and with the relationships between cultures. In addition, it implies that one acquires the competence to learn cultures autonomously. Putting culture at the core of language education means preparing students to be culture learners.

We hope to have made it clear why current societal developments compel us to move away from a teacher-led language-and-culture pedagogy to a student-centred learner autonomy approach. We also hope to have demonstrated what criteria can be observed when revising curricula and developing language-and-culture courses aimed at the development of intercultural communicative competence and learner autonomy. We have tried to explain why both the cultural contents and the culture teaching approaches of hitherto used language-and-culture courses deserve serious scrutiny.

It is our conviction that, in the multicultural international world in which we live, foreign language competence will gain in importance. Therefore, the teaching of communicative competence must be continued at the same high level as it is done now. It is however also high time that language educators realise that speaking a foreign language always means entering a cultural world that may to a lesser or a larger extent be different from one's own. Therefore, all language education should always also be intercultural education.

6. References

Allen, W.W. (1985) Toward cultural proficiency. In: A.C. Omaggio (Ed.) *Proficiency, Curriculum, Articulation: The Ties That Bind*. Middlebury (VT): Northeast Conference, 137-166.

Appudurai, A. (1996) *Modernity at Large: Cultural Dimensions of Globalization*. Minneapolis: University of Minnesota Press.

Atkinson, D. (1999) TESOL and culture. *TESOL Quarterly* 33, 4: 625-54.

Ausubel, D., Novak, J. & Hanesian, H. (1978) *Educational Psychology: A Cognitive View*. New York: Holt, Rinehart & Winston.

Benson, P. (2001) *Autonomy in Language Learning*. Harlow: Pearson Education.

Bourdieu, P., Passeron, J.C., Nice, R. & Bottomore, T. (1998) *Reproduction in Education, Society and Culture*. London: Sage.

Byram, M. (1997) *Teaching and Assessing Intercultural Communicative Competence*. Clevedon: Multilingual Matters.

Byram, M. & Fleming, M. (Eds.) (1998) *Language Learning in Intercultural Perspective.* Cambridge: Cambridge University Press.

Byram, M. & Zarate, G. (1994) *Definitions, Objectives, and Evaluation of Cultural Competence.* Strasbourg: Council of Europe.

Byram, M. & Zarate, G. (1997) *The Sociocultural and Intercultural Dimension of Language Learning and Teaching.* Strasbourg: Council of Europe.

Cain, A. & Briane, C. (1994) *Comment collégiens et lycéens voient les pays dont ils apprennent la langue. Représentations et stéréotypes.* Paris: Institut National de Recherche Pédagogique.

Clifford, J. (1992) Traveling cultures. In C. Grossberg, C. Nelson & P. Triechler (Eds.) *Cultural Studies.* New York: Routledge, pp. 96-116.

Council of Europe, Council for Cultural Co-operation. Education Committee. Modern Languages Division (2001) *Common European Framework of Reference for Languages: Learning, Teaching, Assessment.* Cambridge: Cambridge University Press.

Craik, F.I. & Lockhart, R.S. (1972) Levels of processing: A framework for memory research. *Journal of Verbal Learning and Verbal Behavior* 11, 671-84.

De Corte, E. & Geerligs, C.T. & Lagerweij, N.A.J. (1981) *Beknopte didaxologie. (Concise didaxology).* 5th revised edition. Leuven: Leuven University Press.

Doyé, P. (1991) Erziehung zur internationalen Verständigung als Aufgabe des Fremdsprachenunterrichts. Ein Beitrag zur politischen Bildung. In P. Doyé (Hrsg.) *Großbritannien. Seine Darstellung in deutschen Schulbüchern für den Englischunterricht.* Frankfurt/Main: Diesterweg & Georg-Eckert-Institut für Internationale Schulbuchforschung, 11-20.

Krashnick, H. (1988). Dimensions of cultural competence: Implications for the ESL curriculum. *TESL Reporter* 21(3): 49-55.

Little, D. (2000) Autonomy and autonomous learning. In: M. Byram (Ed.) *Routledge Encyclopedia of Language and Culture.* London: Routledge, 69-72.

Met, M. (2000) Content-based instruction. In: M. Byram (Ed.) *Routledge Encyclopedia of Language and Culture.* London: Routledge, 137-140.

Morgan, C. & Cain, A. (2000) *Foreign Language and Culture Learning from a Dialogic Perspective.* Clevedon: Multilingual Matters.

Müller, B. (2000) Intercultural Communication. In: M. Byram (Ed.) *Routledge Encyclopedia of Language and Culture.* London: Routledge, 295-297.

Müller, B. (2000a) Interkulturelle Didaktik. In: M. Byram (Ed.) *Routledge Encyclopedia of Language and Culture.* London: Routledge, 303-307.

Neuner, G. & Krüger, M. & Grewer, U. (1985) *Übungstypologie zum kommunikativen Deutschunterricht.* Berlin: Langenscheidt.

Pratt, M.L. (1991) Arts of the contact zone. *Profession* 91: 33-40.

Risager, K. (1991) Cultural studies and foreign language teaching after World War II: The international debate as received in the Scandinavian countries. In D. Buttjes & M. Byram (eds) *Mediating Languages and Cultures: Towards an Intercultural Theory of Foreign Language Education.* Clevedon: Multilingual Matters, 33-46.

Scardamalia, M. & Bereiter, C. (1991) Higher levels of agency for children in knowledge building: A challenge for the design of new knowledge media. *Journal of the Learning Sciences* 1, 1: 37-68.

Scardamalia, M. & Bereiter, C. (1994) Computer support for knowledge building communities. *Journal of the Learning Sciences* 3, 3: 265-83.

Scollon, R. & Scollon, S. (1995) *Intercultural Communication.* Oxford UK & Cambridge USA: Blackwell.

Sercu, L. (2000) *Acquiring Intercultural Communicative Competence from Textbooks. The Case of Flemish Adolescent Pupils Learning German.* Leuven: Leuven University Press.

Sercu, L. (2000a) Exercise types and grading. In M. Byram (ed) *Routledge Encyclopedia of Foreign Language Teaching and Learning.* London: Routledge, 214-6.

Sercu, L. (2002) Autonomous learning and the acquisition of intercultural communicative competence. Some implications for course development. *Language Culture and Curriculum*, 15 (1): 61-74.

Wenden, A. (1995) Learner training in context: A knowledge-based approach. *System* 23(2), 183-194.

Wood, D. & Wood, H. (1996) Vygotsky, Tutoring and Learning. *Oxford Review of Education*, 22(1), 5-10.

Researching the acquisition of intercultural communicative competence in a foreign language. Setting the agenda for a research area.

Lies Sercu, Leuven University, Belgium

1 Introduction

This chapter provides an overview of the research literature pertaining to the acquisition of intercultural competence in foreign language education, and sets the agenda for future research. It is organised into 3 sections pertaining to the main areas of research in the field. In the first section we examine work that has been done to develop the theoretical foundations of the field of intercultural competence teaching in foreign language education. Two main strands of research will be elaborated. The first strand concerns research which has revealed the many ways in which language and culture are entwined. The second strand concerns work that has contributed to a more adequate definition of 'intercultural experience' and 'the intercultural person'. The second section shifts the chapter's attention from theoretical to applied research. It discusses some approaches that have been developed to teaching intercultural communicative competence (ICC) as well as the basic premises on which they rest. In the third section, we direct our attention towards empirical research regarding culture-and-language teaching-and-learning. We organise our review on the basis of a number of variables that appear to affect the acquisition of intercultural communicative competence in an instructional setting, namely the setting, the teacher, the learner, the learning materials and assessment.

2 Theoretical research: Conceptual developments

This section examines a number of concepts central to the understanding of intercultural communicative competence. First, it documents some major developments with respect to the way in which language educationists have viewed 'culture' over the years. Next, it focuses on the insights provided by research of intercultural communication regarding the many levels at which language and culture are integrated. Finally, it presents work that has focused on developing the notions of 'intercultural competence', 'intercultural experience' and 'the intercultural speaker'. All conceptual shifts described in this section have led to important shifts in the definition of the objectives and the contents of foreign language education.

Views of culture in foreign language education

An important body of theoretical writings in the area of culture-and-language teaching has been concerned with the definition of 'culture'. The way in which culture has been viewed in foreign language education has changed over the years. Earlier models (Nostrand, 1974; Brooks, 1975) tended to view culture as a relatively unvarying and static entity made up of accumulated, classifiable, observable, thus eminently teachable and learnable "facts". This perspective focused on small 'c' and/or big 'C' culture. Such a received common-sense view of culture reflected the conviction that the truth regarding the essence of a particular culture or people can be passed on.

The more recent models see culture as dynamic and variable. They look at the underlying value orientations and shared meanings (Taylor, 1971) which underpin a social group's behaviours and the "social representations" (Farr and Moscovici, 1984) its members have in common. These models recognise the variability of behaviour within the target cultural community, the participative role of the individual in the creation of culture, or the interaction of language and culture in the making of meaning (Moore, 1991; Atkinson, 1999). This major transformation in perspective has also been mirrored in conceptual shifts, from culture-specific to culture-general models of intercultural competence, from cultural absolutes to cultural variations (within and across cultures), and from culture as distinct from language to culture as integral to language.

Views regarding the integration of language and culture

By its very nature, foreign language teaching is predicated on the conviction that because we are all humans, we can easily understand each other provided we share the same code; all we have to do is learn that code and use it accurately and appropriately. In foreign language education, this belief has been most fruitful in promoting functional and pragmatic approaches to the teaching and learning of foreign languages around the world. From this perspective, culture is often seen as mere information conveyed by the language, not as a feature of language itself; cultural awareness becomes an educational objective in itself, separate from language.

During recent years, several researchers have furthered our thinking about the relation of language and culture in language teaching (see e.g. Blum-Kulka *et al.* 1989). Although there is no one-to-one relationship between anyone's language and his or her cultural identity, language is *the* most sensitive indicator of the relationship between individuals or between an individual and a given social group (Kramsch, 1998). Language users bring to any verbal encounter blueprints for action that have developed through their socialisation or acculturation in a given society. From childhood on they have learned to realise certain speech acts, such as thanking, greeting or complimenting, in a culturally appropriate manner, like saying 'thank you' in response to receiving gifts, and 'goodbye' as a way of closing encounters. They have also learned to use different registers and speak differently to people of different ranks. Language users have not only learned to interpret signs and to act upon them; they have also learned to expect certain behaviours of others as well. They have learned to take on various institutional and interactional roles and to act them out, also linguistically, in accordance with what is considered appropriate behaviour within their culture. They have come to master the conversational styles typical of their culture. They know what prosodic patterns (intonation and timing) to use, what topics are taboo in social conversation and what opening topics to select from. They have acquired the meanings of words in accordance with the particular world views taken by their discourse community. They know what to believe in, what values to live by, what goals to strive for in life, how to move their bodies, how to perceive themselves in relation to their parents or grandparents, how to deal with time, how to respect people's privacy, etc.

This enumeration shows that cultural differences may not only manifest themselves at the sociolinguistic or pragmatic levels of communicative competence - where they might be most obvious. They may also show at the lexical, grammatical or phonological levels of the language. A number of reference schemes have been developed which provide an overview of the levels at which language and culture are integrated (Müller, 1995; Scollon & Scollon, 1995). They are the result of research into intercultural communicative situations. This research is referred to as discourse analysis of communicative events, where people from different cultural backgrounds engage in face-to-face communication. The current focus is on how people handle differences in linguistic behaviour and its various effects. The analyses result in descriptions of culturally specific ways of expressing and interpreting the situated linguistic action of the coparticipants. These schemes mention the lexicon (including culture-specific meanings, prototypes, culture-specific interrelations and their interpretations by different coparticipants); speech acts (culture-related preferences in form, condition, sequence, frequency and distribution); discourse conventions (conversation patterns, including the length of opening/concluding remarks, use of argument/ counter-argument, routines of turn-taking related to the situational context); topics (different rules for the choice of topics and recognition of taboo); register (different functional varieties of speech, expressing interpersonal relations depending on the situation itself, the status, age, rank, or gender of the coparticipants); para-verbal phenomena (interpretation of prosody, rhythm, volume, pauses); non-verbal expressions (facial expressions, gestures, proxemics, eye contact); communicative style (direct/indirect realisation of speech acts; degree of explicitness in speaking; relationships of verbal and non-verbal expression; rules of interruption, simultaneous talk, self portrayal); culture-specific actions (including rituals) and action sequences (stereotyped interpretation of actions like the wine-tasting procedure before a toast, the emitting of laryngeal sound after taking a swig of beer, or other 'strange' forms of expressing courtesy or religion (Knapp & Knapp-Potthoff, 1990).

Views of intercultural competence: the intercultural person coping with intercultural experiences

The previous paragraphs have focused on defining culture and culture in language. In that sense they have been concerned with the knowledge that learners have to acquire in order to become interculturally competent persons. This section defines the nature of intercultural experiences and examines what characteristics a person needs to be able to cope with intercultural experiences. These insights, stemming mainly from psychologists and sociologists, have affected the way in which intercultural competence has been defined in foreign language education.

Intercultural experience

In literature on the subject, the intercultural experience is described as an uncomfortable one, requiring the revision of beliefs, concepts and attitudes that one has hitherto taken for granted. The process includes changes in attitudes, beliefs, identity and values (Berry *et al.*, 1992). It requires people to revise their social identity, to reconsider the ideas they have held about out-groups, to reconsider their position towards the outgroup, since they have now themselves become members of the outgroup. One is required to revise what one has acquired in the course of socialisation (Berger & Luckmann, 1971) into one's own culture. The range of feelings experienced varies from anger and anxiety to excitement and relief. The emotions come from many sources: fear of encountering something new, excitement at the discovery of new and different ways of thinking, relief through self-expression, anger that a deeply held belief may have been challenged. The common factor is the element of surprise which is the cornerstone of the intercultural experience. There are those who may respond with envy or embarrassment, others with pleasure and appreciation. One of the consequences of intercultural experiences may be that individuals retrench themselves in their pre-exposure beliefs and resist attempts to look at their own cultural systems from the point of view of the 'other'. They may experience a high level of what is called acculturative stress, and experience feelings of marginality and alienation, identity confusion and heightened psychosomatic symptom levels, high levels of anxiety and depression. (Sen Gupta, forthcoming)

The intercultural person

Being able to cope with intercultural experiences and intercultural stress requires that a person possesses a number of intercultural competencies and characteristics. These characteristics and competencies have been identified as the willingness to engage with the foreign culture, self-awareness and the ability to look upon oneself from the outside, the ability to see the world through the others' eyes, the ability to cope with uncertainty, the ability to act as a cultural mediator, the ability to evaluate others' points of views, the ability to consciously use culture learning skills and to read the cultural context, the understanding that individuals cannot be reduced to their collective identities. (Sen Gupta, forthcoming; Alred, forthcoming)

Intercultural competence

Evolutions in foreign language education of the views of intercultural competence reflect the above insights regarding the nature of intercultural experiences and the competencies needed to cope with them. The learning goals have shifted from the memorisation of cultural facts (including sociolinguistic conventions for language use) to higher order learning outcomes including: the acquisition of interactional competence and to learning how to learn about culture. Recent conceptual models of the learning of intercultural competence distinguish between knowledge, competencies and skills, and attitudes, i.e. the cognitive, behavioural and affective domains of learning. This is a distinction based on the pioneering work of psychologists such as Bloom (1964) and interculturalists (see Damen, 1987, for a extensive review of culture learning models). It is a conceptual perspective finding increased recognition among foreign language educators (Seelye,1994; Buttjes & Byram, 1991; Byram & Morgan, 1994; Byram & Zarate, 1997). Recent models also increasingly make the distinction between culture-specific and culture-general knowledge and skills. Culture-specific learning refers to the acquisition of knowledge and skills relevant to a given "target culture", i.e. a particular group or community. Culture-general knowledge and skills, on the other hand, refer to knowledge that is more generalizable in nature and transferable across cultures. This body of knowledge includes, among other things, the concept of culture, the nature of cultural adjustment and learning, the impact of culture on communication and interaction between individuals or groups, the stress associated with intense culture and language immersion (culture and language fatigue), strategies for coping with stress, the role of emotions in cross-cultural, cross-linguistic interactions, and so forth. Culture-general skills include the capacity to display respect for and interest in the culture, the ability to be a self-sustaining culture learner and to draw on a variety of resources for that learning, tolerance and patience in cross-cultural situations, control of emotions and emotional resilience, and the like (Lustig & Koester, 1996, Kelley & Myers, 1995).

3   Applied research: The development of teaching approaches

In the recent past quite a number of different instructional approaches have been put forward by language teachers and researchers as approaches favouring the acquisition of ICC. (see for example, Roberts, 1995; Byram & Fleming, 1998; Davcheva & Docheva, 1998; Morgan & Cain, 2000; Byram, Nichols & Stevens, 2001). These teaching approaches can be broadly classified under three headings, namely (1) approaches that focus on cultural contents and invite learners to relate the foreign culture to their own in an intercultural way (intercultural culture teaching approaches); (2) culture exploration approaches, which stimulate learners to autonomously investigate particular aspects of the foreign culture, and (3) linguistic awareness of culture approaches, which aim to integrate the teaching of language and culture and to enhance learners' metacognitive awareness of intercultural issues. In actual teaching, many approaches are found which combine aspects of these three types.

(1)   Approaches that focus on cultural contents

Risager (1998) distinguishes between 'the foreign cultural approach', 'the intercultural approach', 'the multicultural approach' and 'the transcultural approach', and considers these approaches in a chronological perspective. Though these approaches all focus primarily on the acquisition of cultural knowledge, and not on the acquisition of culture learning skills or intercultural interactional competence, they don't do so in exactly the same way, departing from different concepts of culture and language. According to Risager, the first approach, which "has been the dominant paradigm with foreign language teaching in Western countries from the last century until the 1980s" (Risager, 1998: 244) is strongly called into question in the pedagogical debate today and has been replaced by either the intercultural or the multicultural approach. Since it is assumed that these approaches are sufficiently well-known, they will not be further commented on here. The oncoming transcultural approach then "takes as its point of departure the interwoven character of cultures as a common condition for the whole world: cultures penetrate each other in changing combinations by virtue of extensive migration and tourism, world-wide communication systems for mass and private communications, economic interdependence, and the globalisation of the production of goods (Hannerz, 1992). A driving force as regards this approach is the growing importance of cross-cultural personal contacts between learners (and teachers and families, etc.), especially in situations where the target language is used as a lingua franca." (Risager, 1998: 248-249)

(2)   Culture exploration approaches

Out of dissatisfaction with traditional approaches to culture teaching, researchers working with adult foreign language learners have developed alternative approaches where learners do not learn *about* another set of cultural practices, but *with* and *through* those practices (Barro *et al.*, 1998: 79), turning to anthropology for inspiration (Ellen, 1984; Hammersley & Atkinson, 1995). These approaches have come to be known as ethnographic approaches to culture learning (Gottlieb Berney, 1999). 'Fieldwork', 'participant observation', 'the language learner as ethnographer' are terms which can typically be found in descriptions of these programmes. The notion of the language learner as *ethnographer* aims to combine the experience of the ethnographer in the field and a set of conceptual frameworks for cultural analysis with the best practice from communicative and immersion language learning. These programmes will typically combine work in the classroom with exploratory work outside the classroom. Home ethnography may be combined with fieldwork abroad. The method employed in fieldwork is usually termed *participant-observation*. As the concept indicates, this method consists of two separate and yet connected approaches. Participation, on the one hand, means that the ethnographer, in order to understand life as it is lived in a specific place, leaves his or her own world and for a time becomes part of another 'reality'. Only from a position inside the other reality is it possible to get real insight. Observation, on the other hand, implies that the ethnographer maintains a distance to the life in which he or she is participating. Only by observing and reflecting while participating is it possible to make sense of what is experienced.

(3) Linguistic awareness of culture approaches

These approaches aim to integrate the teaching of language and culture and to enhance learners' metacognitive awareness of intercultural issues and of the many levels at which language and culture are entwined (Knapp-Potthoff & Liedke, 1997). Their point of departure is that cultural differences are hidden in linguistic manifestations. If the interactors do not perceive the linguistic indicators or manifestations, there will be constant misunderstandings. Therefore, this approach proposes a cumulative consideration of key linguistic problems. The idea behind the technique is to consciously consider types of communication problems in intercultural contact (illustrated by different episodes, critical incidents or situations experienced by the learners themselves) and teach strategies for solving them. This framework applies to the set of categories that have been elaborated earlier in this chapter, namely lexicon; speech acts; discourse conventions; topics; register; para-verbal phenomena; non-verbal expressions; communicative style; culture-specific actions and action sequences. Trainers introduce these linguistic categories, using examples of critical incidents (Wight, 1995; Dant, 1995; Bennett, 1995) where these categories explain misunderstandings. They emphasise that the examples use contrast-cultures and that no attempt is being made to reach conclusions about the 'typical' communicative behaviour of members from either culture. Thus in this phase of training, trainers are not concerned with how authentic or typical certain forms of behaviour are. Rather, they are aiming at systematically working out a checklist of linguistic categories that represent a carefully selected choice of factors which threaten intercultural situations. This list will enable them to systematically analyse intercultural situations in search of possible linguistic reasons for misunderstandings. At the same time, they will acquire the necessary meta-linguistic basis for exchanging hypotheses about discourse features in intercultural situations.

4   Empirical research

The key question to ask of any teaching practice, namely 'How does this particular practice help learners to acquire the objectives set?' remains to be answered with respect to many of the above-mentioned approaches. Many practitioners (and researchers) rely on their intuition or experience as practitioners to claim and trust that their approaches work and effectively contribute to promoting the acquisition of ICC with their learners. Yet, if we want to enhance the effectiveness of intercultural foreign language teaching, research is needed which empirically demonstrates which approaches are most effective under which circumstances with which learner groups. It is only when it can be shown that a particular instructional strategy is advantageous to a larger population than to the group of learners who happen to be in one teacher's foreign language class, that it will be possible to systematically improve intercultural communicative competence teaching practice.

Substantiating claims regarding the effectiveness of particular teaching approaches presupposes that we understand how intercultural communicative competence in a foreign language is acquired, what factors affect the acquisition process, what factors appear to provide an explanation for the variation in learning, what combinations of factors appear to explain the variance in the dependent factor, namely intercultural competence. Therefore, in the third section, we direct our attention towards empirical research. We examine what research literature has revealed regarding culture learning in a foreign language education context. We organise our review on the basis of a number of variables that appear to affect the learning of culture: setting, teacher, learner, materials, and assessment.

Some words of warning are appropriate here. A first word of warning concerns the fact that the number of empirical studies investigating the acquisition of intercultural competence in a foreign language education is still very limited, and at any rate far more limited than that of studies investigating second language acquisition. Much of the literature reported on here addresses primarily language learning, and does not have culture learning as its main focus. A second word of warning concerns the many comments that can be noted regarding the inappropriateness of the research methodology employed in studies investigating intercultural learning in foreign language education. At present, many different data collection procedures are used, of which some find their origin in psychology, others in sociology, linguistics, anthropology or educational sciences, and of which some could be termed quantitative and others qualitative. Experimental, causal-comparative or correlational research designs are found next to, for example, ethnographic, case study or action research. It is clear that the field would benefit from a meta-investigation of research studies, providing insights into the advantages and disadvantages of particular research strategies for investigating particular intercultural learning problems. Finally, one can say that research into the acquisition of intercultural competence has been hampered by the number of factors involved and the complexity of their interaction. In each individual case, biographical, affective, cognitive and circumstantial variables come into play, with students' previous language learning and aptitude affected by their age, motivation, attitudes, personality characteristics, learning styles and strategies, as well as by elements such as location of school, type of instruction, the number of teaching periods available for language learning, the status of foreign languages in the curriculum, the degree of contact with native speakers, degree of familiarity with foreign cultures, etc. etc. Many studies show high individual variation. Few studies have been able to substantiate causal relationships between independent variables and intercultural competence.

4.1 Setting variables

Two principal settings for language programmes can be distinguished: the naturalistic setting of the field and the formal, structured setting of the classroom. In the theoretical literature, a combination of classroom culture learning and experiential learning in the field are advocated as the best approach to promote the acquisition of intercultural communicative competence (Byram, 1989). However, till now research has not been able to demonstrate that this avocation can be maintained.

The 'study abroad' literature yields the most abundant research on the importance of context on culture learning. It demonstrates that the effects of a 'study abroad' experience or of classroom learning on culture learning are complex in nature and more complex than previously thought. The evidence is consistent that study abroad promotes language learning in certain ways (Coleman, 1997; Freed, 1995, 1998; Teichler 1997). The research findings are much less clear on the impact of study abroad on culture learning, although certain outcomes - greater self-confidence, an increase in global awareness, enhanced cultural self-awareness (Carlson *et al*, 1991), and positive attitudes toward other culture groups - are consistently found to be associated with overseas learning experiences. However, the research also suggests that one negative experience abroad can also dominate the person's perspective about the new culture, impede language acquisition and culture learning (Freed, 1991, 1995), or reinforce negative generalisations (Byram *et al.*, 1991, Sercu, 2000). Thus, it can be said that, the naturalistic setting, of and by itself, does not guarantee increases in either language or culture learning beyond what can be provided by the classroom. But if the study abroad cultural immersion experience is positive and the learner has the proper motivation and background, study abroad can significantly enhance culture learning.

Structured settings: culture in classroom learning
Perhaps because of the many difficulties involved in studying classroom settings and their effect on culture learning, there is a remarkable scarcity of empirical or descriptive studies dealing with the real world of the classroom. Empirical classroom data are rare. The situation for immersion classrooms or second-language classrooms is somewhat more promising than that for foreign language classrooms.

Research on immersion classrooms has focused largely on language learning (see Cummins, 2000 for an overview), though more recent research also focuses on the acquisition of intercultural competence which is deemed essential for attaining the level of proficiency with respect to academic language skills. Thomas & Collier (2000) report on a longitudinal research project which has examined many different types of school programs provided for (ethnic minority group) students, in all regions of the US over the past fifteen years, with respect to their effectiveness for promoting the acquisition of academic language skills.

Although the number of empirical studies investigating the effectiveness of instructed intercultural communicative competence learning is small, the amount of speculative theorising about language and culture learning in classroom settings is considerable. Most researchers consider that there are both disadvantages and advantages to language and culture learning in the classroom. As regards the disadvantages, many theorists argue that classroom-based learning is cognitive and deductive in nature, relying far too much on rule-ordered pedagogy. Accordingly, learning becomes superficial; students simply memorise the material without integrating it into a larger cultural knowledge base, or reflecting on their previous beliefs and attitudes (Jurasek, 1995; Robinson & Nocon, 1996). Also, there is only so much foreign culture that can be "brought" into the classroom, and preserving authenticity under these conditions is a challenge in itself (Kramsch, 1993; Baumgratz-Gangl, 1991). Other authors have theorised that the classroom as an artificial community can provide some unexpected benefits for language and culture learning (Mitchell, 1988; Damen, 1987; Kramsch, 1993). In particular, they hypothesise that the classroom is a protective environment where students can feel free to make mistakes without any lasting repercussions.

There has also been some theorising concerning differences between the second and the foreign language learning classroom. The second language classroom such as the ESL classroom in the U.S. or the FLE (Français Langue Etrangère) in France, does create a unique learning environment which differs from the foreign language classroom not only in terms of student composition but also with regard to motivation and perspective. While foreign language students are more likely to take the course voluntarily, second language students may be required to take the class (e.g. new immigrants or international students who are provisionally admitted pending successful completion of the ESL course). While the foreign language teacher is generally from the same culture as the students, the second language teacher, generally a native speaker of the language being taught, is likely to be of a different culture than the students. And the students themselves are likely to be culturally diverse. One important consequence of the cultural homogeneity between teacher and student in FL classrooms is that neither educator nor pupil need consciously attend to the ways in which they are engaged in "cultural transmission" (Ferdman, 1990, p. 189), an omission which can hinder the culture learning process. In second language classrooms, other problematic dynamics occur such as fear of being assimilated into the target culture (Ryan, 1994) and anxiety about the teacher, who is the representative of that culture.

4.2 Teacher variables

The role of the teacher in bridging languages and cultures cannot be denied. In this section we examine a number of teacher variables that impact culture learning and affect the acquisition of intercultural communicative competence.

A first variable concerns teachers' beliefs. Researchers in the field of teacher thinking have demonstrated that teachers' beliefs affect their teaching behaviour. These beliefs may regard not only their profession as a whole and their role as teachers of language and culture, but also the subject matter, the objectives to attain, the priorities to set, the assessment procedures to use (Nespor, 1987; Pajares, 1992; Woods, 1996). Research regarding foreign language teachers has provided insights into teachers' conceptions of 'culture' in foreign language education and their understanding of the objectives of foreign language education (Ryan, 1994; Byram & Risager, 1999; Sercu et al., forthcoming). Teachers' definitions of culture appear to be static (Stodolsky & Grossman, 1995) and very broad, embracing many aspects of daily life and of big 'C' culture (Robinson, 1985; Lessard-Clouston, 1992). In 1984, Knox reported that teachers in college courses tended to emphasise small "c" (daily life) culture, while with secondary teachers, instruction on topics of touristic highlights, geography and current events was more frequent. As regards the ways in which teachers define the goals of foreign language education, research has revealed that (Wolf & Riordan, 1991; Byram & Risager, 1999; Sercu, 2001; Sercu et al., forthcoming) teachers tend to define the objectives of foreign language teaching in linguistic terms, rather than in cultural terms. To them, it is more important that learners acquire linguistic competence in the foreign language than that they acquire a certain degree of familiarity with foreign cultures or that foreign language education promotes tolerance towards other cultures. The reasons which teachers mention for not getting round to culture teaching more often include: lack of time, lack of familiarity with the target culture, insufficient understanding of how 'intercultural competence' can be taught, inadequate teaching materials (Sercu, 2001).

A different strand of research has been concerned with the culture which teachers often unconsciously carry into the second language classroom. Falsgraf

(1994) investigating an immersion classroom, concludes that metacultural and metalinguistic instruction is not necessary since teaching through the second language provides sufficient input for the acquisition of implicit culture. Several studies have looked at teachers' perspectives regarding cultural diversity. According to Haberman & Post (1990), for example, teachers who want to "actively seek to maintain and enhance subgroups", but also "see some danger to subgroups from individuals and the general society" (p. 33) would appear to be more receptive to the kind of cross-cultural instruction and interaction that leads to the development of intercultural competence.

4.3 Learner variables

Learner variables further complicate ICCA research, and they are more numerous than the variables ordinarily distinguished in SLA research. Age, aptitude, motivation, cognitive style and learning strategies are important variables to account for in ICCA research too, as are degree of familiarity with cultures; range of cultures a learner is familiar with; experience of foreign cultures; attitude towards foreign cultures, or purposes for learning the foreign language (tourist, professional, immersion).

Much of the research has focused on the way in which attitudes towards foreign communities and peoples change in the course of foreign language education (Byram *et al*, 1991, Sercu, 2000), or on learners' motivation to study the foreign language (and culture). Gardner's (1985) model, distinguishing between instrumental and integrative motivation, has been particularly influential in foreign language education. Gardner looked at L2 motivation from a social perspective, regarding it largely as a function of intergroup relations and as a powerful factor to enhance or hinder intercultural communication and affiliation. Schumann's acculturation model (1986) suggests three strategies taken by adult learners: total adoption of the target culture (assimilation), preservation of the home culture (total rejection of the target culture), and "acculturation," which he defines as learning to function in the new culture while maintaining one's own identity. In the foreign - unlike the second - language classroom, the situation is slightly different, in that the need for assimilation or acculturation is practically non-existent, especially at beginning levels and in languages such as French or German where, as Byram and Morgan (1994) suggest, "understanding the target culture is appreciated ... but generally only as a support to linguistic proficiency" (p. 7). This finding is supported by Martin and Laurie (1993) who also found that the learners' reasons for studying the foreign language were more related to linguistic than cultural interests. In a second language situation, by contrast, where the cultural reality is readily encountered, a different set of responses to culture learning may occur, ranging from a desire to get to know one's neighbour to a deliberate effort to keep members of the other culture at a safe distance (Robinson - Stuart & Nocon, 1996). The research on motivation and attitudes seems to gravitate around the notion of 'contact' and its role in the embryonic stages of intercultural development. While causality is far from being unidirectional, more studies point to contact improving attitudes than vice-versa.

A number of other learner factors have been examined, among them learning style (Reid, 1987; Dirksen, 1990), intelligence, previous language background, language aptitude, and strategy use. Gardner and MacIntyre (1993) detail a "Socio-education model" of second-language acquisition which suggests that all of these factors—and perhaps many others—influence linguistic and non-linguistic (presumably cultural) outcomes in formal and informal language acquisition contexts.

4.4 Teaching materials as a variable affecting the learning process

This section examines research that has been concerned with investigating teaching materials as a variable affecting the culture learning process. The research has emphasised textbooks, since textbooks have repeatedly been shown to continue to be the guiding principle in many foreign language classrooms, at least at the beginner and intermediate levels. Alternative materials and methods often appear to teachers to be more time consuming, less efficient, and more difficult to use.

Four different research strands can be distinguished. The first strand of research is concerned with investigating the cultural contents of foreign language textbooks (Byram, 1993, Doyé, 1991; Sercu, 2000). These investigations have shown that to date the cultural contents tend to be limited to culture-specific information on the foreign culture(s) traditionally associated with the foreign languages taught. The dimensions of the target culture typically dealt with are, in decreasing order of predominance in many foreign language courses: leisure activities in the foreign country, tourist highlights & Culture, geography, transportation and commerce. Many textbooks adopt an outsider, tourist perspective on the target culture, and tend not to present insider views of the foreign culture, namely the views of people living in the target culture. The information in textbooks lacks complexity. (Ueber and Grosse, 1991, Wieczorek, 1994). The texts were found to be limited not only in the depth of cultural information but also in the range of topics and cultures depicted. The information is found to be often presented from the point of view of the author(s) only. The information is mostly positively biased, presenting an attractive picture of the foreign culture (Sercu, 1998).

There are far fewer studies that describe and evaluate the culture teaching approaches adopted in foreign language textbooks. Sercu (2000) is a notable exception. She demonstrates that foreign language textbooks to date seem to include mostly culture learning tasks that can be classified as apperception and reproduction tasks, requiring only low levels of involvement with the cultural contents offered.[1]

The second strand of research concerns impact studies. Perhaps because of the difficulty to isolate textbooks from all other potentially influential factors in the learning environment and in the learners' daily lives, the number of impact studies is very limited. Some researchers have speculated about possible effects. Sercu's (2000) analysis of, on the one hand, learners' perceptions and attitudes regarding the foreign cultures associated with the language they are learning, and, on the other, the cultural contents and culture teaching approaches of the textbooks these learners use demonstrates that the potential of textbooks for promoting learners' intercultural competence is limited. As Kramsch (1987) points out, textbooks that use the culture contrast approach are not necessarily better than textbooks that use the traditional foreign-culture approach. In the culture contrast approach, learners are asked to contrast their subjective views of their own culture with generalities presented about the foreign culture. But because readers rarely have sufficient understanding of their own culture, they are unable to critically assess the concepts being presented and they reduce the comparative process to a low-level comparison of facts. Similar ideas have been presented by Moore (1991). In the absence of knowledge about "*cultural antecedents*" (Triandis, 1972) learners are left to interpret the text on the basis of a priori assumptions, and, as a result, equate the culture under study with their own.

The third strand of research has been concerned with developing learning materials especially with the purpose of promoting both the acquisition of communicative competence and intercultural competence in a foreign language. In Germany, 3 textbook series have received particular attention. *Sichtwechsel neu* (Bachmann *et al.*, 1995) aims at developing a cognitive understanding of intercultural mechanisms and an awareness of culture being a socially constructed and dynamic system of meaning manifesting itself in language. *Sprachbrücke* (Mebus *et al.*, 1987) tries to promote learners' awareness of the culture-specific meaning of words by including the perspective of an extraterrestrial creature. Being from a different planet, *Lunja* continually enquires into the meaning of words, as s/he does not understand their culture-specific meaning. Whereas both *Sichtwechsel* and *Sprachbrücke* were designed for use in German language classes around the world, *Typisch deutsch!?* (Behal-Thomsen *et al.*, 1993) was written for the specific situation of American students learning German and uses a culture-and-language contrast approach geared to the particular context found in German-American language-and-culture learning-and-teaching. These books have been evaluated in Reiß (1997) with respect to the number and the types of stereotypes they contain. Working with a detailed scheme of different types of stereotypes,

---

[1] Since the results of this study have been included in an earlier chapter they will not be reiterated here.

she demonstrates that these three different textbook series are more successful than other textbooks in avoiding stereotypes and realising an intercultural approach to foreign language teaching, but that important differences exist between them.

A fourth strand of research is concerned with the analysis of other types of learning materials than textbooks. These other materials may include authentic materials, additional materials, such as videos or audiotapes or ICT-supported learning materials. While there is a large and growing body of theoretical writing concerned with promoting the use of authentic materials (Baumgratz-Gangl, 1991; Kane, 1991; Kramsch, 1993), there is very little actual research that has attempted to study the effects of authentic materials on either linguistic or cultural competency. Kienbaum, Russell and Welty (1986) found that students appreciated the view of the target country's cultural and social reality offered through the instructors' personal slides and interviews with citizens. The students responded favourably to the current events selections and gained a better understanding of their own cultural assumptions and values through articles and editorials related to the United States. Sercu (2000) has shown that when teachers use additional materials, even though these may have been chosen for cultural reasons, this does not necessarily mean that teachers will adopt a different approach to the teaching of intercultural communicative competence. Kramsch (1991) and Robinson (1981) also remind us that the use of authentic materials needs to be accompanied by an understanding of how one derives meaning from them. The danger of inaccurate or monocultural interpretations of the materials is always present. This applies to computer-assisted learning programmes and the internet as well. Though the computer scenario can provide added contextual cues while involving the student as one of the characters in the scene, and may allow for more active learner involvement with the cultural materials offered, here too, it is not self-evident that computer-programmes promote more intercultural competence or provide more adequate representations of foreign cultures (Kramsch & Andersen; 1999).

4.5 Assessment as a variable affecting the learning process

It is axiomatic among educators that what is tested is what is taught, and what is taught is what is tested. Research regarding the assessment[2] of intercultural communicative competence has been concerned with documenting current and developing future assessment procedures.

As research has demonstrated, teachers either do not test culture learning or, when they do so, they test culture solely in terms of the acquisition of cultural

---

[2] The term 'assessment' is generally used to cover all methods of testing and assessment, although some teachers and testers apply the term 'testing' to formal or standardized tests such as the Test of English as a Foreign language (TOEFL), and 'assessment' to more informal methods. Here, 'assessment' and 'tests' are used interchangeably.

knowledge (Seelye, 1994). Valette (1986) argues that the focus on discrete elements of cultural knowledge is preferred by many teachers for practical reasons: it is easy to prepare, test, and score. Partly to avoid the uncertainty that comes when taking into account the cultural diversity of the target culture, teachers often choose to focus their tests on the Big C culture (e.g. architecture, geography, and artistic traditions) associated with the presumed centre of the target culture. Recently, teachers have started experimenting with alternative ways to assess their students' culture learning. As Royer (1996) reports, her assessment techniques include audio recordings, performances, written essays, observation of group work, and group projects.

In order to compensate for the shortcomings of the cognitively oriented testing procedures administered in foreign language classrooms, researchers have proposed alternative tests, which focus on the more attitudinal and behavioural dimensions of intercultural competence as well as on its cognitive knowledge dimension. As the survey of test initiatives taken will show, some researchers strive for objectively valid and reliable tests, while others have developed alternative assessment procedures or techniques combining both objectively and subjectively scorable test types. Alternative assessment procedures refer to informal assessment procedures, such as writing-portfolios, learner diaries or interviews with teachers, which are often used within the classroom.

The culture assimilator model, for example, places the reader in real-life situations (Brislin *et al.*, 1986) Each episode is followed by three to four specific answers from which the students are asked to select what they think is the best explanation of that particular cross-cultural situation. The Intercultural Perspective-Taking Scale developed by Steglitz (1993) demonstrates another use of the critical incident, one which leads to more culture-general assessment. Here, the students read the story and then write an essay explaining their interpretation of what is occurring in the cross-cultural encounter. The teacher or coder rates the essay according to the degree to which the student (1) incorporates cultural variables into the analysis and (2) reflects upon how the culturally different person in the story might be construing events. King (1990) developed a cultural awareness test similar to the assimilator called cultural mini-dramas. These dramas incorporate the performance of linguistic as well as 'small c' culture practices, which can be observed by the teacher. Other interesting assessment techniques include the use of videotaping of cultural role plays (Falsgraf, 1994) and interactive computer programs that prompt students with various verbal and non-verbal cues (Baugh, 1994). Some European educators and researchers (Kordes, 1991; Meyer, 1991) have argued for the use of cross-cultural mediation tasks that would enable the teacher to assess a learner's culture-general skills such as empathy, tolerance, the ability to suspend judgement, and the adoption of someone else's point of view. Damen (1987) diagrams out four types of evaluation techniques for culture learning: self-report, enactments (such as role-plays or simulations), productions of materials (essays or letters), and observation by the teacher or other peers when the student is demonstrating specific cultural skills.

Two more instruments deserve mention here: the Cross-Cultural Adaptability Inventory (CCAI) (Kelley & Meyers, 1999) and the Intercultural Development Inventory (IDI) (Hammer, 1999). The CCAI is a 36-item paper and pencil, culture-general assessment instrument which measures four qualities hypothesised by the authors to be associated with intercultural competence: emotional resilience, flexibility and openness, perceptual acuity (the ability to read verbal and non-verbal cues), and personal autonomy. The Intercultural Development Inventory is a 70-item paper and pencil instrument intended to measure the respondent's degree of "intercultural sensitivity" along a six-stage developmental continuum: the stage of denial, of defence, of minimisation, of acceptance, of cognitive adaptation and of behavioural adaptation.

5   Conclusion: Research challenges

The overview of research findings shows that much work has been done in the area of culture learning in a foreign language education context, but that many research challenges remain. By way of conclusion we want to call for two research agendas here.

The first agenda we call for is for basic research which is devoted to developing the theoretical foundations of the field, and which continues to address the many setting and learning variables affecting the intercultural communicative competence acquisition (ICCA) process. This would help establish a more thorough understanding of what the learning of intercultural communicative competence involves. An important issue to address in this respect is the identification of the different developmental stages learners pass through and the definition of indices of development. Defining indices of development for the different components of intercultural communicative competence is indispensable if one wants to map progress and relate that progress to particular instructional practices. Research directed towards the identification of the different variables affecting the acquisition of intercultural competence, as well as the relationships between these variables, constitutes another important research challenge. The criticism that has been passed on the (unsystematic use of) methodology employed in a number of research studies deserves researchers' attention too. A meta-investigation of research studies, providing insights into the advantages and disadvantages of particular research strategies for investigating particular intercultural learning problems, might help to provide methodological direction to the field.

Future research should depart from new concepts of intercultural communicative competence and take account of its cognitive, affective and behavioural components.

The second research agenda should be constructed of theory-driven qualitative and quantitative applied research studies which concentrate on improving our understanding of the effect of choosing from among particular instructional design features, particular learning materials, particular assessment procedures. Teachers' expectations about what ICCA research can tell us at this point must be modest. At the moment, research reveals to a limited extent what learners do and know at particular points in their learning process. It has not yet, however, reached the point where we can say with assurance how they have come to do and to know these things, and we are further still from saying what teaching practices should therefore be followed. For one thing, applied research should be concerned with the development of new approaches to teaching and assessing intercultural competence. For another and in the absence of empirical data on culture teaching classrooms, it is essential that more empirical classroom data be collected. Empirical studies should depart from up-to-date concepts of culture and intercultural competence. They should observe both traditional culture teaching practices, making use of traditional textbooks in a traditional way, as well as classrooms in which newer types of culture teaching are in operation such as task-based exploratory approaches to culture learning, classrooms that make use of intercultural foreign language textbooks, or classrooms that integrate computer-supported instruction. These studies will shed additional light on culture teaching in different learning settings, and may help to identify a fixed set of descriptors that can be used to define the characteristics of different culture teaching approaches and assessment procedures. In this way, valid and reliable research regarding the effect of particular teaching approaches on learning becomes possible. These studies will also help to identify the major explanatory factors of variance during culture learning.

Finally, we want to suggest a role for both teachers and researchers in developing the field. To our mind it is important that practitioners continue to develop educational approaches which they feel are effective and adequate for their particular learner groups. It is, however, also crucial that teachers and researchers co-operate in trying to demonstrate empirically what exactly is happening in classrooms, what exactly are the effects of particular features of specific teaching strategies on learners' rate of development, on developmental sequences or on learners' ultimate level of attainment. Action research, in which teachers investigate the effects of their teaching in their classrooms, needs to be combined with other types of applied research, where academics surpass the individual case as they strive to discover generalisable patterns in the acquisition of intercultural communicative competence.

6 References

Alred, G. (forthcoming) Becoming a better stranger: A therapeutic perspective on intercultural experience and/as education. In G. Alred, M. Byram & M. Fleming (Eds.) *Intercultural Experience and Education.* Clevedon: Multilingual Matters.

Atkinson, D. (1999) TESOL and culture. *TESOL Quarterly 33*(4): 625-654.

Bachmann, S., Gerhold, S., Müller, B.-D. & Wessling, G. (1995) *Sichtwechsel Neu - Mittelstufe Deutsch als Fremdsprache.* Stuttgart: Klett.

Barro, A., Jordan, S. & Roberts, C. (1998) Cultural practice in everyday life: the language learner as ethnographer. In M. Byram & M. Fleming (Eds.) *Language learning in intercultural perspective.* Cambridge: CUP, 76-97.

Baugh, I.W. (1994) Hypermedia as a performance-based assessment tool. *The Computing Teacher 22*: 14-17.

Baumgratz-Gangl, G. (1991) Relating experience, culture and language: a French video project for language teaching. In D. Buttjes & M. Byram (Eds.) *Mediating languages and cultures.* Clevedon: Multilingual Matters, 228-239.

Behal-Thomsen, H. *et al.* (1993) *Typisch deutsch!? Arbeitsbuch zu Aspekten deutscher Mentalität.* Berlin: Langenscheidt.

Bennett, M. (1995) Critical incidents in an intercultural conflict-resolution exercise. In S. Fowler & M. Mumford (Eds.) *Intercultural sourcebook: Cross-cultural training methods. Volume 1.* Yarmouth: Intercultural Press, 147-156.

Berger, P. & Luckmann, T. (1971) *The social construction of reality: A treatise in the sociology of knowledge* (1971-print. First published in 1966). Garden City (NY): Double Day.

Bloom, B. (1964) *Stability and change in human characteristics.* New York: John Wiley.

Blum-Kulka, S., House, J. & Kasper, G. (Eds.) (1989) *Cross-cultural pragmatics: requests and apologies.* Norwood, NJ: Ablex.

Brislin, R. W., Cushner, K., Cherrie, C. & Yong, M. (1986) *Intercultural interactions: A practical guide.* New York: Sage Publications.

Brooks, N. (1975) The analysis of language and familiar cultures. In R. Lafayette (Ed.) *The cultural revolution in foreign language teaching. Reports of the Northeast Conference on the Teaching of Foreign Languages.* Lincolnwood, IL: National Textbook, 19-31.

Buttjes, D. & Byram, M. (Eds.) (1991) *Mediating languages and cultures: towards an intercultural theory of foreign language education.* Clevedon: Multilingual Matters.

Byram, M. (1989) *Cultural studies in foreign language education.* Clevedon: Multilingual Matters.

Byram, M. (Ed.) (1993) *Germany. Its representation in textbooks for teaching German in Great Britain.* Frankfurt/Main: Diesterweg & Georg-Eckert-Institut für Internationale Schulbuchforschung.

Byram, M. (1997) *Teaching and assessing intercultural communicative competence.* Clevedon: Multilingual Matters.

Byram, M., Esarte-Sarries, V. & Taylor, S. (1991) *Cultural studies and language learning. A research report.* Clevedon: Multilingual Matters.

Byram, M. & Esarte-Sarries, V. (1991) *Investigating cultural studies in foreign language teaching. Clevedon:* Multilingual Matters.

Byram, M. & Morgan, C. et al. (1994) *Teaching-and-learning language-and-culture.* Clevedon: Multilingual Matters.

Byram, M. & Zarate, G. (1994) *Definitions, objectives, and evaluation of cultural competence.* Strasbourg: Council of Europe.

Byram, M. & Zarate, G. (1997) Defining and assessing intercultural competence: Some principles and proposals for the European context. *Language Teaching 29*: 239-243.

Byram, M. & Fleming, M. (Eds.) (1998) *Language learning in intercultural perspective.* Cambridge: CUP.

Byram, M. & Risager, K. (1999) *Language teachers, politics and cultures.* Clevedon: Multilingual Matters.

Byram, M.& Nichols, A., Stevens, D. (Eds.) (2001) *Intercultural competence in practice.* Clevedon: Multilingual Matters.

Carlson, J. et al. (1991) Study abroad: The experience of American undergraduates in Western Europe and the United States. Occasional Papers on International Education Exchange Research Series.

Coleman, J. (1997) Residence abroad within language study. *Language Teaching 30*(1): 1-20.

Cummins, J. (2000) Learning to read in a second language: Fact and fiction. In S. Shaw (Ed.) *Intercultural education in European classrooms.* Stoke on Trent, UK/Sterling, USA: Trentham Books, 37-62.

Damen, L. (1987) *Culture learning: The fifth dimension in the language classroom.* Reading, MA: Addison-Wesley.

Dant, W. (1995) Using critical incidents as a tool for reflection. In S. Fowler & M. Mumford (Eds.) *Intercultural sourcebook: Cross-cultural training methods. Volume 1.* Yarmouth: Intercultural Press, 141-146.

Davcheva, L. & Docheva, Y. (1998) *Branching out. A cultural studies syllabus.* Sofia: British Council.

Dirksen, C. (1990) Learning styles of mainland Chinese students of English. *IDEAL 5*: 29-38.

Doyé, P. (1991) *Großbritannien. Seine Darstellung in deutschen Schulbüchern für den Englischunterricht.* Frankfurt/M.: Diesterweg & Georg-Eckert-Institut für Internationale Schulbuchforschung.

Ellen, R 1984. *Ethnographic research: a guide to general conduct*. London: Academic Press
Falsgraf, C. D. (1994) *Language and culture at a Japanese immersion school. Unpublished doctoral dissertation*. University of Oregon.
Farr, R. M. & Moscovici, S. (Eds.) (1984) *Social Representations*. Cambridge: CUP.
Ferdman, B. (1990) Literacy and cultural identity. *Harvard Educational Review 60*(2): 181-204.
Freed, B. F. (Ed.) (1991) *Foreign language acquisition research and the classroom*. Lexington, MA: D.C. Heath and Company.
Freed, B.F. (Ed.) (1995) *Second language acquisition in a study abroad context*. Amsterdam/Philadelphia: John Benjamins.
Freed, B.F. (Ed.) (1998) *Special issue of Frontiers: the Interdisciplinary Journal of Study Abroad*, Fall 1998.
Gardner, R. (1985) *Social psychology and second language learning: the role of attitudes and motivation*. London: Edward Arnold.
Gardner, R. C. & MacIntyre, P. D. (1993) Students' contributions to second-language learning. Part II: Affective variables. *Language Teaching 26*: 1-11.
Gottlieb Berney, M. (1999) Field studies: Individual and group trips, expeditions and hunts. In S. Fowler and M. Mumford (Ed.) *Intercultural Sourcebook: Cross-cultural training methods. Volume 2*. Yarmouth: Intercultural Press, 175-184.
Haberman, M. & Post, L. (1990) Cooperating teachers' perceptions of the goals of multicultural education. *Action in Teacher Education 12*(3): 31-35.
Halliday, M.A.K. (1989) Context of situation. In M. A. K. Halliday & R. Hasan (Eds.) *Language, context, and text*. Oxford: Oxford University Press, 3-12.
Hammer, M. (1999) A measure of intercultural sensitivity: The intercultural development inventory. In S. Fowler & M. Mumford (Eds.) *Intercultural sourcebook: Cross-cultural training methods. Volume 2*. Yarmouth: Intercultural Press, 61-72.
Hammersley, M. & Atkinson, P. (1995) *Ethnography: Principles in practice. 2nd. Edition*. London: Routledge.
Hannerz, U. (1992) *Cultural complexity. Studies in the social organization of meaning*. New York: Columbia University Press.
Jurasek, R. (1995) Using ethnography to bridge the gap between study abroad and the on-campus language and culture curriculum. In C. Kramsch (Ed.) *Redefining the boundaries of language study*. Boston: Heinle & Heinle, 221-251.

Kane, L. (1991) The acquisition of cultural competence: An ethnographic framework for cultural studies curricula. In D. Buttjes & M. Byram (Eds.) *Mediating languages and cultures*. Clevedon: Multilingual Matters, 239-247.

Kelley, C., & Meyers, J. (1995) *Cross-cultural adaptability inventory*. Minnetonka, MN: NCS Assessments.

Kelley, C. & Meyers, J. (1999) The cross-cultural adaptability inventory. In S. Fowler & M. Mumford (Eds.) *Intercultural sourcebook: Cross-cultural training methods. Volume 2*. Yarmouth: Intercultural Press, 53-60.

Kienbaum, B.E., Russel, A.J. & Welty, S. (1986) *Communicative competence in foreign language learning with authentic materials: Final project report*. (ERIC Document Reproduction Service No. ED 275200).

King, C.P. (1990) A linguistic and a cultural competence: Can they live happily together? *Foreign Language Annals 23*(1): 65-70.

Knapp, K. & Knapp-Potthoff, A. (1990) Interkulturelle Kommunikation. *Zeitschrift für Fremdsprachenforschung 1*: 62-93.

Knapp-Potthoff, A. & Liedke, M. (Eds.) (1997) *Aspekte interkultureller Kommunikationsfähigkeit*. Munich: Iudicium.

Knox, E. (1984) Report of the teaching of French civilization. *French Review 56*(3): 369-378.

Kordes, H. (1991) Intercultural learning at school: Limits and possibilities. In D. Buttjes & M. Byram (Eds.) *Mediating languages and cultures*. Clevedon: Multilingual Matters, 17-30.

Kramsch, C.J. (1987) Foreign language textbooks' construction of foreign reality. *The Canadian Modern Language Review 44*(1), 95-119.

Kramsch, C. (1991) The order of discourse in language teaching. In B.F. Freed (Ed.) *Foreign language acquisition research and the classroom*. Lexington, MA: D.C. Heath and Company, 191-204.

Kramsch, C. (1993) *Context and culture in language teaching*. New York: Oxford University Press.

Kramsch, C. (1998) *Language and culture*. Oxford: OUP.

Kramsch, C. & Andersen, R. (1999) Teaching text and context through multimedia. *Language Learning & Technology 2*(2): 31-42.

Lessard-Clouston, M. (1992) Assessing culture learning: Issues and suggestions. *The Canadian Modern Language Review 48*(2): 326-341.

Lustig, M.W., Koester, J. (1996) *Intercultural competence: Intercultural communication across cultures. 2nd edition*. New York: Harper-Collins.

Martin, A.L., Laurie, I. (1993) Student views about contributions of literary and cultural content to language learning at intermediate level. *Foreign Language Annals 26*(2): 188-207.

Mebus, G., Pauldrach, A., Rall, M. & Rösler, D. (1987) *Sprachbrücke. Deutsch als Fremdsprache*. Munich: Klett.

Meyer, M. (1991) Developing transcultural competence: Case studies of advanced language learners. In D. Buttjes & M. Byram (Eds.) *Mediating languages and cultures.* Clevedon,: Multilingual Matters, 136-158.

Mitchell, R. (1988) *Communicative language teaching in practice.* London: Centre for Information on Language Teaching.

Moore, J. (1991) *An analysis of the cultural content of post-secondary textbooks for Spanish: Evidence of information processing strategies and types of learning in reading selections and post-reading adjunct questions. Unpublished doctoral dissertation.* University of Minnesota, Minneapolis.

Morgan, C., Cain, A. (2000) *Foreign Language and Culture Learning from a Dialogic Perspective.* Clevedon: Multilingual Matters.

Müller, B.-D. (1995) Steps towards an intercultural methodology for teaching foreign languages. In L. Sercu (Ed.) *Intercultural competence: A new challenge for language teachers and trainers in Europe. Volume 1.* Aalborg: Aalborg University Press, 71-116.

Nespor, J. (1987) The role of beliefs in the practice of teaching. *Journal of Curriculum Studies 19*(4): 317-332.

Nostrand, H.L. (1974) Empathy for a second culture: Motivations and techniques. In G. A. Jarvis (Ed.) *Responding to new realities.* The American Council on the Teaching of Foreign Languages Foreign Language Education Series. Skokie, IL: National Textbook, 263-327.

Pajares, M. (1992) Teachers' beliefs and educational research cleaning up a messy construct. *Review of Educational Research 62* (3): 307-332.

Reid, J.M. (1987) The learning style preferences of ESL students. *TESOL Quarterly 21*: 87-111.

Reiß, S. (1997) *Stereotypen und Fremdsprachendidaktik.* Hamburg: Verlag Dr. Kovač.

Risager, K. (1998) Language teaching and the process of European integration. In: M. Byram & M. Fleming (Eds.) *Language learning in intercultural perspective. Approaches through drama and ethnography.* Cambridge: Cambridge University Press, 242-254.

Roberts, C. (1995) Language and cultural learning. An ethnographic approach. In: A. Aarup-Jensen, K. Jaeger & A. Lorentsen (Eds.) *Intercultural Competence. A New Challenge for Language Teachers and Trainers in Europe. Volume II: The Adult Learner.* Aalborg: Aalborg University Press, 89-99.

Robinson, G.L. (1981) *Issues in second language and cross-cultural education: The forest through the trees.* Boston: Heinle & Heinle.

Robinson, G.L (1985) *Cross-cultural understanding: Processes and approaches for foreign language, English as a second language and bilingual educators.* Oxford: Pergamon.

Robinson-Stuart, G. & Nocon, H. (1996) Second culture acquisition: Ethnography in the foreign language classroom. *The Modern Language Journal 80*(4): 431-449.

Royer, K. (1996) Summative authentic assessment in the French classroom. *The Clearing House 69*(3): 174-176.

Ryan, P.M. (1994) *Foreign language teachers' perceptions of culture and the classroom: A case study. Unpublished doctoral dissertation*I. University of Utah, Salt Lake City.

Schumann, J.H. (1986) Research on the acculturation model for second language acquisition. *Journal of Multilingual and Multicultural Development 7*: 379-392.

Scollon, R. & Scollon, S. (1995) *Intercultural Communication*. Oxford UK/Cambridge USA: Blackwell.

Seelye, N. (1994) *Teaching culture: Strategies for intercultural communication 3rd edition*. Lincolnwood, IL: National Textbook Company.

Sen Gupta, A. (forthcoming) "Changing the focus". A discussion of the dynamics of the intercutural experience. In In G. Alred, M. Byram & M. Fleming (Eds.) *Intercultural Experience and Education*. Clevedon: Multilingual Matters.

Sercu, L. (1998) Learning culture from foreign language textbooks. Reality or illusion? *Internationale Schulbuchforschung/International Textbook Research 20*: 275-293.

Sercu, L. (2000) *Acquiring intercultural communicative competence from textbooks. The case of Flemish adolescents learning German*. Leuven: Leuven University Press.

Sercu, L. (2001) La dimension interculturalle dans la vision pédagogique en langue étrangère. Analyse comparative des conceptions professionnelles des enseignants d'anglais, de français et d'allemand. In G. Zarate (Ed.) *Langues, xénophobie, xénophilie dans une Europe multiculturelle*. CRDP de Basse-Normandie, 169-180.

Sercu, L. (2002) Autonomous learning and the acquisition of intercultural communicative competence. Some implications for course development. *Language Culture and Curriculum*, 15 (1): 61-74.

Sercu, L. et al. (forthcoming) *Teaching intercultural communicative competence. Language teachers' beliefs and practices. A comparative investigation in 9 countries*. Clevedon: Multilingual Matters.

Steglitz, I. (1993) *Intercultural perspective-taking: The impact of study abroad. Unpublished doctoral dissertation*. University of Minnesota, Minneapolis.

Stodolsky, S.S, & Grossman, P.L. (1994) The impact of subject matter on curricular activity: An analysis of five academic subjects. *American Educational Research Journal 32*(2): 227-249.

Taylor, C. (1971) Interpretation and the sciences of man. *The Review of Metaphysics* 25(1): 3-51.
Teichler, U. (1997) *The ERASMUS experience. Major findings of the ERASMUS evaluation research.* Luxembourg: Office for Official Publications of the European Communities.
Thomas, W., Collier, V. (2000) Accelerated schooling for all students: Research findings on education in multilingual communities. In S. Shaw (Ed.) *Intercultural education in European classrooms.* Stoke on Trent, UK/Sterling, USA: Trentham Books, 15-36.
Triandis, H.C. (1972) *The analysis of subjective culture.* New York: Wiley.
Ueber, D.M., Grosse, C.U. (1991) The cultural content of business French texts. *The French Review* 65(2): 247-255.
Valette, R.M. (1986) The culture test. In J. M. Valdes (Ed.) *Culture bound: Bridging the cultural gap in language teaching.* New York: Cambridge University Press, 179-197.
Wieczorek, J.A. (1994) The concept of "French" in foreign language texts. *Foreign Language Annals* 27(4): 487-497.
Wight, A. (1995) The critical incident as a training tool. In S. Fowler & M. Mumford (Eds.) *Intercultural sourcebook: Cross-cultural training methods. Volume 1.* Yarmouth: Intercultural Press, 127-140.
Wolf, W.C., Riordan, K.M. (1991) Foreign language teachers' demographic characteristics, in-service training needs, and attitudes towards teaching. *Foreign Language Annals* 24(6): 471-478.
Woods, D. (1996) *Teacher cognition in language teaching. Beliefs, decision-making and classroom practice.* Cambridge: CUP.

The acquisition of intercultural communicative competence.
Some guidelines for better results on the 'intercultural competence' level.
Lieve De Wachter & Annemie Decavele, Leuven University, Belgium

1   Introduction

Foreign language learners have to acquire a considerable number of skills, attitudes, values and savoirs in order to become interculturally competent users of that language. In this 'acquisition process', the foreign language teacher plays an extremely important role. More particularly, the teacher has to guide the foreign language learner as efficiently as possible through the process of acquiring the different 'savoirs'.

In order to be able to do that, teachers have to develop a number of essential insights. They should among others understand how students' learning styles differ and how such preferences affect their acquisition of intercultural competence. Also, they should be able to recognise learners' different 'intelligences' and respond to them. Therefore, they should first of all be aware of their own multiple intelligence profile.

At the same time, the foreign language teacher should understand how cultural background and attitudes towards foreign cultures may affect language learning. Awareness of these differences is a prerequisite for the development of materials and strategies that are fully in tune with and take account of the needs of specific groups.

This chapter discusses the above-mentioned requirements for the foreign language teacher and also presents and discusses a number of techniques that may be used in the multicultural foreign language classroom to create an atmosphere conducive to learning in general and to acquiring intercultural competence in particular.

2   The 'savoirs' process

In the previous chapter, Lies Sercu has made it clear that gaining intercultural communicative competence amounts to much more than the combination of communicative competence and cultural awareness would suggest. She maintains that "an intercultural speaker is determined to understand, to gain an inside view of the other person's culture, and at the same time to contribute to the other person's understanding of his/her own culture from an insider's point of view." To express this 'inside view' in an intelligible way, Sercu uses Byram's conceptual framework comprising 5 'savoirs' (savoirs, savoir-apprendre, savoir-comprendre, savoir-être, savoir-s'engager). This 'savoir'-model appears to be a very useful tool to represent the learner's intercultural competence development.

As all foreign language teachers in multicultural classrooms will acknowledge, the different learning cultures of students may influence the way they progress through the savoir-process. It is true that most students first learn to 'savoir-apprendre' and 'savoir-comprendre' before they manage to become culturally competent on the 'savoir-être' and 'savoir-s'engager' level. However, the ways in which students progress may differ largely because of differences in individual and culturally conditioned learning styles.

For the student, learning how to become 'interculturally competent' could be measured by the progress that is being made on the savoir level. At the same time, it is clear that in order to make progress in acquiring the 'savoirs', learners need not only to gain a certain insight into the target culture, but will also need to forge a sense of their own cultural identity, to develop concepts about the construction of culture, and to understand that there is more than one way of 'living' in the world.

In this process, foreign language teachers play an extremely important role. For foreign language teachers, it certainly helps to go through such an intercultural learning process themselves on one or more occasions. Foreign language teachers who have mastered several foreign languages themselves will usually have a better understanding of what 'phases' a foreign language student has to pass through while learning the language. Teachers who themselves have learned a new language are in a position to realise what it takes to truly understand a foreign culture from within and to relate one's own cultural identity to that foreign culture.

In this sense, we think there is an important distinction between foreign language teachers teaching their own mother tongue and teachers teaching a foreign language they have had to master themselves first. In the first case, the mastery of the language will usually be better than in the second, but, with regard to a teacher's mother tongue, it is certainly more difficult to reflect upon the language and upon the 'savoir' process. Therefore, we are of the opinion that language teachers teaching their mother tongue should make a special effort to reflect upon the process the students have to pass through.

Ideally, teachers should have an inside view into all the home languages and cultures of the students in their class. In practice, this is usually impossible, especially when working with large heterogeneous groups.

3   Class practice

Knowing that students should pass through successive phases of the 'savoir process' in order to become interculturally competent in a foreign culture is one thing. Turning the ambition to guide students through this learning process into practice, appears to be quite another. How can one design teaching materials that take account of students' learning and promote their acquisition of intercultural competence? How can one select appropriate contents and teaching-and-learning approaches?

The guidance which teachers can obtain from curricular documents tends to be minimal. As Lies Sercu puts it with respect to the Council of Europe's Modern Languages project, "It [Common European Framework of Reference] does, however, fail to demonstrate how course developers could proceed if they wanted to design materials which aim to teach these intercultural savoirs and communicative competence in an integrated way." Teachers often feel insufficiently prepared for teaching both the foreign language and intercultural competence to a group of students, whether this group is homogeneous or heterogeneous.[1]

We believe teachers can become competent teachers of language and culture when they constantly reflect on the degree of success and failure in the approaches they use to promote students' acquisition of intercultural competence. As we see it, foreign language teachers should operate on different 'levels' at the same time, being aware of what their own strong sides and limitations are: they should constantly put themselves to the test as well. Moreover, they should be able to recognize and analyse their students' 'profiles', both on a personal and on an intercultural level.

In what follows we will first present the multiple intelligences theory and explain (1) how it can be used to gain a better understanding of the learners' culture-and-language learning processes and (2) how it can be applied to designing learning-and-teaching environments that are conducive to language-and-culture learning in multicultural language classrooms.

4 Multiple Intelligences Theory

Intercultural communicative competence comprises abilities that are acquired differently by people with different individual intelligences. Behaving in an interculturally correct way in a foreign culture clearly has to do not only with mastering the vocabulary and grammar of a foreign language, but also with personality and character development and with having an 'open' mind towards the foreign culture.

Gardner's Multiple Intelligences Theory helps us to understand how complex the concept of 'intelligence' is and this insight can help us to understand the complexity of the 'savoir-learning process'. Moreover, teachers should understand this complexity in order to be able to work with it efficiently.

Foreign language teachers often wonder at the concept of intelligence as a static construct. Most of them have the experience that students demonstrate so

---

[1] We will not go into detail on the difficult concept of "homogeneity" here. We realize that a group is never genuinely "homogeneous" in the strict sense of the word. What is usually meant with "homogeneous" groups is that there is a conformity in nationality, or in educational background. In this article, we will clearly define what we mean with a "homogeneous" as opposed to a "heterogeneous" group.

many different individual strengths and skills, that it is almost impossible to determine 'the most intelligent' student.

Gardner's *Multiple Intelligences Theory* (1985) proposes distinct intelligence capacities that result in many different ways of knowing, understanding and learning about the world. (Gardner, 1985; 1993)

In his original framework, Gardner identified seven intelligences. He later added an eighth. The list is certainly not meant to be exhaustive. The point is rather that each person has raw biological potential that can be sculptured in different ways. The intelligences Gardner identified are the following:

- BODILY-KINESTHETIC INTELLIGENCE: the ability to use the body to express ideas and feelings and to solve problems (including physical skills such as coordination, flexibility, speed and balance)
- INTRAPERSONAL INTELLIGENCE: the ability to understand yourself – your strengths, weaknesses, moods, desires and intentions (including such skills as understanding how you are similar to or different from others, knowing about yourself as a teacher, as a learner, knowing how to handle your feelings)
- INTERPERSONAL INTELLIGENCE: the ability to understand another person's moods, feelings, motivations and intentions (including such skills as responding effectively to other people in some pragmatic way)
- LINGUISTIC INTELLIGENCE: the ability to use words effectively both orally and in writing (including such skills as remembering information, convincing others, talking about language itself)
- LOGICAL-MATHEMATICAL INTELLIGENCE: the ability to use numbers effectively and reason well (including such skills as understanding the basic properties of numbers and principles of cause and effect)
- MUSICAL INTELLIGENCE: the ability to sense rhythm, pitch and melody (including such skills as the ability to recognize simple songs and to vary speed, tempo and rhythm in simple melodies)
- SPATIAL INTELLIGENCE: the ability to sense form, space, colour, line and shape and to graphically represent visual or spatial ideas
- NATURALIST INTELLIGENCE: the ability to recognize and classify plants, minerals and animals and to recognize cultural artefacts

It is obvious to everyone who observes human beings and human behaviour from time to time that no intelligence develops on its own. On the contrary, intelligences always work together in complex ways; only some people appear to have reasonably high levels of functioning in most intelligences whereas others seem to lack the most rudimentary aspects of a certain intelligence.

Students with a strongly developed linguistic intelligence will usually not have many problems with learning the foreign language up to a certain level.

However, this does not automatically imply that they can also manage to behave in an interculturally competent way within the foreign language culture. There is a need for more than simply linguistic intelligence. It is the teacher's task to stimulate other intelligences among his students.

By applying well chosen devices and techniques in the foreign language classroom (cf. infra) some teachers succeed in developing several of their students' underdeveloped intelligences. This may help the students to function well when they encounter the foreign culture.

So, for example, a person whose logical-mathematical intelligence has been strongly developed, will probably have few problems with using numbers effectively and with reasoning well. This type of student will have no problems with understanding and studying grammar rules and even with applying these rules in exercises. But this does not automatically imply that this student has developed his interpersonal intelligence as well! Traditional class practice often still starts from the assumption that students who can do their grammar and vocabulary exercises well, have mastered the language sufficiently. They are traditionally considered good learners.[2] But if this logical-mathematical intelligence is not complemented by a strongly developed interpersonal intelligence, it is doubtful whether these students can function at all in the foreign language environment. Students with an underdeveloped interpersonal intelligence will usually not be able to understand why people in the target culture react the way they do and will frequently feel hurt, simply because they are not able to see the 'rationale' in people's behaviour. Two examples will further clarify what we mean.

Our wide experience with Chinese students studying Dutch as a foreign language teaches us for example that many of them have a strongly developed logical-mathematical intelligence and sometimes also well-developed spatial and musical intelligences: these students manage to see the logical relationships between rules and they can also easily remember word lists in a certain order; moreover they are able to sense rhythm, speed, pitch and melody quite well.[3] The latter shows e.g. when students are asked to repeat words, word patterns or sentences in the 'language lab'. However, quite a few of these students seem to have more difficulty with the concept of 'interpersonal intelligence' the way western people experience it, e.g. when they need to show empathy for another person or respond to other people in a sensitive and pragmatic way. In homogeneous Chinese language classes therefore, teaching how to become culturally competent in a foreign culture, is a very difficult job for the western

---

[2] We will elaborate on the concept of `good learner' when we introduce Krashen's notions of `monitor' and `affective filter' further on in this article.
[3] Of course we realize that it is dangerous to generalize over cultures as we do here. However, it turns out that learning styles may largely differ in different cultures and this cannot but have an effect on the individual learning profiles of students in the foreign language class.

foreign language teacher as students often do not seem to realize what the problem is: they do not have the examples of students of other countries or cultures in their class who have developed different intelligences in different ways. In this type of homogeneous group, the teacher is the only link with the foreign culture. Consequently, he has to deal with the difficult and complex task of intermediating effectively between the source and the target culture. The role of the language teacher should at the same time be open and supportive, but he should also encourage the students to expand their mindsets and outlooks: he has to provide learners with the means to analyse their own culture and understand and relate to the social world inhabited by their interlocutors.

Of course, a more or less homogeneous group of American students studying Dutch as a foreign language is also bound to experience difficulties at some point with interculturally 'correct' communication. American students will probably not meet with the same problems most Chinese students deal with. In classroom situations, foreign language teachers may sometimes notice that e.g. Asian people tend to keep quiet when spoken to whereas Americans speak up more easily. These differences in attitude can be partly related to over-using or under-using the 'monitor' (cf. infra). Usually, American students seem to have quite well developed 'interpersonal intelligences' and equally well developed 'intrapersonal intelligences', since they are used to analyzing themselves and their feelings, speaking up for themselves and being communicative. But here again, it will become clear that the 'Flemish', 'Belgian', 'Dutch' or even 'Western European' interpretations of culturally competent behaviour are very different from their own. To give just one example: American students readily use the phrase "Dag, hoe gaat het?" (Hello, how are you doing?) as an introduction to a conversation with a complete stranger. For the latter, this speech act can easily be experienced as a rather aggressive way of introducing oneself because in Flanders few people say more than 'Hallo' (Hello), or 'Hoi' (Hi) when they meet someone new. Furthermore, Belgian people often regard Americans as 'loud' or 'noisy' and this sometimes makes intercultural interaction more difficult, as Belgians will easily shut up in the face of American boisterousness.

Of course these are partly stereotypical generalisations, although class practice reveals that students often experience things this way. In the foreign language classroom, misconceptions like these can be discussed, for example, by making use of 'Taalriedels' as a teaching device: 'Taalriedels' are simple riddles and/or rhymes which offer the opportunity to talk about the ways you are similar to or different from others, how to express your feelings and how to respond effectively to other people in a pragmatic way.

Some American students also have the tendency to express themselves and their opinions by using the loaded verbs: 'to love' and 'to hate'. This too can lead to misunderstandings that can be avoided by discussing the associations these words have and their implications and effect in the target culture and language.

(cfr. The negotiation techniques mentioned below) In this way, the teacher can help students to realize that their ways of perceiving and representing the world may be different from the way other people understand it. This is an important realization that may not only lead to the development of more and different intelligences, but also to proceeding further through the 'savoir-process': it is our experience that once students have understood how their cultural patterns differ from the patterns of the target culture (savoir-comprendre), they usually succeed in taking a big step towards 'savoir-être' and 'savoir-s'engager'.

5 The teacher's multiple intelligence profile

An effective application of multiple intelligence theory in foreign language teaching is only possible if the teachers learn more about their own multiple intelligence profile themselves and draw conclusions from this. So at all times, teachers should critically examine and evaluate themselves. For it is obvious that "the types of learning activities teachers select are often directly related to their experiences in the real world. The choices they make as teachers, in turn, can affect the multiple intelligence profiles of the [foreign language] students in their classes. As a [foreign language teacher], you also naturally choose classroom activities that complement your own multiple intelligence profile." (Christison, 1998; 6-7) As Christison explains, the choices teachers make when teaching can affect the extent to which students are able to develop their intelligences. We are convinced that in order to accommodate as many different intelligence profiles as possible, it is important that teachers use an eclectic method, mixing and varying several kinds of activities. Language students and language teachers can then benefit from instructional approaches that help them reflect on their own learning. (Christison, 1998: 7 ; Marzano *et al.*, 1988)

In the above, we have tried to make it clear that getting an insight into the multiple intelligence profile of both teachers and students alike is an essential condition for facilitating intercultural competence. Also, the development of multiple intelligences will certainly help the foreign language student to proceed further in his or her exploration of the different savoirs. But although multiple intelligence development is an essential condition for intercultural communicative competence, it is certainly not a sufficient one. In the next paragraphs, we will elaborate on some other vital factors.

6 Multiple intelligences and the learning-and-teaching environment

In a learning-and-teaching environment, it is extremely important that students can develop their intelligences in order to facilitate the transition through the savoir-process. It is the teacher's task to create a class atmosphere in which the necessary intelligences can best be developed.

Traditionally, a 'good learner' is considered to be someone who pays attention to grammatical form. But, obviously, a 'good' learner is a concept filled in by the teacher and influenced by cultural values. Western teachers still often link thorough grammatical knowledge with a 'good' mastery of the language. However, this does not necessarily reveal anything about the intercultural communicative competence of students.

Most foreign language teachers realize how important it is for students to feel comfortable in a classroom. People that are stressed or feel anxious can experience mental blocks. This phenomenon is often referred to in terms of an 'affective filter' which prevents language and other information from entering and being assimilated into the students' knowledge constructs. The more students are able to relax in class, the easier it will be for them to pass through the process of foreign language acquisition and through the different savoirs. Both Gardner and Krashen mention such an affective component. (Gardner 1985 and 1993; Krashen 1981; see also Mason and Schultz.)

It is quite obvious that learners with high motivation, self-confidence, a good self-image and a low level of anxiety are better equipped for success in second language acquisition. "Low motivation, low self-esteem, and debilitating anxiety can combine to 'raise' the affective filter and form a 'mental block' that prevents comprehensible input from being used for acquisition of language and culture." (Schultz 2001) Consequently, for optimal learning the affective filter must be low. If the strength of their affective filters is high, learners will not seek language and culture input, and therefore, will not be open to language and culture acquisition.

Therefore, it is the teacher's task to keep the language-learning environment relaxed yet alert, by providing activities that offer appropriate language and culture material and, at the same time, help 'lower' the affective filter. A student who feels at ease has a low affective filter and will consequently be less defensive, thus more open towards, another language and culture.

In traditional classroom situations, it is often still the teacher who dominates the interaction. He is the starting point of the whole process: he decides on the topics of discussions, on the way in which interactions are to take place and on who should speak. This can be explained by the fact that his culture and personal methodological preferences (often depending on his own 'favourite intelligences', cf. supra) control and influence the class environment. In this kind of situation, optimal classroom communication is difficult to obtain. The teacher and everything he stands for linguistically and culturally, can be experienced as intimidating and hard to live up to.

Apart from the teacher's attitude, there may be other factors that disturb the interactive communication process. One of them is inappropriate language material, which does not appeal to the students' culture and mentality or reflect their reality. This may discourage them from communicating. Obviously, it is the teacher's task to find a good balance between language material students feel at ease with, and language material that is perhaps unknown but that stimulates the intercultural communication process. For example, most Chinese students would be very happy if presented only with word lists, grammar rules and language lab drills, but of course, foreign language teachers should not limit themselves to these. The only way for Chinese students to learn more about interculturally competent behaviour, is by being confronted with authentic listening and reading materials, 'creative' exercises – exercises requiring debate and consultancy, etc.

Some students, for example many Asians, also fear 'losing face' in public. Students who do not understand the material are sometimes hesitant to admit it, when they are not only confronted by the teacher but, at the same time, observed by the whole group. In some cultures, communicating the fact that you are ignorant of something, is simply not done as it is considered something to be ashamed of.

In this respect, it is important for the teacher to get a clear picture of the profiles of his students in order to tune into their foreign language needs. Learners seem to be better motivated by teaching techniques they can, to some degree, associate with. Consequently a consideration of culture is essential. An approach which students do not feel comfortable with may be counterproductive. This again suggests the importance of an eclectic way of working where different methods are blended together and are applied to stimulate and appeal to a wide range of persons, cultures and systems. A more detailed study of strategies commonly used by particular cultural groups would be helpful to elaborate a variety of techniques.

In the following section, we will offer some strategies which we believe have potential to break through the possible restraints in foreign language classrooms and to create a dynamic and 'open' class environment. This will lead not only to smoother language acquisition, but also to improved intercultural communicative competence.

7 Some strategies that may facilitate the exploration of the multiple intelligences in a class environment

Asher's Total Physical Response (TPR) method links language learning to physical actions. (Asher 1982 and Zandbergen 1995) Practitioners of this method claim that it is pedagogically advantageous to allow students to keep silent as long as they want to by giving them the choice of when to produce one word utterances or short sentences. TPR is regarded as a very social way to learn a language. During the whole process students have to help and support one another via action and interaction. This didactic procedure permits introverted persons or students whose cultures differ widely from the source culture, to take their time and discover the language before actually 'speaking' it. In our classes, we ascertain that Chinese students, who often have difficulties grasping the beginning and ending of words and sentences in Flemish, enjoy this receptive way of dealing with the language and culture.

Another strategy that is closely linked to the previous one is the use of a negotiation technique, in which the teacher tries, as a coach, to involve the whole group in the clarification process of words and concepts instead of explaining things immediately himself.

Since different strategies evoke different responses in students from different cultures, the teacher should ideally have a good notion of all the diverse cultures of students in his class. We have noticed, for example, that in our homogeneous American groups, the element of 'competition' evokes a certain 'drive' which, to a large extent, stimulates language and culture acquisition. This might be explained as follows: "In the USA, natural differences and performances are the factors taken to be substantial, because they produce different individual results that, through competition, allow us to make distinctions." (Pinheiro Neves 2000, p.342)

A homogeneous Indonesian group however, seems to benefit more from collaborative exercises. Competitive exercises for the latter seem to be counterproductive.[4] A strategy in which each student is involved and in which the opinion of everyone is equally significant is the 'information gap'. This could be done as follows: in a group of four students each student has one part of a comic strip. It is only by putting together the four constituent parts that the meaning of the joke or of the comic strip can be understood. At the same time, divergent interpretations might come to the surface and can be discussed or discovered within each group. In our experience, cultural values often determine students' interpretations. For example, the cultural assumptions in the Hagar comic strip – immensely popular in Belgium – are apparently difficult to grasp by students from non-Western cultures. By confronting students with an information gap, the teacher creates a reason for them to reflect upon their own and the target culture and explain to each other why they interpret the comic strip the way they do. This type of exercise gradually creates a respectful atmosphere that might lead to more cultural self-reflection, which is a basic necessity for better intercultural communication in the target language.

As previously mentioned, 'Taalriedels' can be used as a teaching device to stimulate the exchange of typical cultural speech acts (Deen and Van Veen 1994). The riddles deal with daily activities such as 'visiting someone', 'meeting a friend on the street' and 'thanking somebody'. 'Taalriedels' are very melodious riddles accompanied by suggestive and illustrative drawings, which offer the teacher the opportunity to focus on specific cultural habits. They can be very effective in triggering students to speak about differences in culture. Fluency of speech implies that a part of the speaker's language use is automatic. 'Taalriedels', which are based on American Jazz Chants, help students learn to use formulaic

---

[4] On several occasions teachers of the Insitituut voor Levende Talen have been teaching Dutch in Indonesian universities on invitation of the Dutch Taalunie. Their findings appear to be useful for teaching practice.

expressions and so, by offering chunks of language that students can learn as wholes, contribute to the production of more creative communication. We have experienced that this method fits into the musical intelligence profile of, for example, many Indonesian students and meets the expectations of their group-oriented mentality. The aim of 'Taalriedels' is, in the first place, to promote correct pronunciation, intonation and rhythm, which are the skills that correspond most closely to a musical intelligence profile.

The above mentioned strategies offer a number of advantages: they reduce the dominance of the teacher over the class, they promote collaboration among learners, they create a more comfortable, relaxed atmosphere, they enable the teacher to work more as a facilitator or consultant and they can promote learner responsibility and autonomy. However, their crucial advantage is that they can increase the amount of student participation time in the classroom and the exchange of language and culture between them. In these exchanges between students, several skills can be developed, such as understanding how you are similar to or different from others, how to understand another person's moods, feelings, motivations and intentions, as well as how to respond effectively to other people in a pragmatic way. Needless to say, such activity supports the extension of the intrapersonal, interpersonal, musical and linguistic intelligences.

When teachers manage to create a safer class climate by using similar techniques and strategies, such a place is often a productive environment for promoting and fostering intercultural communicative competence. In other words, in such class climates, students usually manage to communicate with each other in socially acceptable ways and, at the same time, become more aware of cultural traits.

8 Conclusion

We hope that it has become clear that foreign language teachers should realise that each activity can be approached from an intercultural perspective. Teachers should be aware that their task is to stimulate students to gain deeper insight into the target culture. At the same time, they should offer the students a place to develop a sense of their own cultural identity in order to 'see' that there is more than their own perspective in life. It is only by passing through this phase that students will manage to proceed through the 'savoir process' and increase their intercultural communicative competence.

To summarize, we can say that two of the teacher's most important tasks in foreign language teaching are to develop the learner's multiple intelligence profile and to stimulate a positive attitude in the learner towards the target language and culture. One of the pedagogical consequences of what we have said is that the teacher will not only have to function as a teacher but also as a learner. This helps to create the basic conditions for a multi-dimensional dialogue.

We hope to have made it clear that in order to acquire the necessary 'savoirs' for intercultural communicative competence, several strategies can be combined in an eclectic methodology. In this context, the teacher is invited to step out of the classroom spotlight, and shift the focus onto the students. In order to succeed, a teacher will not only have to evaluate the students' output but, at the same time, he will have to keep on evaluating his own performances.

9 References

Anderson, P., 1995. Walkabout Grammar. In: Headway, Teacher's Magazine, 4.

Armstrong, T., 1994. Multiple Intelligences in the classroom. Alexandria, VA: ASCD.

Asher, James J. 1982. *Learning another language through actions*. Los Gatos, CA: Sky Oaks Productions.

Christison, M.A., 1998, 'Applying Multiple Intelligences Theory in Preservice and Inservice TEFL Education Programs', in: *English Teaching Forum*

Deen, J. and C. van Veen, 1994. Taalriedels. Een cursus spreekvaardigheid Nederlands als tweede taal. Wolters-Noordhoff, Groningen.

Gardner, H., 1985. Frames of mind: the theory of multiple intelligences. New York: Basic Books.

Gardner, H., 1993. Multiple intelligences: the theory and practice. New York: Basic Books

Krashen, S., 1981. Second Language Acquisition and second language learning. Pergamon Press Inc.

Marzano, R., R. Brandt, C. Hughes, B. Jones, B. Presseisen, and S. Rankin, 1988. Dimensions of thinking: A framework for curriculum and instruction. Alexandria.

Mason, T., Didactics-11: Critique of Krashen: The Affective Filter Hypothesis on http://perso.club-internet.fr/tmason/WebPages/LangTeach/Licence/CM/OldLectures/L11.

Pinheiro Neves, L.M., 2000. Putting mericracy in its place: the logic of performance in the United States, Brazil and Japan. In: Critique of anthropology, 20/4:333-358.

Schültz, R., 2001. Stephen Krashen's Theory of Second Language Acquisition. http://www.sk.com.br/sk-krash.html.

Sprenger, R., 1994. Body Grammar. In: Headway, Teacher's Magazine, 1.

Zandbergen, E., 1995. Taal koppelen aan lichamelijke actie met Total Physical Response. In: Samenwijs, 15 (9), May.

Part IV

Learner Autonomy in Foreign Language Education

Learner Autonomy in Foreign Language Learning and Teaching

Eus Schalkwijk, Kees van Esch, Adri Elsen, Wim Setz
University of Nijmegen, The Netherlands

1 Introduction

In many industrial countries, secondary education is undergoing change. One of these changes involves the implementation of learner-centred educational models to which the concepts of 'learner autonomy' (LA) and 'learning to learn' are central. For the past two decades there has been growing academic interest in learner autonomy in the fields of language learning and language teaching. As a result, both language teachers and language learners are increasingly put into situations in which learners are expected to be responsible for and to be able to direct their own language learning. Furthermore, in order to prepare student teachers for their future roles, learner autonomy should be fostered in foreign language teacher training.

When foreign language learners or educators are asked what learner autonomy is, one is likely to get a variety of response. These responses will reflect very different beliefs about what learner autonomy is or should be and in every answer different aspects will be stressed: the pupil's freedom, the (new) roles of the teachers, the learning strategies the learner has to use, collaborative learning, (self-) evaluation or a combination of these aspects. We will elaborate on these aspects later on in this chapter. Nevertheless, we would like to present a definition of learner autonomy, right away. According to Little (1997: 94): "Humans are autonomous with respect to a particular task when they are able to perform that task (i) without assistance, (ii) beyond the immediate context in which they acquired the knowledge and skills and on which successful task performance depends, and (iii) flexibly, taking account of the special requirements of particular circumstances". This definition serves as a good starting point for the way we perceive learner autonomy.

What are the origins and what is the background of learner autonomy? And what are the reasons for emphasising learning autonomy? A first point of view that can help to answer these questions focuses on the relationship between learner autonomy and human agency. An agent is a person who acts. In order to act, there must be initiation. One cannot initiate action without exercising one's power to do so (see paragraph 2.1). A second point of view concerns the relationship between learner autonomy and society. In a review of literature on the topic, concepts of self-determination soon became prominent (see paragraph 2.2). A third, and last point of view regards the relationship between learner autonomy and learning. A number of important orientations from educational psychology on learning and motivation attracted our interest. They are useful in exploring concepts of learner autonomy in human learning (see paragraph 2.3).

After exploring these three perspectives, we then will turn to educational practice in foreign language teaching and language teacher training. We will give some definitions of learner autonomy, talk about the implications of learner autonomy for foreign language learning and teaching and say something about the new roles teachers need to adopt (see paragraph 3.1). We then try to explain why learner autonomy should be a guiding principle in foreign language teacher training and suggest some ways of how this could be done (see paragraph 3.2). The chapter will be rounded off by a summary and some conclusions.

2 Origins of and reasons for Learner Autonomy

2.1 Learner Autonomy and human agency

Philosophers have long been interested in human agency and personal autonomy. An agent is a person who acts. Action must be intitiated. One cannot initiate action without exercising one's power to do so. Human beings have authority over themselves for the simple fact that they can initiate their own actions. From this view, personal autonomy is seen as a mere form of self-government. The authority we have over our actions is but a formal feature of agency. This does not imply that whenever we act, the forces that move us are manifestations of our own power as agents. Our motives are not necessarily related to the decision-making power that moves us to act. Agents determine how to act, but the job can be done without completely being in control.

Philosophers have concentrated on the relationship between the agent's power and the power of the forces that move him or her by attempting to answer two essential questions. What motives are attributable to the agents themselves and what motives can be seen as external? What distinguishes motives on which the agent has conferred authority from the motives whose power has reduced authorisation to a mere formality? Philosophers have proposed different accounts of a human being's special relation to personal motives. Buss (2002) mentions four more or less overlapping approaches to personal autonomy: coherentist, reasons-responsive, responsiveness to reasoning and incompatibilist. The four approaches may help us unravel some of the complexities between a person's motives and the power to act.

Coherentist approaches

In a coherentist approach, it is argued that human beings can only be called autonomous agents if they accept their motives, identify with them, approve of them, or believe they make sense in relation to any long term commitments or plans they may have. The approach assumes a reflexive attitude towards the motives that make a person act. If a person endorses and accepts these motives, that person is called an autonomous agent. Actions occur with the permission of the agent, if not necessarily at his or her command. If people do not accept or identify with the motives that make them act, then these motives are caused by external forces in conflict with their personal autonomy.

Reasons-responsive approaches

According to philosophers advocating a reasons-responsive conception of autonomy, human beings are not seen as autonomous agents unless their motives, or the mental states that produced them, are responsive to a wide range of reasons for and/or against behaving as they do. It is considered that human beings who fail to appreciate and evaluate a variety of reasons for action are unlikely to govern themselves well. Ignorance of "... a pattern of actual and hypothetical recognition of reasons (some of which are moral reasons) that is understandable to some appropriate external observer" is seen as a serious threat to self-government. (Fischer and Ravizza, 1993:90)

Responsiveness-to-reasoning approaches

According to responsiveness to reasoning theorists, people govern themselves if they have the capacity to evaluate their motives by relating them to whatever else they believe in or desire, and adjust these motives in response to their evaluations (Buss, 2002:4). Responsive-to-reasoning accounts, with their focus on the reasoning process, often suggest that self-government requires the capacity for self-transformation and development. On this assumption, autonomous agents are capable of changing their minds when they discover good reason to do so in the course of their reasoning. It is important to note that changes of mind caused by sensitivity to reasoning do not automatically lead to a growth in autonomy of the agent in question.

Whether a person reasons correctly or wrongly is norm-referenced and determined by the reasons or criteria that underlie a particular norm. The norms that govern the reasoning process seem to be shaped both by internal and external forces. An implicit plea is made to investigate what forces are involved and how they interact in the course of the reasoning process.

Incompatibilist approaches

A fourth view of personal autonomy is generally referred to as incompatibilist. According to this account it is impossible to validly distinguish between internal and external forces that influence a human agent's intention-forming process. Incompatibilists feel that autonomy is incompatible with determinism. One of the more rigorous expressions of the incompatibilist position is to be found in Kane (1996). According to Kane, the wish to be an autonomous agent is the desire to have "the power to be the ultimate producer of [one's] own ends ... the power to make choices which can only and finally be explained in terms of [one's] own [will]". "No one," he argues "can have this power in a determined world." (Kane, 1996:254).

Summary and conclusion
We started this chapter with Little's definition of autonomy. The four accounts of human agency help to clarify and specify his definition and our conception of what learner autonomy is. The definition started with the claim that a human being is autonomous in relation to a task if he can perform his task "without assistance". This means that the agent him- or herself initiates the action. Whether this is seen as autonomous action depends on how we define human agency. As we have seen there are four main accounts of autonomous action. Are we to take sides and favour a particular account of autonomy, or is there an alternative? The matter can be resolved if we take a person's motives into consideration. This is what coherentists do. Having studied a person's motives and checked whether he or she endorses them, it is important to find out whether agents have selected their motives from a wide range of reasons. Next, we ought to pay due attention to the quality of a person's reasoning process. Responsiveness of the autonomous agent to improving the quality of reasoning and the selection and choice from a wide range of reasons might well be decisive in calling one person more autonomous than another in a particular situation. The *motives*, wide *range of reasons* and the *quality of reasoning* are important variables in studying learner autonomy. If they prove to be stable, they could be used in formulating criteria. Autonomy is not something you either have or do not have. You have it in varying degrees, depending on the situation or social context you are in. The settings of foreign language acquisition and use often include formal educational contexts. Incompatibilist accounts of personal autonomy have sensitised us to the fact that external factors negatively interfere with personal autonomy. However, dismissing autonomy as a construct would do no justice to the potential of a person's motives, quality of reasoning and ability to construct and select from a wide range of reasons for her autonomy. The remainder of the definition we started with refers to acquisition and transfer contexts and flexibility.

2.2   Learner Autonomy and society
Four different culture orientations
Every society has its own views and ideas about how it should function. In sociological terms these views and ideas are often referred to as culture orientations. A society may have its own specific culture orientation at a certain point in time, which influences how people think and act in different ways and provides guidelines for their daily actions. As a rule, various culture orientations co-exist within a society, but the prevailing orientation is typically the most influential during a given period of time. For the Netherlands within a European

context, Matthijsen (1972) distinguishes four culture orientations that have influenced periods within the past millennia:

- The *aristocratic culture orientation*. Its central notion is that the leadership of a state can only be entrusted to an elite of high-ranking people (nobility or patricians).
- The *theocratic culture orientation*. Characteristic of a society that considers God the ultimate authority and is primarily oriented towards priests ruling as direct servants of God.
- The *meritocratic culture orientation*. People derive social status from their individual abilities and achievements.
- The *democratic culture orientation*. The direct or indirect government of a state by the people is at the centre. The individuals in society decide who rules. The democratic orientation explicitly incorporates a model of self-determination. An important aspect of this autonomy model is that groups and individuals have the opportunity to develop their talents or abilities. The common factor in the first three orientations is that power in society is beyond the reach of ordinary persons. Power is in the hands of select groups of privileged individuals such as nobility and clergy. In the fourth orientation, the individual has social and political status irrespective of ability or achievement. Moreover, interest in the individual is not limited to newly gained social and political status. Societies are concerned with creating opportunities for their members to develop their potential. This aspect of autonomy is most clearly visible in a democratic culture orientation.

Self-determination in historical perspective

In Europe as well as in the Americas, the concept of creating opportunities for self-determination has gradually gained acceptance and, in turn, influenced education, as the following historical examples will illustrate.

Athens was one of the city-states in ancient Greece. The city-states were governed by aristocratic elites, and the aristocratic culture orientation was dominant. In the course of the 5th century BC, Athens developed into Greece's largest maritime power (Boyd, 1964). A new upper middle class of free citizens arose. Within this class, the autonomy model increasingly secured influence. Its ideal was the power of free citizens who were aware of their responsibilities and capable of shouldering them. In practice, the right to self-determination was reserved for a select percentage of the male population. Slavery had not yet been abolished.

The dominant aristocratic culture orientation was increasingly questioned in Greek society. According to Bemal (1969), a civilian democracy emerged for the first time in history. This led to the demand for a different type of education.

The sophists, a new class of travelling professional teachers, appeared and challenged existing conventions and dogmas. Traditions (such as the aristocrats' right to rule by virtue of birth) were called into question and presented as fabrications of the human mind. In those days for the first time, education in Athens became geared toward the preparation of young male adults for life in society. These young men were not only educated in the art of rhetoric and argumentation, they also received lessons in logic and ethics.

During the Middle Ages in Europe, the aristocratic and the theocratic culture orientations were alternately dominant. There were feudal class societies in which the church was very influential. The rural economy was greatly dependent on a large group of serfs. The development of trade and industry lead to the rise of the bourgeoisie in the cities (Bemal, 1969). The bourgeoisie became increasingly involved in a struggle for power with the ruling nobility and clergy. Many of the first scientists and scholars tried to legitimise the dominant aristocratic or theocratic culture orientations. Their task was to confirm by reasoning what religion already claimed as an indisputable truth (Störig, 1964). The rise of cities and the bourgeoisie gradually led to a need for science and knowledge and for education aimed at the practical needs of societies.

Toward the end of the 18th and early in the 19th centuries, Europe was confronted with an explosive population growth resulting, among other things, in great poverty, unemployment, and famine (Matthijssen, 1982). This proved fertile for the development of a new economy based on industrialisation, new production methods, and market-oriented thinking. Industrialisation had far-reaching effects on the lifestyle of the people. A meritocratic culture orientation emerged, aimed primarily at economic benefit. Social status was measured in terms of individual abilities and achievements. This culture orientation became increasingly dominant and strongly influenced ideas about education. The industrial revolution linked education to the demands of trade and industry. Education was increasingly seen as training for professional practice.

In the second half of the 19th and first half of the 20th centuries, the training concept of education came under attack. It was argued that education exclusively geared to the benefit of economic evolution could result in an undesirable technocracy in societies. The inspiring goal of self-determination was proclaimed once again. It was man who controlled science and its technical applications and not the other way round. Concerns with well-being and ethics should figure more prominently.

Early in the 20th century, thinkers such as Dewey (Pragmatism in America), Montessori, and Peterson (German Reform Pedagogy) were elaborating on the ideas of Rousseau and Comenius whose ideas were critical of the established system of education (see Röhr, 1991). They saw a great gap between education and the life of the child and advocated the exploration of a child's ability and potential for self-development. Their most important points of criticism were that the process of education was aimed at the acquisition of knowledge as an objective in itself and that many curricula were organised and graded in accordance with the abstract learning principles of logic. In addition, they found that the transfer of knowledge was impersonal and authoritarian and that the pupil was forced into passivity and immobility (see van der Meer & Bergman, 1975).

In the 20th century, dominance by the meritocratic culture orientation increased even further as a result of the two world wars. Following each world war, every aspect of society was dominated by post-war reconstruction, economic growth, and technical progress. The dominant influence of rationality in technocratic societies caused concern and doubt among an increasing number of intellectuals (see Marcuse, 1968; Illich, 1979). An orientation toward autonomy began to increase again in the seventies, due in part to the influence of the activist movements (e.g. revolts by students against the Vietnam war and the Cold war) until the pursuit of models of autonomy once again dominated educational frontiers.

The nature of education was often passionately debated in the light of changing social perspectives, resulting in movements concerned with all forms of education on both national and international levels. During the seventies, great interest arose in concepts such as learner autonomy within various forms of socially-committed project education bearing remarkable similarities to the ideas of the educational reformers described above. Among other things, this interest was a reaction to classic behaviourism. Rejection of behaviourist determinism translated into a general opposition to the establishment and a search for alternatives. An important objection against the established system of education was its one-sided emphasis on cognitive development. For critics, the system of education was too rigid, both because of the strict separation of primary and secondary education and the system of ability streaming and tracking from the first year of secondary education onwards. Moreover, links between school learning and the life experiences of the child were generally missing. Among other criticisms levelled at the education system were the ineffectiveness of formal education in abolishing social inequality of opportunities and, ultimately, a failure to stimulate and fulfil the needs of learners for independence, responsibility, and participation. For a summary of these criticisms we refer to critics such as Freire (1972, 1996), Illich (1979), and Rogers (1983).

In the early 1980s, people lost interest in socially-oriented project education in which explicit attention was paid to the social relevance of educational content. Once again, education became profession-oriented and geared toward the development of professional skills and practical thinking.

Summary and conclusions

To summarize and to conclude, we saw that the need for learner autonomy stems from what is in essence a democratically oriented vision of education. Sometimes a more democratic orientation develops as a reaction against a dominant orientation, as was the case with the aristocratic, theocratic, and meritocratic cultural orientations identified above. Only the democratic culture orientation incorporates a model of self-determination, and it is this orientation that has increasingly gained influence in Europe within the past few decades. In the Netherlands, it has resulted in an educational reform geared at fostering a concept of learner autonomy that includes both meritocratic and democratic traits.

In the following sections, we will offer an additional perspective on learner autonomy. We will review briefly some general theories of learning and motivation. This second perspective helps explain current notions held by teachers and learners with regard to self-direction in learning how to communicate in a foreign language.

2.3   Learner Autonomy and learning

Humanistic psychology

With respect to theories and notions of human learning, cognitive and constructivist views were most notable in the latter half of the twentieth century. More recent versions of these views on learning still resonate in discussions of independent learning. This certainly applies to the renewed interest in the model of direct teaching advanced in the 1980s (Rosenshine, 1976). The demonstrated effectiveness of direct teaching seems to account for its renewed popularity, especially in the field of cognitive performance (Rosenshine & Stevens, 1986; Good & Brophy, 1991).

Humanist psychologists acknowledge that stimulus-response reactions may play a role in learning processes. However, they feel that behaviour and experience are primarily initiated by the individual and not caused exclusively by external incentives reinforcing certain responses. Humans have the principal and unique capability to make choices and to distinguish themselves from one another. Responsibility for the choices they make lies with them. Humanist psychology thus emphasises the ways in which learners perceive their environments. In education, humanist psychologists attribute an important role to a learner's thoughts, feelings, and motivation. Two representatives of humanist psychology who have been explicit on educational matters are Maslov (1970) and Rogers (1983).

A cognitive perspective

A behaviourist point of view excluded mental explanations for behaviour and changes in behaviour. Behaviourists were unable to provide explanations for a great many everyday practical human activities, and this led to the rise of cognitive psychology. For example, Chomsky (1959) argued that the behaviourist theory fails to account for the phenomenon that children come to know more about the structure of their native language than would be possible if this knowledge was based solely on the language input they are exposed to.

Cognitive psychologists saw learning as an individual process of collecting information and storing it in the brain. Subsequently, they developed an interest in learning strategies. However, the affective and social aspects of learning generally remained outside their scope of inquiry. In the 1980s, cognitive psychologists focused on meta-cognition; the question of how aspects of the learning process can be regulated became important.

Sociocultural theory

Sociocultural theorists have approached human learning from yet another perspective, emphasising that a child grows up in a social world and that learning occurs in part through interaction with others. This continuous interaction allows children to attribute meaning to the world around them. Vygotsky (1978; 1986; see also Wertsch, 1985) stresses the importance of language in human interaction. Through language culture is transmitted, mental processes are made explicit, and human learning can take place. Vygotsky rejected the idea that subject matter can be divided into separate small units that are transferred as isolated knowledge and skills. Subject matter has to be meaningful and be presented in all its complexity. Vygotsky saw an important role for the teacher who leads the learning process in the right direction and, at the same time, pays attention to peer and other forms of co-operative learning. By interacting with the learner, the teacher or fellow learners serve as mediators, helping a learner find ways to stay within an area Vygotsky called the *zone of proximal development* (ZPD). He defined this zone as "the distance between the actual development level as determined by independent problem solving and the level of potential development as determined through problem solving under adult guidance or in collaboration with more capable peers." (Vygotsky, 1978, p.86). Applied to foreign language learning, ZPD refers to the difference between what a language learner can do with assistance and what he or she can do without guidance. For reasons of brevity, we refer to Lantolf (in this volume) who presents an extensive review of other important aspects of sociocultural theory which have significant implications for learning and teaching.

Constructivism

Cognitive psychology has contributed significantly to the development of constructivism. Several theories on learning (e.g. Bartlett, 1932; Neisser, 1967; Wolff, 1994) build on the common assumption that every individual uses prior knowledge and experiences to process, store, and retrieve new information in his or her own subjective way. These theories about information processing provide the cognitive underpinning of constructivism. Constructivism has many variants.

However, they share the claim that human perception is a construct of mental activity in which the environment, "society," or "the other" play essential roles. Learning is considered a continuous process in which learners acquire new knowledge in their own subjective ways, process it, and locate it in the existing structures of their knowledge, experiences, and beliefs. In this way, learning can be seen as a continual process of construction and reconstruction (Boekaerts & Simons, 1995; Lowyck & Verloop, 1995).

Affective Factors in Learner Autonomy

Let us now consider the affective sides of learning in more detail. Discussions on learner autonomy have often started from the premise that learners are intrinsically motivated to assume and develop responsibility. In the Netherlands, these aspects came to the fore in the 1990s, when the first direct experiences with aspects of learner autonomy in education were reported by teachers and learners. Teachers in particular indicated that they believed or had experienced that many pupils were insufficiently motivated to assume more responsibility for their own learning. The distinction made between intrinsic and extrinsic motivation is helpful here. According to Lens (1993) intrinsic motivation means that learners are motivated because of the activity itself, because they enjoy it or find it rewarding. Extrinsic motivation, on the other hand, refers to motivation because of an external reward such as a good grade given by the teacher. The activity itself can be experienced by the learner either as pleasant or as unpleasant.

Learner autonomy requires learners who are primarily intrinsically motivated. The learner should experience and learn that he is the cause and initiator of his own learning behaviour (DeCharmes, 1984); Ryan & Grolnick, 1986) and that he feels responsible for it (Wang, 1981). It thus is important that the learner transform his intentions into behaviour and can, at an early stage, recognise and deal with any obstructions in the areas of action or emotion. Within this framework, Kuhl (1985) uses the notions of action-orientation and situation-orientation. Learners who are situation-oriented waste time in the execution of their tasks as a result of indecisiveness in the orientation stage and volatility in the execution stage. Learners who are action-oriented, on the other hand, take initiatives quickly in the orientation stage and persevere in the execution stage.

Summary and conclusions

Humanistic psychology has emphasized the importance of thoughts, feelings and motives in making individual choices and in taking responsibility for these choices. Attention has increasingly come to be focused on the learner in the learning process along with affective factors such as motivation that is commonly regarded as a 'condition sine qua non' for realising learner autonomy. Cognitive psychologists and constructivists have explored the cognitive and social dimensions of the individual's learning process which encompasses such factors as the prior knowledge, experiences, and beliefs of the learner. Such insights have led to more attention being given to meta-cognition and to a fundamental change in learner' and teacher' roles as a prerequisite for learner autonomy. We have stressed two aspects of sociocultural theory, namely the importance of language in human interaction and how, in interaction with the learner, the teacher and/ or co-learner can serve as mediators to make development possible. Referring to the affective sides of learning, we have focussed on the distinction between intrinsic and extrinsic motivation, concluding that, for learner autonomy to be realised, the learner must be primarily intrinsically motivated. This means that, in spite of external constraints and difficulties, he should learn that he is the cause, the initiator and the one who is responsible for his own learning. In the next section, we will turn to educational practice in foreign language learning and teaching and to language teacher training.

3 Learner Autonomy in Foreign Language Learning and Teaching

3.1 The autonomous foreign language learner and the roles of the teacher
Definitions of Learner Autonomy in Foreign Language Learning and Teaching

According to Holec (1981, 1988), foreign language learner autonomy involves learners who are both willing and able to assume responsibility for their own language learning. They do so by making their own choices of objectives, didactic materials, and processes. Similarly, for Little (1994), learner autonomy is a permanent objective in language teaching and learning. His definition of autonomy seems equally applicable to that of language learning as it fits in with the democratic cultural orientation: the learner has to learn how to keep developing his language learning knowledge and skills independently in order to reach a further stage of autonomy. "Humans are autonomous with respect to a particular task when they are able to perform that task (i) without assistance, (ii) beyond the immediate context in which they acquired the knowledge and skills and on which successful task performance depends, and (iii) flexibly, taking account of the special requirements of particular circumstances" (Little, 1997, p.94).

Two other aspects of learner autonomy should be stressed. First, there is the social aspect (Slavin, 1995; Kagan, 1993; Dam, 1994) underlying successful teacher-learner and learner-learner co-operation. Second, there is the aspect of individualisation and orientation of the individual learner (Nunan, 1988; Narcy, 1994). No two learners learn in the same way. A third aspect of learner autonomy, related to the ones above, is the learner's orientation toward the learning process. Wolff (1994) explicitly links this aspect to constructivism. In processing information, every learner starts from his/her own prior knowledge and prior experiences in his/her own way. All we perceive in a foreign language is a "construct" of our own mental activities in interaction with the surrounding environment. A focus on the learning process of the learner also implies that, in developing learner autonomy, a great deal of attention has to be paid to learning strategies. Research on learning strategies has resulted in concrete proposals for the learning and teaching of foreign languages, e.g. Naiman et al. (1978), Wenden & Rubin (1987), O'Malley & Chamot (1990), and Oxford (1990).

The ideal autonomous foreign language learner

Together with Rampillon (1994), the principles described above serve to create the ideal autonomous foreign language learner: a learner who is motivated to learn, knows his/her own capacities and limitations and tries to surmount them, formulates his/her own learning targets, initiates the learning process and keeps it going, determines how he/she learns best, keeps track of the subject material, and evaluates his/her learning results to find ways they can be improved.

In order for these ideals to become a reality, a number of requirements must be met. Schools have to be organised so that learners can work independently, either alone or in groups; study corners, a library, and computers have to be available at all times. Course materials have to be in accordance with or adjusted to principles of learner autonomy. Learning to learn how to communicate in a foreign language implies that communication in the foreign language has to be encouraged and instructions for learning tasks made clear. Study guides help increase learner autonomy. Course materials, didactic procedures, and forms of (self-) evaluation should encourage independence and self-control. Co-operation with others has to be promoted and efficient use made of information and communication technology.

Roletaking by the teachers

An important condition which also has to be met in fostering learner autonomy is that the teacher adapt to another role, namely that of instructor, supervisor, and coach. As Widdowson (1990) justifiably remarks, learner autonomy does not imply that the teacher no longer directs or 'teaches' the learner. More than ever before, the foreign language teacher will have to serve as a guide who helps learners to take increasing levels of responsibility for their own learning processes. This can be done by helping learners organise and plan their learning and develop new and better modes of language learning. The teacher monitors how learners learn before, during, and after they carry out learning tasks, encouraging them to think about how their planning and execution proceeded and the improvements that could be made.

Putting learner autonomy into practice shifts teacher roles from directing to coaching, from executing to preparing, from exclusively assessing the product to assessing both product and process. Let us have a close look at these roles.

Firstly, the role of a coach. The teacher who wishes to instil autonomy and responsibility in his pupils, will be a coach and advisor or tutor, rather than the leader and director of the learning process. Actually, he will usually be the initiator and organiser of the learning process and its evaluation, rather than its leader.

With respect to foreign languages, there is the additional role of being a conversation partner to enable communication in the foreign language, and to put it into practice. Promoting learner autonomy will also entail the teacher devoting much more time and attention to developing and adjusting learning tasks and, consequently, to managing and preparing classes.

Finally, the third role of assessing product as well as process, means that he must not be exclusively concerned with what his pupils have to learn, but also with how they should learn it. This means in point of fact, that he will have to pay a lot more attention to learning strategies and to improving the learners' approaches to learning tasks. In short, the teacher's role will not be less prominent, but will definitely be different.

Implications of learner autonomy for foreign language learning and teaching

Earlier, we argued that learner autonomy is closely related to a democratic culture orientation with its inclusion of self-determination. Next, we showed how, in learning theories, increased attention came to be focused on the learner in the learning process along with affective factors such as motivation. In the Netherlands, as in many other European countries, some of these insights have been incorporated into theoretical notions of foreign language teaching didactics. Theory tries to provide answers to the question of how learners learn to learn how to communicate in a foreign language. We consider fostering learner autonomy in foreign language learners to be among the most recent developments in communicative language learning and teaching. The didactics of foreign language learning and teaching have undergone numerous changes. We have the distinct impression that, in the Netherlands, traces of past developments will be evident in the beliefs of both teachers and learners on how foreign languages are best taught and learned. Despite the development of more communicative approaches to language teaching and learning, traces of the grammar-translation method are still found in language curricula, didactic materials, and lessons. The audio-lingual method was supported by a behaviourist perspective on learning (Savignon, 1983, 1997; Van Els et al., 1984). Structuralists were of the opinion that the structure of oral or written expressions of language could be described in an objective way. In the Netherlands, there are still schools where the language classroom remains as envisioned by the structuralists.

Within communicative language teaching, language is seen as a system for the interpretation, expression and negotiation of meaning (Savignon 1983, 2002 and this volume), with the primary function of interaction and communication.

The underpinning theory of learning is that the activities carried out should involve real communication, meaningful tasks, and language which is meaningful to the learner. In communicative language teaching, the teacher is the facilitator of the communication process, participants' tasks, and texts. The teacher is the process manager whereas the learner is a negotiator, an interactor, who is both giving and receiving.

The road towards more successful foreign language learners and teachers has never been a bed of roses. Some secondary school pupils, who we have interviewed, agree that some subjects are more suitable for this new didactic approach. They feel it works for English and French, but they are convinced that it will not work for German. They claim their teacher of German is not the kind of person to give away control. Besides, the class feels they are going to fail all his tests if they have to do without his explicit grammar teaching. In response to a question in a discussion with a university teacher trainee, six out of fourteen youngsters said that they would like to have less freedom because they admitted they lacked the discipline required to work and learn on their own. The remaining eight felt the level of freedom was just right, but they added that teacher instruction and guidance were still very important. They did not want to have more freedom and choice. "Whenever a subject is dealt with by the teacher in front of the class, it is easier to get good marks," some of the young learners claimed. The statement did not surprise their teacher of French. "It is a matter of getting used to new ways of teaching. That is why I feel it is important that teachers make explicit why they opt for a particular didactic approach. In the Netherlands, we have made our learners dependent on marks and grades, causing them to distrust didactic procedures that differ from the usual. More freedom and responsibility will work only if the learners actually experience that they are becoming better language learners and language users, by making sure the advantages are seen and felt" (Schalkwijk, Van Esch, Elsen, Setz, 2002: 166).

3.2 Foreign Language Teacher Training

It is not only for the practical reasons outlined above that learner autonomy should be a guiding principle in foreign language teacher training; the decision is prompted by theory as well. In a previous article (Van Esch, Schalkwijk & Sleegers, 1996), we claimed that student teachers' subjective educational theories should be the starting point for a training programme aimed at teaching them to learn autonomously. We also claimed our didactic approach was experience-driven. It is aimed at a confrontation between student teachers' subjective educational theories and their practical knowledge, and other sources of knowledge (cf. Kelchtermans, 1993). This didactic principle was based on a constructivist view of learning. Cognitive psychology has made an important contribution to the development of constructivism. In 1932, Bartlett formulated his 'schema' theory. He claimed his research showed that people remember stories and are able to reconstruct them on the basis of their own schemata – individual constructs of relevant knowledge, memory and experience – and do not simply reproduce the original stories (Bartlett, 1932). This means that prior knowledge and expectations are added to elements of the story in the reconstruction process.

Wolff (1994) provides insight into how constructivism originated, listing contributions made by textual analysis theory, literary theory and by cognitive psychology, and considers the implications of this theoretical position for foreign language teaching. He describes constructivism as a psychological and philosophical theory of perception and understanding, linking it to reception aesthetics and textual linguistics of the 60's and 70's. In reception aesthetics, mainly developed by Jauss (1970) and Iser (1975), the (literary) text is 'recreated' by every reader. The same text thus acquires a new meaning unique to the particular reader. The contribution made by textual linguistics (cf. De Beaugrande & Dressler, 1981) consists of insights into the way readers reconstruct every text into a coherent whole.

As mentioned before, one of the foundational premises common to constructivist theories of learning is that we learn about the world subjectively as we process new information and construct new knowledge internally on the basis of existing knowledge and experience. Consequently, learning is an individual process, which is different for each student teacher. This means that in training foreign language teachers, each student teacher's initial situation will have to be considered. This also means that, although final requirements must of course be met, goals, subject matter and methods will have to be fine-tuned to each student teacher's abilities, and it means a lot of attention will have to be paid to individual choices and responsibilities in the learning process. This is the only way to ensure that teachers are at least willing and able to continue growing and developing after their initial education. As a result, our tendency to determine all subject matter beforehand and the way in which student teachers should process it has become far less strong than it used to be.

In an earlier publication (Van Esch, Schalkwijk & Sleegers, 1996), we also argued that future foreign language teachers should have some insight into their learning processes and be able to direct them in order to coach their pupils properly in becoming autonomous foreign language learners. It is important to state, as Wolff (1994) does, that the theoretical basis for learner autonomy is found in constructivism. There are clear parallels between the principles of constructivism and those of learner autonomy. The use of authentic material in learner autonomy approaches to foreign language learning, for instance, can be recognised as the counterpart to the constructivist principle of complex learning matter, and communication in the foreign language is the concrete demonstration of the principle of an authentic learning environment. And the emphasis on information processing and the learning process is related to constructivist explanations of how knowledge is processed.

During their training programmes, future foreign language teachers will have to be prepared for this new role and the new tasks by putting learner autonomy into practice and by learning to take responsibility for their learning processes.

This can be achieved first of all through the design and the organisation of the programme. In designing it according to the principles of learner autonomy, and phasing it into the stages of orientation, application and elaboration, one can encourage student teachers to learn to work autonomously. It is also vital that they learn to co-operate with other student teachers and are enabled to gradually transform strong direction by the educator into self-direction and individual responsibility during the last stage of the programme.

In the initial situation, it is important to address the subjective educational theories the student teacher has, and to offer new subjects only when the student teacher is ready for them. This does not alter the fact that the student teacher has to be challenged too.

As regards institutional didactic procedures, by carrying out learning tasks, just as their pupils do, the prospective teachers will get a clearer idea of the learning strategies necessary to work efficiently. Moreover, constant individual, as well as collective, reflection on teaching practice will teach them to link practice to their own and other people's theories, thus taking a further step in the learning process.

By acquiring skills, knowledge, and insight into testing learning results and evaluating learning processes, student teachers learn not only to monitor correctly and readjust their pupils' learning processes, but they will also gain a clearer view of their own progress, and develop more autonomy and responsibility for the ways in which they learn. Such a capacity for autonomy will increase student teachers' chances of a successful start in the teaching profession and will help to ensure their professional development in the course of their careers.

Finally, by becoming acquainted with the theory and the practice of learner autonomy in practical research, student teachers are enabled to make choices in researching a particular aspect of it, and develop approaches to classroom investigation guided by the principles of learner autonomy.

Summary and conclusions

Learner autonomy in foreign language learning and teaching is a relatively recent development, aligning with the democratic culture orientation. The concept embraces several different aspects and principles: responsibility, freedom of choice, interaction and cooperation, and attention to the learning process by emphasizing the use of strategies and metacognition.

In the search for the ideal autonomous foreign language learner, we stated that a number of requirements must be met. Besides the organization, the course materials, didactic procedures and forms of self-evaluation, an important condition of increasing learner autonomy lies in the teacher himself. The misconception about learner autonomy that has influenced response to it, as an approach, from educators over the last decennia, is that learner autonomy implies that the role of the teacher must be minimized. Instead of minimizing his or her role, the teacher must gradually adopt other roles: coach and advisor or tutor, initiator and organizer of the learning process and its evaluation and, especially with regard to foreign languages, a promoter of interaction and communication in the foreign language. A closer look at foreign language teaching practice makes it clear that to instil autonomy and responsibility, teachers must be aware not only of the potential, but also of the contextual and individual constraints. Despite these constraints, the question as to whether the autonomy of learners can be increased, and to what degree, depends on their teachers' motivation, willingness and preparation. An important way to realise this process is to take small steps and for teachers to relinquish their control and responsiblity over the learning situation gradually, while giving increasing scope for learners to excercise control and responsiblity (cf. also Van Esch & St. John, 2003, p. 16-17).

We concluded that future teachers must be prepared for these new roles. As has been pointed out by constructivism, they must learn to acquire insight into their own beliefs and their own learning processes in order to be able to prepare for their new roles in fostering learner autonomy among their students.

Another conclusion was that initial teacher education itself must be designed and organized according to principles of learner autonomy, such as gradually handing over control and responsiblity to student teachers, enhancing cooperation and interaction between them, and including the self-assessment of their own products and processes. In the last chapter of this book, we will describe some practical examples of how to put these principles into practice in initial teacher education.

Whether learner autonomy can be introduced in the way we are proposing depends on factors such as the contexts of teacher training institutions and the school systems in different countries, as well as on the learning and teaching theories of (future) foreign language teachers. There are important conditions required to successfully implement learner autonomy in the foreign language classroom and, besides a teacher's control and good classroom management, these include a firm theoretical basis and the willingness to introduce this innovation. But a fundamental change in the perspective of teachers and learners is also needed: teachers must become learners themselves and their learners must be engaged in practising key principles of learner autonomy, such as learning by doing, cooperation and peer- and self-evaluation. Perhaps above all, there is a need for empirical data about changes in teacher and learner perspectives and in concrete teaching practice when principles of learner autonomy are applied. We will discuss this topic further in the next chapter.

4 References

Anderson, J. R. & Bower, G. H. (1980) *Human Associative Memory.* Hillsdale (NJ): Lawrence Erlbaum Associates.

Baker, L., & Brown, A.L. (1984) Metacognitive skills and reading. In D. Pearson, M. Kamil, R. Barr, & P. Mosenthal (Eds.), *Handbook of reading research.* New York: Longman, 353-394.

Barlett, F. C. (1932) *Remembering.* Cambridge: Cambridge University Press.

Bemal, J.D. (1969) *Science in history. Volume I: The emergence of science.* Hannondsworth: C.A. Watts & Col Penguin Books.

Boekaerts, M. & Simons, P. R. J. (1995) *Leren en instructie. Psychologie van de leerlingen het leerproces.* Assen: Dekker & van de Vegt.

Boyd, W. (1964) *The history of Western Education.* London: Adam & Charles Black.

Buss, S. (2002) Personal Autonomy, In *The Stanford Encyclopedia of Philosophy (Winter 2002 Edition)*, Edward N. Zalta (ed.) URL = <http://plato.stanford.edu/archives/win2002/entries/personal-autonomy/.

Chomsky, N. (1959) Review of *Verbal Behavior* by B.F. Skinner, *Language 35/1,* 26-58.

Dam, L. (1994) How do we recognize an autonomous classroom? In *Die Neueren Sprachen,* 93,503-527.

De Beaugrande, R. & Dressler, W. (1981) *Introduction to Text Linguistics,* Longman: New York.

De Charms, , R. (1984) motivation enhancement in educational settings. In Ames, R.E. & Aimes, C. (Eds.) *Motivation in* Education. Vol. 1, pp. 275-31-. New York, NY: Academic Press *I*

Fischer, J.M. & Ravizza, M. (1993) *Perspectives on Moral Responsibility*, Ithaca: Cornell University Press.

Freire, P. (1972, 1996) *Pedagogy of the oppressed.* Harmondsworth: Penguin.

Good, T. L., & Brophy, J. E. (1991) *Looking in classrooms.* New York: Harper Collins.

Holec, H. (1981) *Autonomy in Foreign Language Learning,* Oxford: Pergamon Press.

Holec, H. (1988) *Autonomy and Self-directed Learning: Present Fields of Application,* Strasbourg: Council of Europe.

Illich, I. (1979) *Deschooling society.* Harmondsworth: Penguin.

Iser, W. (1975) Die Wirklichkeit der Fiktion. In R. Warning (Ed.) *Rezeptionsästhetik, Munich: Fink.*

Jauss, H. R. (1970) *Literaturgeschiche als Provokation,* Frankfurt: Suhrkamp.

Johnson, D. W., & Johnson R. T. (1989). *Cooperation andcompetition: theory andresearch.* Edina, MN: Interaction Book Company.

Kagan, S. (1993) *Cooperative learning.* San Juan Capistrano, CA: Resources for Teachers.
Kane, R. (1996) *The Significance of Free Will,* New York: Oxford University Press.
Kelchtermans. G. (1993) *De professionele ontwikkeling van leerkrachten basisonderwijs vanuit het biografisch perspectief,* Academisch Proefschrift, Katholieke Universiteit Leuven.
Kuhl, J. (1985) Volitional mediators of cognition-behavior consistency: Self-regulatory processes and action versus state orientation. In J. Kubl, & J. Beckman (Eds.), *Action control: From cognition to behavior.* Berlin: Springer-Verlag, 23-35.
Lens, W. (1993) *Studiemotivatie: theorie voor de praktijk op school en thuis.* Leuven: Universitaire Pers Leuven.
Little, D. (1994) Learner autonomy: A theoretical construct and its practical application. *Die Neueren Sprachen,* 93,430-442.
Little, D. (1997) Language awareness and the autonomous language learner. *Language Awareness,* 6, 2-3, 93-104
Lowyck, J. and Verloop, N. (1995) *Onderwijskunde. Een kennisbasis voor professionals,* Groningen: Wolters-Noordhoff.
Marcuse, H. (1968) *De eendimensionale mens: Studies over de ideologie van de hoog industriële samenleving.* Bussum: Brand.
Maslov, A. H. (1970) *Motivation and personality.* New Vork: Harper & Row.
Matthijssen, M. A. J. M. (1972) *Klasse-onderwijs: sociologie van het onderwijs.* Deventer: Van Loghum Slaterus.
Matthijssen, M. A. J. M. (1982) *De elite en de mythe: een sociologische analyse van de strijd om onderwijsverandering.* Deventer: Van Loghum Slaterus.
Narcy, J. P. (1994) Autonomie: Evolution ou révolution? *Die Neueren Sprachen,* 93: 442-454.
Naiman, N., Frohlich, M., Stem, H., & Todesco, A. (1978) *The good language learner.* Toronto: The Toronto Institute for Studies in Education.
Neisser, U. (1967) *Cognitive Psychology,* New York: Appleton
Nunan, D. (1988) *The learner-centered curriculum.* Cambridge: Cambridge University Press.
O'Malley, M. J., & Chamot, A. U. (1990) *Learning strategies in second language acquisition.* Cambridge: Cambridge University Press.
Oxford, R. L. (1990) *Language learning strategies: What every teacher should know.* New Vork: Harper Collins.
Rampillon, U. (1994) Autonomes Lemen im Fremdsprachenunterricht- ein Widerspruch in sich oder eine neue Perspektive? *Die Neueren Sprachen,* 93, 455-466.
Rogers, C. (1969, 1983) *Freedom to learn.* New York: Merill Publishing Company.

Röhr, H. (1991) *Die Reformpädagogik: Ursprung und Verlaufunter internationalem Aspect.* Weinheim: Deutscher Studien Verlag.

Rosenshine, B., & Stevens, R. (1986) Teaching functions. In M. C. Wittrock (Ed.), *Handbook of research on teaching.* New Vork: MacMillan, 376-391.

Ryan, R. M., & Grolnick, W. S. (1986) Origins and pawns in the classroom: Self-report and projective assessments of individual differences in children's perceptions. *Journal of Personality and Social Psychology, 50,* 550-558.

Savignon, S. J. (1983) *Communicative competence: Theory and classroom practice.* Reading, MA: Addison-Wesley.

Savignon, S. J. (1997) *Communicative competence: Theory and classroom practice.* Second Edition. New York: Mc.Graw-Hill.

Savignon, S. J. (2002) Communicative Language Teaching: Linguistic Theory and Classroom Practice. In: Savignon, S.J. (Ed.) *Interpreting Communicative Language Teaching.* New Haven & Londen: Yale University Press, 1-29

Schalkwijk, E., Esch, C. van, Elsen, E. and Setz, W. (2002) Learner Autonomy and the Education of Language Teachers: How to Practice What Is Preached and Preach What Is Practiced. In Savignon, S.J. (Ed.) *Interpreting Communicative Language Teaching.* New Haven & Londen: Yale University Press, 165-191.

Simons, P. R. J., & Zuylen, J.G.G. (1994) *Actief en Zelfstandig Leren in de Tweede Fase.* Tilburg: Mesoconsult.

Slavin, R. E. (1995) *Cooperative learning: Theory, research, and practice.* Boston: Allyn & Bacon.

Störig, H. J. (1964) *Kleine Weltgeschichte derPhilosophie.* Stuttgart: W. Kohlhammer-Verlag.

Van der Meer, Q. L., & Bergman, H. (1975) *Onderwijskundigen van de twintigste eeuw.* Amsterdam-Groningen: Intermediair / Wolters.

Van Els, T.; Bongaerts, T.; Extra, G.; Os van, C.; Janssen-van Dieten, A. & Oirsouw van, R (tr.). (1984). *Applied linguistics and the learning and teaching offoreign languages.* London: Edward Arnold.

Van Esch, C. , Schalkwijk, E. & Sleegers, P. (1996) Zelfstandig Ieren in de opleiding van leraren, in *VELON Tijdschrift voor Lerarenopleiders* 17,4: 24-30.

Van Esch, K. & St. John, O. (eds) (2003) *A Framework for Freedom. Learner Autonomy in Foreign Language Teacher Education.* Peter Lang Verlag: Frankfurt am Main.

Vygotsky, L. S. (1978) *Mind in society: The development of higher psychological processes.* Cambridge, MA: Harvard University Press.

Vygotsky, L. S. (1986) *Thought and Language.* Cambridge, MA: MIT Press.

Wang, M.C. (1981) 'Development and consequences of student's sense of personal control'. In J. M. Levine, & M.C. Wang (Eds.), *Teacher and student perceptions.* Hillsdale, NJ: Lawrence Erlbaum, 213-247.

Wenden, A., & Rubin, J. (1987) *Learner strategies in language learning.* New Jersey: Prentice Hall International.

Wertsch, J. V. (1985) *Culture, communication, and cognition: Vygotskian perspectives.* New York: Cambridge University Press.

Widdowson, H. (1990) *Aspects of language teaching.* Oxford: Oxford University Press.

Wolff, D. (1994) Der Konstruktivismus: Ein neues Paradigma in der Fremdsprachendi- daktik. In *Die Neueren Sprachen* 93, 5: 407-429.

Effecting Change: research into Learner Autonomy in Foreign Language Learning and Teaching

Kees van Esch and Adri Elsen
University of Nijmegen, The Netherlands

1   Introduction

In the previous chapter we explored the origins of learner autonomy from three different perspectives: (1) learner autonomy and human agency, (2) learner autonomy and society and (3) learner autonomy and learning. Relating learner autonomy to foreign language education, we reviewed definitions of learner autonomy. In these definitions, learner autonomy is a pedagogical construct in which different aspects can be emphasized such as willingness, responsibility, cooperation and individualisation. We also discussed the implications for foreign language learning and teaching and for foreign language teacher training. We particularly highlighted the new roles and tasks for foreign language teachers. It was argued that a focus on learner autonomy should lead to guiding principles in foreign language teacher training. A number of suggestions were offered.

The present chapter focuses on research into learner autonomy in foreign language learning and teaching. The chapter consists of four sections, each examining distinct contributions based on investigations and operationalizations of learner autonomy.

First, we will pay attention to theoretical research. The literature reviewed particularly focuses on the political and ideological dimensions of learner autonomy. The psychological and philosophical dimensions discussed in the former chapter are less prominent.

Second, we will discuss applied research into different aspects of learner autonomy in foreign language learning and teaching, such as the problems and conditions related to applying learner autonomy, learner and teacher beliefs about autonomy, the role of motivation, learner strategies, group work, cooperation and interaction, and (self-)assessment and evaluation.

Third, we will investigate the relationship between learner autonomy and teacher autonomy and discuss implications for initial and in-service foreign language teacher training.

We will end this chapter with some conclusions and suggestions for further research in different areas of learner autonomy.

2   Researching the validity of the construct
Learner autonomy, a Western construct?

Little (1999) mentions essential characteristics of learner autonomy. He subsequently reasons that the construct and its development is largely independent of communities or systems of formal learning, such as Western societies based on Christian humanism or Eastern societies based on Confucianism. Essentials of learner autonomy are that "the basis of learner autonomy is acceptance of responsibility for one's own learning, that the development of learner autonomy depends on the exercise of that responsibility in a never-ending effort to understand what one is learning, why one is learning, how one is learning and with what degree of success; and the effect of learner autonomy is to remove the barriers that so easily erect themselves between formal learning and the wider environment in which the learner lives" (Little, 1999, p.11). In opposition to the view that learner autonomy is a Western construct, and, as such, an inappropriate pedagogical goal in non-Western societies, he offers two arguments. The first is his claim that learner autonomy is a minority pursuit that does not flow naturally or inevitably from a particular cultural basis or educational system. The second is the feeling that learner autonomy is always enhanced when critical thinking and independence of mind are favoured. He considers learner autonomy as "a universal human capacity that has always existed independently of particular pedagogies". In formal education, it is "a special case of a more general human capacity for autonomous behaviour", which in the developmental domain is achieved "with infinitely varying degrees of explicitness.". He also believes that "explicitness in planning, implementation and evaluation is fundamental to the development or LA from the very beginning" (Little, 1999, p.17). His conclusion is that although empirical research to demonstrate the efficacy of learner autonomy is welcomed, the construct works by definition. It is a conclusion hard to find fault with. Yet, we feel such a conclusion might too easily lead to a *laissez-faire* attitude and possible negligence. Our point of view is that empirical research on the efficacy of (aspects of) learner autonomy in various settings continues to be necessary in order to learn more about its relevance to education and the specific ways in which it can be fostered in second or foreign language learners.

Following the line of Little (1999), Aoki and Smith (1999) investigated and commented on the cultural context of learner autonomy. After reviewing misconceptions of "culture", they discuss misconceptions of learner autonomy. They oppose claims that learner autonomy offers a new methodology, that it entails individualism and that it depends on psychological and cultural considerations. In spite of the supposed collectivist character of Japanese society (cf. Hofstede, 1991,1998), a society which, according to Aoki and Smith (1999), has never been homogeneously collectivist, they conclude that learner autonomy can also be a successful pedagogical approach in non-western societies. Evidence was provided from two Japanese EFL classes.

Towards a political and 'postcritical' understanding of learner autonomy

In contrast to the more culturally oriented approaches of Little (1999) and Aoki and Smith (1999), Benson (1997) opts for an approach that is politically oriented. He discusses three basic versions of autonomy serving as 'ideal' constructs. The first is a technical version, in which the act of learning a language takes place outside the framework of an educational institution and without the intervention of a teacher. In this version the most important issue of learner autonomy is how to equip the learners with the skills and techniques they need to cope with such situations. A second version of autonomy is psychological. It considers learner autonomy as a capacity- a construct of attitudes and abilities - that allows learners to take more responsibility for their own learning and in which autonomy is developed by internal transformation within the individual learner. The third version is political. At issue is how far a learner has control over the processes and contents of learning. A political version of autonomy highlights the importance of creating structural conditions that enable learners to not only control their own learning but also partly determine the conditions of learning.

Benson reviews three loosely-defined theories of learning, i.e. *positivism*, in which knowledge is considered as the more or less accurate reflection of objective reality, *constructivism*, in which knowledge is seen as the co-construction of meaning, which helps each learner to construct extended versions of reality, and finally *critical theory*, in which knowledge is constructed rather than acquired within social contexts and constraints, often conflicting ideologies. Benson elaborates on the political version of learner autonomy and on critical theory. In critical theory, learning in general and the learning of foreign languages in particular are dependent on and determined by political and social conditions (cf. also Pennycook, 1997 and 2001). Therefore, Benson (1997) proposes to concentrate on the social and political context in which second or foreign language learning takes place, and on the roles and relationships of the people who interact both inside and outside of the classroom. Benson feels the learner must adopt a critical attitude towards learning goals, content of learning (e.g. materials and learning tasks) and didactic procedures, in short towards all areas in which autonomy can be promoted. Benson's political version of autonomy (1997) has origins similar to the critical pedagogy of e.g. Giroux (1981), Mclaren (1989) and Kanpol (1994, 1997). They also criticize formal education, acknowledge the political aspects of schooling and curricula, and attempt to encourage students to develop their own democratic alternatives..

Critical pedagogy is not without its opponents. Pennycook (2001) has summarised critiques of critical pedagogy. It has been accused of remaining at the level of 'grand theorizing', unrelated to pedagogical practice. It tends to be prescriptive, i.e. telling teachers what to do, often without being explicit. And, according to the critics, critical pedagogy has been concerned more with North-American individualistic idealism than with effecting social change (Pennycook, 2001: 130-132). Pennycook acknowledges the criticisms, but, at the same time, recognizes the merits of critical pedagogy, such as offering insight into and understanding of educational theory and adopting a constructively critical approach to language and education. Therefore, he argues for what he calls a "postcritical pedagogy" of language education, which "attempts to deal with the postcolonial challenge of dealing with the Other, the poststructuralist requirement to understand how discourses operate across multiple sites, constructing our world and subjectivities, and the postmodern challenge to deal with the particularities and complexities presented by trying to take differences seriously". (Pennycook, 2001: 140).

The postcritical approach to foreign language learning and teaching advocated by Pennycook is strongly related to the so-called "postmethod" pedagogy of Kumaravadivelu (2001). It was proposed in response to the alleged limitations of the concept of *method* and the transmission model of teacher education. Postmethod pedagogy is based on three principles. The first is *particularity*, meaning that "language pedagogy must be sensitive to a particular group of teachers teaching a particular group of learners pursuing a particular set of goals within a particular institutional model embedded in a particular sociocultural milieu". The second is *practicality* that emphasizes the need for teachers to theorize from their practice and practice what they theorize." The third principle is *possibility*, referring to creating opportunities for foreign language learning and teaching "by acknowledging and highlighting students' and teachers' subject positions - that is, their class, race, gender, and ethnicity" and stimulating them to question the status quo that keeps them subjugated" (Kumaravadivelu, 2001: 542).

As an advocate of postmethod pedagogy, Ferreira (2001) criticizes modernist views of learner autonomy. Based on Usher & Edwards (1994), he discusses two alleged modernist conditions for autonomy to be required: objectivity and self-consciousness. Modernists assume objectivity because they believe autonomous learners are able to describe reality as it is and can produce knowledge that is unprejudiced. Self-consciousness is assumed because it is claimed that learners are aware of their own selves and their own values and beliefs. Ferreira doubts whether objectivity and self-consciousness can ever be achieved in their modernist senses, not in the least because many educational systems tend to increase the level of monitoring and control over both teachers' and students attitudes and action. As an alternative, Ferreira (2001) argues for a deconstruction and reconstruction of the concept of learner autonomy. The process of de- and reconstruction first involves awareness of the ways in which pedagogical practices are embedded in the socio-historical contexts of education. Second, it involves a realisation that subjectivity is in reality *inter-subjectivity*, because subjectivity is socially constructed in interaction between individuals that typically include complex systems of information, values and beliefs. The knowledge, skills and competences produced in this interaction are closely related to dimensions of power. Critical reflection on these power dimensions in teacher education, teaching methodology and classroom practices is needed to review pedagogical practices and evaluate concepts such as learner autonomy.

To conclude this section, a political view of autonomy as well as postcritical and postmethod pedagogy help to critically develop and review pedagogical approaches that aim to foster learner autonomy in learners. They particularly help to highlight discuss and negotiate power dimensions, such as particular situational demands or pressures that help or hinder learner independence. However, a version of learner autonomy that is primarily ideological or political may not do justice to the psychological or philosophical dimensions of the essential characteristics we quoted at the beginning of this section, e.g. "...[an] acceptance of responsibility for one's own learning, a never-ending effort to understand what one is learning, why one is learning, how one is learning and with what degree of success; and the removal of the barriers between formal learning and the wider environment in which a learner lives" (Little, 1999, p.11). These dimensions will be discussed in more detail in the next section, which starts with a review of research into the problems of and the conditions needed for successfully applying learner autonomy.

3   Researching autonomy in foreign language learning and teaching
Applying learner autonomy: problems and conditions

There have been so many proposals for applying aspects of learner autonomy to the learning and teaching of foreign language, that it seems impossible to review them all or to present truly representative samples. Therefore, our selection is personal and limited to a small number of applications that each touch upon different areas or aspects of learner autonomy. Some of the examples are interesting because of the methodology used or the empirical data yielded.

A first example refers to some of the drawbacks and opportunities of applying learner autonomy in secondary education. Dam (1994) describes the most important features of one of her autonomous foreign language classrooms and discusses the requirements for implementing learner autonomy in this classroom. She transcribes and describes what has been said by the pupils and what have been her interventions as a teacher and researcher, and discusses these in detail. Her conclusions are that the main requirements of a foreign language classroom are (1) "an *awareness of learning, ...*" (2) "*changes in teacher and learner roles*, ..." (3) "*evaluation* as a recurring activity, being the backbone or pivot of the learning process, ..." and (4) "a *learning environment* equivalent to a workshop or laboratory where things are tried out and investigated, learners are teachers and teachers are learners and the process is basically the content" (Dam, 1994: 525). Based on these requirements and in spite of the problems involved in the application of learner autonomy in the setting of secondary education, Dam and Legenhausen (1999) have carried out the LAALE (Language Acquisition in an Autonomous Learning Environment) project in a school in Denmark and collected relevant empirical data that will be discussed later on in this chapter, when we focus on assessing and evaluating learner autonomy.

In a similar setting in the Netherlands, Van Esch, Schalkwijk and Van Summeren (2000 and 2001), carried out an exploratory investigation of current and good practices of learner autonomy in foreign language learning and teaching, especially related to listening and speaking development. Using three different instruments, lesson observations, video recordings and interviews, they collected data in classes of French and English and drew conclusions about current and good practices of learner autonomy. The results of this study highlighted a number of conditions that seemed to determine failure or success when implementing learner autonomy in the foreign language classroom: a clear orientation by the teacher into *what* to learn and *how* to learn, careful planning by the students, explicit training of the students in how to structure learning tasks well and on how to use learning strategies and reflection on the results of this training, a gradual transfer of control over the learning process from the teacher to the learners, and a change in the roles of the teacher from an assessor and manager of the learning process to a facilitator and resource for the individual learner. Both students and teachers fell short in complying with these conditions due to internal and external constraints such as absence of motivation and willingness, time constraints, a lack of preparation despite in-service training, and insufficient support by school authorities. The results offered an 'early' indication of the reasons for the actual problems in implementing learner autonomy in secondary education in the Netherlands.

A study by O'Leary (2002) carried out in the context of higher education shows that applying principles of learner autonomy to educational practice is no easy matter. Using instruments such as reports, diaries, questionnaires and portfolios, she was able to demonstrate the development of cognitive and meta-cognitive knowledge and skills in the learners. It appeared it was far from easy for the students to learn how to reflect and to see these reflections as essential parts of their learning activities. Moreover, they also experienced difficulties in using the meta-language needed to be able to discuss their learning efforts and results. O'Leary argued for the development of a learner training programme in collaboration with the students and with the help of an electronic learning environment to exchange information, experiences and reflections.

Besides the application of learner autonomy in the context of secondary and higher education, there have been a considerable number of studies on implementing learner autonomy in 'self-access centres' (SACs) or 'self-access language learning centres' (SALLs), mostly by university researchers in New-Zealand, Hong-Kong and Japan. The Kanda University, in Japan, has begun research projects aimed at developing a personal English proficiency curriculum for each student entering the university based on principles of learner autonomy. Carrying out action research into concepts such as individualization, interaction and interdependence in the learning process, they found promising results regarding the application of these concepts (cf. Johnson et al., 2002). Similar projects were carried out in SACs and SALLs in Hong-Kong and New Zealand. The project carried out by Pemberton et al. (1999) was aimed at self-directed English-language-learning and developing learner autonomy among postgraduate students in the SALL at Hong Kong University of Science & Technology. They investigated the effects of workshops in which the students were introduced to the principles of self-access learning and made aware of ways to learn more effectively, This was done by means of inventories of learning styles, diaries, portfolios and advisory sessions. The first results indicated that the students progressed and improved both in language proficiency and in the development of learner autonomy, albeit more in the former aspect than in the latter. The researchers concluded that learner autonomy could have been developed more by giving the students more freedom in choosing materials and activities, adapting the learning process to their preferred learning styles and stimulating more collaborative learning. Other studies on learner autonomy in the SACs and SALLs at Hong-Kong university (cf. Mak & Turnbull, 1999; Miller, 1999 and Fitzgerald, 1999) have yielded interesting findings about (1) how students judge aspects of self-directed learning and learner autonomy with regard to the content and organization of language courses, preferred ways of learning, participation in these courses, advisory sessions and the use of multimedia and (2) the opinions of teachers and students about how to improve these aspects in order to enhance their autonomy as learners. The results yielded by these studies were that the feedback given by students on the different aspects of the SACs and SALLs led to an improvement of the programming and the materials including the use of multimedia, to insights into the role of multimedia in self-access-centres, to an enhancement of the learner- tutor communication, and to recommendations for implementing learner autonomy in other settings than the SACs or the SALLs, such as primary and secondary schools.

To conclude this section, investigating the daily practice of applying learner autonomy in the foreign language classroom both in the formal settings of the school and of the SACs and SALLs, helps us to understand problems students and teachers have to cope with and to find the conditions and requirements needed for a successful implementation of learner autonomy: awareness of the learning process, changes in learner and teacher roles, careful selection and structuring of content, materials and tasks, including the use of multimedia and electronic learning environments. But investigating this practice makes it clear that, in addition to conditions and requirements, there are other aspects that need to be taken into account when applying learner autonomy. Personal factors, such as beliefs and motivation, also affect the process significantly. In the next two sections we will review research on these factors.

Learner and teacher beliefs about learner autonomy

A question studied in several research projects is that of teachers' and learners' beliefs about aspects of learner autonomy. An example of a study of learners' beliefs is Cotterall (1995). She argues for the necessity to probe and assess the learners' readiness for the changes in behaviour and beliefs which autonomy implies, before any intervention of autonomy-oriented approaches to language learning is made. Her study presents data on learner beliefs collected in a study with 139 adult ESL learners in the summer of 1992-1993. The overall aim was to see if subjects' responses to a questionnaire revealed any particular cluster of beliefs. Using a factor analysis, six factors were obtained: (1) Role of the teacher, (2) Role of feedback, (3) Learner independence, (4) Learner confidence in study ability, (5) Experience of language learning (i.e. experiencing being successful in language learning) and (6) Approach to studying. Her conclusion was that these learner beliefs would affect (and sometimes inhibit) learners' receptiveness to the ideas and activities presented in the language class. In her own words: "Learners' beliefs about language learning will profoundly affect their approach to language learning" (Cotterall, 1995: 202). She claims that an awareness of the role of cognitive and affective variables in language learning, of how language functions and of how strategies influence learning can enhance learners' quality of thinking and task engagement. Autonomous learners, she maintains, draw on their experiences of working on tasks, using strategies and solving problems to deepen their understanding of the target language system. "By exploring these beliefs, learners and teachers can hope to construct a shared understanding of the language learning process and of the part they play in it. This awareness is an essential foundation of learner autonomy." (Cotterall, 1995: 203).

Research by Crabbe, Hoffmann and Cotterall (2001) has clearly shown that an awareness of learner beliefs is a decisive factor in successfully implementing learner autonomy. Analysing the discourse of interviews between three learners of a second language at university level and their tutors, the researchers have explored the problems experienced by these learners in immediate and long-term goal setting and in expressing their beliefs about language learning. In their conclusions, they state that goals occupy a central position in the learning process and that "making the goals explicit seems a useful basis for any subsequent discussion of strategic behaviour that might serve those goals". They also claim that "the immediate effectiveness of the session could be measured by how well the learners represent the problem, how committed they are to specific goals, and how aware they are of their beliefs about language learning" (Crabbe, Hoffmann and Cotterall, 2001: 14).

Another example of a study of teachers' beliefs about language learning and learner autonomy is Elsen (due 2004). The study called *Testing for Autonomy* centres around three exploratory case studies of the language testing practice of academically-trained teachers of English in the fourth forms of upper secondary education in The Netherlands in 1999 - 2000. In August 1999, all 500 schools offering general secondary and pre-university education had started implementing curricular and didactic changes that highlighted notions such as learner autonomy and learning how to learn. It was envisaged that closely monitoring three teachers and three different classes in a year of turbulent curricular and didactic reform would provide interesting research data. The study was set up to realize three objectives, namely (1) to explore the variables of informal assessment and evaluation practice in settings geared at fostering learner autonomy in foreign language learners, (2) to highlight relevant theory, and (3) to make recommendations for future research and for training programmes for educators on how to create positive washback of language tests in learning to learn how to communicate in English.

The data consisted of teacher and learner questionnaires, teacher and learner interviews, classroom observations, and nine sample language tests the teachers had designed and used. After gathering, transcribing and analysing the data, its preliminary findings were generalized to theory and analysed for a second time. The design proved to be useful for the exploration of complex constructs in classroom practice, such as learner autonomy, learning how to learn, communicative language ability and test washback and is likely to yield relevant results when replicated in similar studies.

The variables explored relate primarily to the teacher. Learner data have been used to illustrate and corroborate some aspects of teacher rhetoric. The data analysis moved from open codes, to predominant categories of codes, to variables generalized to theory, to a final examination of data. The study led to a number of important conclusions. The first is that educational change geared at curricular didactic reform should not be introduced top-down. Teachers' beliefs, strengths and weaknesses should explicitly be taken into account. Teachers should be engaged and facilitated as experts in their fields. The second conclusion is that educational policy did not do justice to theory and empirical research data when educationists "encouraged" teachers to develop alternative didactic procedures geared at fostering autonomy in learners when they learn how to learn to communicate in English. It led to theoretical and practical notions that were unclear and ambiguous to the school managers and teachers who were expected to implement these changes. To varying degrees, this goes for all of the notions on which the study concentrated, i.e. learner autonomy, learning how to learn, communicative language ability and test washback. A third conclusion is that educational politicians and supervising institutions fail to fully recognise that educational reform takes years and years before it is successfully implemented. In some ways, they abuse the autonomy that was democratically granted to them. Whereas the foreign language learner and teacher are expected to learn from mistakes, other standards seem to apply when it concerns those in power. A fourth conclusion is that fundamental research of complex constructs and classroom research should and could have been the basis on which to design, implement and evaluate the curricular and didactic reforms. Finally, both the three teachers and most of the learners tended to consider language tests as summative assessments of a learning cycle. The tests often involved the reproduction of a limited amount of discrete knowledge or skills. They rarely ever led to extensive evaluations of the teaching and learning process, i.e. of *what* had been tested, *why* this had been done in particular ways, and *how* the results of the tests should be interpreted in view of the learners learning how to communicate in English.

Elsen argues that settings conducive to learner autonomy call for a more extended and dynamic view of language testing, based on specific objectives that are preferably shared by the teacher and the learners. The more explicit and challenging the objectives are, the easier it will be for the teacher and the learners to evaluate the targeted learning at some given time. Learners should be engaged in identifying and formulating criteria that help them assess and evaluate their own learning results. The creation of such settings may also involve teachers in exploring concepts, such as formative assessment and evaluation, test washback and construct validation. Elsen states that a training programme on assessment and evaluation is most likely to be successful if it relates to and starts with what the teachers believe in and what they feel they are good at.

The three studies mentioned above plead for a shared understanding of the teaching and learning process. Teacher and learner beliefs should be discussed and made explicit at the beginning of a learning process in which the learners themselves are to assume active roles. These beliefs should lead to clear objectives and to learning that can be targeted and modified or extended by the learners themselves. Any learning results should be open to assessment and evaluation at any given time of the learning process, both by the teacher and by the learners themselves.

Motivation and learner autonomy

In the interviews of Elsen's study (due 2004), motivation turned out to be the factor most frequently mentioned by teachers and students. To investigate the link between autonomy and motivation, Dickinson (1995) has reviewed literature about motivation. After describing autonomy as both an attitude towards learning and a capacity for independent learning and using Keller's definition of motivation as " ...the choices people make as to what experiences or goals they will approach or avoid, and the degree of effort they will exert in that respect" (Crookes & Smith, 1991, p. 389), Dickinson reviews several theories of motivation.

The first one is the extrinsic / intrinsic motivation theory (Deci and Ryan, 1985), which claims that intrinsically motivated learners, i.e. learners who are challenged by learning tasks and interested in their outcomes without any external pressure or situational demand, are much more likely to become effective learners than extrinsically motivated learners, i.e. learners who are mainly motivated by external incentives, such as getting good grades or a certificate. Gardner's (1985) distinction between integrative and instrumental motivation has made an important contribution to the literature about motivation in language learning. According to Dickinson the former is "a subject-specific example of intrinsic motivation" and the latter is related to extrinsic motivation "with its emphasis on rewards for achievement" (Dickinson, 199, p. 170). The relation between this theory and learner autonomy is that intrinsic motivation is enhanced most when learners are given the opportunity to increasingly have a say in what is learned and how this is done.

The second theory reviewed is the attribution theory that links motivation to the reasons responsible for success or failure in learning, i.e. learners who consider that success or failure is the result of their own efforts to take responsibility are more effective learners than those who attribute success or failure to causes external to themselves or beyond their own ability. The link between this theory and autonomy is the level of control that learners believe they have over their learning. When they attribute their success or failure to their own efforts, they assume this kind of control and exercise their autonomy as learners.

The motivational model of deCharms (1984) was added to the two theories described above. In this model, learners are successful when they control their learning and act as "origins", i.e. they originate their own actions. They don't control their own learning when they act as "pawns", i.e. when they respond to external factors. The Carnegie project was based on deCharms's motivational model. The project was aimed at enhancing the motivation of low income, black, elementary school children in St. Louis and at reducing their "pawn behaviour".

Dickinson (1995) concludes that there is "substantial evidence from cognitive motivational studies that learning success and enhanced motivation is conditional on learners taking responsibility for their own learning, being able to control and perceiving that their learning successes or failures are to be attributed to their own efforts and strategies rather than to factors outside their control. Each of these conditions is characteristic of learner autonomy as it is described in applied linguistics". (Dickinson, 1995, p.172).

Van Lier (1996) has also related the concepts of autonomy and motivation. Instead of assuming a dichotomy between intrinsic and extrinsic motivation, he propagates "an interplay between intrinsic (innate) and extrinsic (environmental) factors" (Van Lier, 1996, p.99). Next, he hypothesizes that in education extrinsic factors tend to dominate to the detriment of intrinsic motivation. Therefore he feels it is necessary to stimulate intrinsic factors, while at the same time, taking into account the pressure of extrinsic demands. He advocates seeking a "responsible course of action which balances intrinsic and extrinsic resources and constraints, and the needs and goals of the individual with the needs and goals of society." (Van Lier, 1996, p. 99). There appears to be a close link between achievement and self-determination in the sense that "... feedback from others can enhance a person's knowledge of success, but only if the person feels that the behaviour was self-determined, and the context was one which facilitated autonomy." (Van Lier, 1996: 120).

Dickinson (1995) and Van Lier (1996) have made clear that there is a strong relationship between motivation and learner autonomy but that, in order to understand this relationship, we have to take into account other variables. One important variable is control over learning: if successes and failures can be attributed to personal efforts instead of factors outside their control, learners will become more autonomous. Another variable is the context of learning. While in education extrinsic motivation is favoured mostly due to e.g. the context of exam and curriculum requirements and time constraints, leading, as is often the case, to "pawn" behaviour (see DeCharms, 1984), intrinsic motivation in the learner must be stimulated to realise responsibility, "origin" behaviour and learner autonomy. Paraphrasing the conclusion in section 2.1 of Chapter 10 about the four accounts of human agency and their relation to learner autonomy, we maintain that, in order to become more autonomous, the learner must seek a balance between the constraints and problems of the external context and internal factors, such as his (intrinsic) motivation, control over learning and his own efforts.

Learning strategies and learner autonomy

Learning strategies are generally divided into three types, although it is not always easy to distinguish clearly between them (cf. e.g. O'Malley & Chamot, 1990, Wenden & Rubin, 1987). The first type of strategy encompasses metacognitive strategies, which refer to knowledge about cognitive processes and the regulation of cognition, executive control or self-management through, for example, the strategies of planning, monitoring, and evaluating. The second type covers *cognitive* strategies. They refer to the steps or operations used in learning, problem solving or the execution of tasks that require direct analysis, transformation, or synthesis of learning materials. The third type includes *socio-affective* strategies, which involve the social and affective components in learning.

Due to the nature of metacognitive strategies, most studies link these strategies to learner autonomy. One of the first examples is Holec (1987), who transcribed and analysed interviews between adult learners of English and their counsellors in a non-school setting in order to find out how foreign language learners manage their learning processes and how they change as learners over time. He found that these learners were not particularly good learners in the sense that they successfully managed their learning processes and that the counsellors needed to become more interested in the learner qua learner in order to develop self-directed learning, learning to learn, learner strategies as well as language learning resource centres. According to Coterall (1999), studies on strategies can be put on a continuum that ranges from self-directed to more or less interventionist approaches. Holec's study is an example of a non-interventionist approach since his learners are what he called "freelance" learners (Holec, 1987: 155). Holec's study gave way to an enormous increase in studies of the relationship between learning strategies and learner autonomy, which emphasised the use of learning strategies – especially metacognitive strategies – when developing the capacity for self-directed learning and autonomy. This practical and instrumental approach belongs to a "technical version of learner autonomy" (Benson and Voller, 1997: 25).

An example of an interventionist approach that relates both to cognitive and metacognitive strategies is Cohen (1999). He advocates direct teaching of strategies or strategies-based instruction (SBI). The aims of SBI are to teach learners explicitly how, when and why strategies can be used to learn a foreign language, and to integrate these strategies into foreign language classroom practice. In a study, he compared the results of 55 intermediate learners of Norwegian and French, who had received either SBI or a regular ten-week language course. His instruments were a pre-treatment questionnaire, speaking tasks, the Strategy Inventory for Language Learning (SILL: Oxford, 1990) filled in before and after the research period, and verbal report data while filling in the SILL. The results were somewhat confusing. On the one hand, there were no significant differences in the overall mean performance of the students grouped together on any of the three tasks. Yet, on the other hand, a better performance of the experimental group on the third task and a general increase of the use of task-specific strategies were reported by the students in the SILL and the verbal reports.

A less interventionist and a more awareness-raising approach was adopted by Nunan, Lai and Keobke (1999). They carried out three different research projects. Nunan investigated how the abilities of sixty undergraduate Arts students at the University of Hong-Kong were affected by strategy training and reflection on and monitoring of their own learning. The results were that the opportunities for self-monitoring, self-assessment, and strategy-training changed students' learning behaviour from a more linguistic focus to a more communicative focus, from a more product-oriented approach to a more process-oriented approach and towards greater control of their own learning process. The second project was carried out by Lai. It was carried out with 30 undergraduate students from various backgrounds and levels and aimed at investigating the effect of guided critical reflection on the capacity to organise their learning of listening to English. These students, who had assessed themselves as poor to mediocre listeners of English, succeeded in stimulating learner control and in improving planning, selection, monitoring and evaluation strategies. The training materials used were self-report questionnaires, journals and diaries, which helped them to reflect on their own learning. The third project, carried out by Keobke, had students focus on their learning processes by providing navigation training within an electronic learning environment. To overcome the contradiction between a traditional classroom with a pre-established curriculum, materials and learning activities and a learner-centred curriculum, Keobke's students were free to satisfy their own needs and follow their own paths with the help of hypermedia and hypertext and so become more autonomous. The project also led to the expected increase of control over the learning processes by the learners themselves.

In the midst of an ever-increasing interest in metacognitive strategies such as planning, monitoring and evaluation and in cognitive strategies related to learner autonomy, Wenden (1995) mentioned a lack of attention to knowledge about cognition, especially task-based knowledge. She claimed that the effect of metacognitive strategies will be rather limited, unless they are firmly based on knowledge. The aspects of task-based knowledge Wenden explores are the purpose, demands and kind of task. Wenden cites ample research of these three aspects and argues for "a task-based and knowledge-based approach to the development and implementation of learner training and strategy training to promote autonomy". This implies the need to recognize that what she calls "the learning software" should comprise both the strategies of learning and the knowledge essential for that learning process (Wenden, 1995: 190, resp.192).

Other issues in learner strategies in relation to learner autonomy are the preference of learners for certain strategies and its implications for foreign language learning. In a review of the literature about the 'order of popularity', McDonough (1999) found evidence for an order of frequency of strategy use in the literature he reviewed on this subject. Studies by O'Malley et al. (1985) and O'Malley & Chamot (1990) showed that repetition, note taking, cooperation and clarification requests were the most popular cognitive strategies used by beginners and intermediate learners of English, and that elaboration, keyword, deduction, grouping and recombination appeared to be the less popular ones. But the differences were not established as statistically reliable and the problem was that the use of strategies was not linked to specific skills and knowledge. If this had been the case, the order of frequency of strategy use would have been different. Nevertheless, the problem remains that such results are not necessarily statistically and methodologically reliable either. In their studies on reading, Block (1986) and Sarig (1987) found that strategies of monitoring and self-evaluation are less frequent than strategies of coherence detection, clarification, and simplification. Carrell (1989) found that local strategies such as word-attack skills and word identification were more important for English-speaking learners of Spanish, whereas Spanish-speaking learners of English in the USA preferred global strategies such as coherence detection and top-down determination of overall meaning and interpretation. The problem was, as Mc Donough states, that in Carrell's investigation (1989), proficiency level, learning circumstance and purpose were confounded and could not be untangled. In her study of strategy use in listening, Young (1996) reported 'summarising' as a more common lower level reception strategy when compared to 'elaboration' or 'planning'. For writing, Jones and Tetroe (1987) found that 'planning' required a greater cognitive load than other strategies. Cohen (1991) mentioned that in their evaluations, excellent writers only reported using the strategy of mental note, while other students also referred to vocabulary, grammar, and the mechanics of writing. Schmitt (1997) reviewed the research on vocabulary learning strategies and carried out a study of strategy use by Japanese learners of English, indicating that these learners initially prefer repetition and memorisation strategies and then pass to interactive strategies and metacognitive elaboration. McDonough (1999) pointed out the methodological problems involved in research on strategies (mostly observational studies via think-aloud protocols, language corpora and questionnaires, and only a few controlled experiments), which make it impossible to generalize and draw definite pedagogical implications. From the studies he reviewed, McDonough adduced the following seven explanations for the differences in frequency of strategy use, order of popularity and order of appearance over time: cognitive complexity of strategies, maturation of the learners, proficiency level, the power of the strategies, the types of tasks, culture and training of the learners and L2 use.

McDonough's explanations show the great amount of variables involved when we attempt to measure the effectiveness of learning strategies in reliable and convincing ways. They also show how little we know about the effectiveness of strategy use for each and every individual learner. Nevertheless, we believe that a learner should be given the opportunity to learn about and practise particular learning strategies, and afterwards evaluate the effects with the teacher. We consider this mutual evaluation and discussion of the targeted learning as an essential component of fostering learner autonomy. Deliberate choice from a variety of strategies helps both the learner and the teacher focus on the learning process. The fact that strategy use may sometimes painfully highlight a lack of knowledge on the learner's part can also be seen as an opportunity to adjust and reformulate learning targets in cognitive domains.

Group work, interaction and discourse in learner autonomy

As pointed out in the first chapter on learner autonomy in this book, the social aspect underlying successful teacher-learner and learner-learner co-operation is a very important element in the development of learner autonomy. Smith (2001) investigated this aspect of learner autonomy in a Japanese setting, which is generally seen as more favourable to group-based approaches as opposed to more Western-oriented individualistic approaches. He described and interpreted the data from classes of 39 first-year students taking an English listening course. They were asked to reflect on and to evaluate group activities aimed at developing self-directed learning and to take responsibility for the contents and ways of learning. The results were that these activities led to an increase in self-direction and autonomy among the Japanese learners.

Legenhausen (2001) studied the interaction in the target language of learners of English in a Danish comprehensive school. He compared the developmental patterns of communication and linguistic aspects of student-to-student talk after one year and five months of English with those after four years of English. Contrary to what is generally found in research about classroom foreign language discourse in compulsory school settings, i.e. that the learners do not achieve high levels of sophistication, the results of this study prove that the discourse of learners in the autonomous classroom setting can be characterised as authentic, verbally complex and sophisticated.

Coyle's (2002) study gives evidence of the possibility of reaching high levels of interaction in foreign language classroom settings geared to promoting autonomy. From a socio-cultural theoretical stance (cf. Chapter 1,2 and 3 of this volume) and using methodological triangulation, based on Van Lier's (1996) semantic spaces, to co-construct learning environments from different perspectives, she analysed foreign language (French and Spanish) classroom discourse in two contrasting comprehensive schools. The instruments she used were document analysis, questionnaires, interviews, field notes, and observations of lessons and student tasks. She identified linguistic and strategic learner 'moves' through microgenetic analysis of peer and student-teacher interaction at both inter- and intra-mental levels during problem-solving tasks in lessons.

Useful data is provided not only by analysis of discourse in the foreign language classroom, but also by analysis of the discourse in advisory sessions. Advising is an important element in developing learner autonomy and the discourse of advising has increasingly become a focus of research. For example, a study by Pemberton et al (2001) describes the approaches of four advisers involved in a self-directed language learning programme for postgraduate learners. They collected data with help of questionnaires, interviews with selected learners, tape-recording of advisory sessions and of a discussion between the four advisers, diaries of learners and advisers, end-of-programme reports and e-mail communication between learners and advisers. The results indicated that although the advisers differed in the degree to which their advice embodied directives and in their tendency to intervene in the learning process – with the potential danger of undermining the development of learner autonomy – all the advisers used a variety of advising strategies in helping their students to learn independently. The great majority of students reported that advice helped them to learn on their own. The authors advocate the analysis of the discourse of advising as a helpful instrument in promoting self-directed foreign language learning.

Evaluation and assessment of learner autonomy

We have already indicated that assessment of the targeted learning and its ensuing evaluation by the learner and teachers are essential aspects in fostering learner autonomy. The targeted learning should ideally be based on clear objectives and assessment criteria, so that the learners can, to a certain extent, assess and evaluate the learning results themselves.

Although learner autonomy in language learning has been discussed and practised for almost two decades, there is, according to Dam and Legenhausen (1999), a general lack of data when it comes to evaluating its successes and failures in terms of linguistic and other outcomes. As a result, in 1992, these two researchers started the LAALE (Learning Acquisition in an Autonomous Learning Environment) project with six different data elicitation phases, trying to vary the elicitation formats systematically and focus on different language aspects, including self- and teacher evaluation, diaries, vocabulary tests, C-tests, interviews and peer-to-peer talks. The control groups were a Folkeskole in Denmark and a grammar and comprehensive school in Germany. The findings were that the autonomous learners proved to be better in vocabulary range, speaking (they were more involved in high-risk, purposeful and authentic communication) and in C-tests. The correlations between self-rating scores, teacher ratings and external assessments were high (from .74 to .87), leading to the conclusion that, given the general uncertainty as to the validity of test measures, teacher ratings and C-tests measures are no more valid than the self-evaluation of autonomous learners.

Having a different research objective than Dam and Legenhausen's (1999) study, Elsen's study (due 2004) of teacher beliefs about effective foreign language learning and educational change, focuses on their beliefs about testing, assessment and evaluation in a learner autonomy setting. Although foreign language assessment and evaluation were considered important to society as well as to the learner and the teacher, the area appeared to be surprisingly neglected both by testers and test takers. Despite the perceived relevance of language testing to politicians, teachers and learners, a teacher's or learner's assessment and evaluation practice seems too often and too easily determined by the language testing practice he or she has been used to for years and years. As such, it has failed to produce the dynamics needed to create positive washback to the teaching and learning process of each and every learner. His conclusions have already been mentioned in the former section on learner and teacher beliefs in this chapter.

Champagne et al (2001) described the role of assessment and evaluation in learner autonomy in an action research project carried out at the Asian Institute of Technology in Thailand with the help of *Talkbase*, a framework in which the practice of learner autonomy and language learning is realised through tasks which are controlled by the teacher and then through subsequent tasks identified and controlled by the learners themselves. In this project, teacher and learner roles have been redefined for autonomy to be realised. According to the authors "language teaching...has continued to evolve...into maintenance of an environment in which we seek to bring students' thoughts in the open, as step towards their communicative abilities and towards allowing and encouraging their autonomy" (Champagne et al. 2001: 48). In assessing the progress in both communicative and autonomy areas, a variety of instruments has been used: entry-exit interviews, self-assessments and evaluations, portfolios of work (individual and group work), written and graphical work, audio tapes and video tapes made outside the classroom, computer-based presentations, teacher observations of progress, report-backs, individual consultations, field trips, classroom videotapes, participants' perceptions of progress, reflection-on-action, journals and writing feedback sessions. They discussed the value of the different instruments and gave examples of experiences with the use of these instruments in assessing progress of students in both language performance and increase of autonomy. Their conclusion was that assessment should accommodate rigorous methods of self-assessment and evaluation as an integral part of a language learning program.

Lai (2001) argues for an analytical approach to assessing learner autonomy. To facilitate objective measurement, two validated measurement scales were developed to assess learners' self-direction, both at the micro-level of task and at the macro-level of overall organisation of their language learning process. To evaluate process control, i.e. the learner's ability to self-monitor and self-evaluate her learning tasks and/or learning strategies, they asked learners to keep a listening journal for every program they listened to or watched. The learners justified choices of programs and/or activities, set aims for the tasks, reported the contents, identified the problems they encountered, employed or developed relevant strategies to cope with these problems and conducted self-assessments of the listening activities. The learners were expected to provide three entries per fortnight and a total of 15 entries were collected from each learner throughout the entire course term. In a first analysis, only the task aims and the self-assessments were explored. A four-item, five-point rating scale was used. Two items were meant to evaluate the task aims set by the individual learner for each programme or activity chosen by them, and two items related to the self-assessments they had conducted after completing the activity. They found high correlation coefficients (0.915 and 0.832) between the two ratings and, hence, a high reliability. For the second analysis, which focused on self-direction, learners were invited to design a personal course for self-directed learning covering aspects such as setting realistic goals, identifying relevant materials and skills, sub-skills and strategies, engaging in appropriate activities to enhance learning, adopting a specific approach to their learning and conducting self-assessment. To measure the impact of the treatment, a rating-scale comprising 17 items was developed to evaluate each learner's personal course design both at the beginning and at the end of the course. Three teachers were invited, independently, to read through all the entries of personal course design and evaluate their adequacy, usefulness and coherence by rating all the aspects covered in each entry. A seven-point rating scale (0-6) was used to determine the degree to which each statement reflected each aspect. For both the pre-test and the post-test rating scales, the correlation coefficients between the raters turned out to be very high (0.96 for the pre-test scores and 0.92 for the post-test scores). Both the rating scale of process control and the one for self-assessment proved to be valid and reliable.

A first conclusion at the end of this section about assessment and evaluation, is that in spite of projects like those carried out by Dam and Legenhausen (1999), there is still a need for empirical data to compare results in knowledge, skills, beliefs, motivation and attitudes of learners and teachers in learner autonomy settings with those in other foreign language learning and teaching settings. Other conclusions based on Elsen's study (due 2004) are that teacher and learner beliefs about assessment and evaluation must be made explicit, that the testing practice of teachers and learners is very difficult to change and that a more extended and dynamic view of language testing in settings conducive to learner autonomy is required, based on objectives shared by learners and teachers, on training learners in active roles in self-assessment and -evaluation and on helping teachers to develop tools for formative assessment and evaluation. Further conclusions refer to the instruments to assess progress in both language performance and increase of autonomy and to the role of the learners in using these instruments. According to Champagne et al (2001), a variety of instruments are needed, self-evaluation should be prominent and assessment must form an integral part of the language learning program. Finally, Lai (2001) concludes that, to assess learner autonomy, both objective measurement and process evaluation are required.

4 Autonomy in teaching foreign languages?
Relationship between learner and teacher autonomy

More and more attention is being given to the role of the teacher in developing learner autonomy. So, it was not without significance that the Fourth Symposium of the Scientific Commission on Learner Autonomy in Language Learning at the 2002 AILA Congress in Singapore was entitled 'Relationships between Learner and Teacher Autonomy'. The first contribution to the symposium was given by Benson (2002), who has investigated teachers' and learners' notions of control. After reviewing literature on learner autonomy, he found that ideas of control tend to be focused on institutional and classroom learning arrangements within an established curriculum. He found contrary evidence in interviews with 31 undergraduate students at Hong Kong University, who had succeeded in developing relatively sophisticated notions of control of their own learning, in spite of their having been subjected to traditional classroom instruction for up to sixteen years. For these learners, autonomy tends to imply the separation of their learning from the traditional language learning curriculum. To bridge this gap, he argues that we need to move in a direction that better accommodates the perspectives of the learners themselves.

Another contributor, Trebbi (2002) has researched the issue of freedom as consciousness raising in relation to the didactic concept of autonomy. She investigated the context of the Norwegian national curriculum as a vehicle for developing learner autonomy in foreign language learning even if it is conceived within the constraints of a framework decided by the educational authority. She found that the Norwegian teachers have not responded to the change of approach to teaching and learning as envisaged by the designers of the national curriculum. She therefore argues that self-awareness, attitudes and understanding of language learning are crucial for developing the autonomy of the teacher and learner alike, regardless of curricula potentialities or constraints. As such, this conclusion is in line with Cotterall (1995), Crabbe, Hoffmann and Cotterall (2001) and Elsen (due 2004). The contribution by Martínez (2002) was concerned with what student teachers should learn to be able to promote learner autonomy in their future profession. Again, students' beliefs about learner autonomy and language learning and their experiences as learners and student teachers proved to be very important for developing learner autonomy.

To understand the relationship between teacher and learner autonomy, Coterall and Crabbe (2002) interviewed learners and proposed three steps to be taken. The first is to deepen our understanding of the kind of goals and constraints learners face in specific contexts and the consequent strategic behaviour they adopt. The second step is to evaluate the apparent effectiveness of the goals and strategic behaviour in those contexts. The third is to re-examine the role of the teacher in managing the opportunities for the learner in the light of the information gathered.

Daoud (2002) explored the relationship between teacher-initiated action research and teacher autonomy with 20 teachers participating in an action research project, using tools such as recordings of the teachers' oral research reports, feedback questionnaires, classroom observations, and interviews. She found a clear relationship between teacher-initiated action research and teacher autonomy on the one hand, and between teacher and learner autonomy on the other, despite constraints such as teacher overload and the leadership style in the particular context.

In an attempt to avoid self-access centres from becoming places where "learners are left to swim or sink", Pemberton et al. (2002) described the way in which teachers coped with a number of constraints by creating a core team of teachers. The constraints they had to deal with were: supporting self-access language learning, teaching loads and materials-writing responsibilities. A similar way of coping with these constraints was a proposal by Shaw (2002). It was based on an examination of teachers' interactions in two intensive pre-masters programs that involved team teaching as a tool to empower teachers to learn about student learning and act upon that learning.

It would seem that teacher and learner autonomy are enhanced when both teaching and learning are seen as a constant process of construction, deconstruction and reconstruction, which can only be realised effectively, validly and reliably if an approach is discussed elaborately and finally shared with peers.

Learner and teacher autonomy in initial teacher training
At the same 'AILA 2002' congress, there were specific contributions on the implications of enhancing learner autonomy for initial and in-service teacher training. We have already mentioned O'Leary (2002), who argued for the development of a learner training programme in collaboration with the students and with the help of an electronic learning environment to exchange information, experiences and reflections. Other projects have implications for learner autonomy in initial teacher training as well. In a Brazilian context, Fernandes (2002) ethnographically investigated beliefs held by future teachers of English about decision taking related to their own learning and examined the relationship between student discourse and pedagogical praxis. Nicolaides (2002) has also researched beliefs and praxis in relation to the development of learner autonomy within the formal educational context. Both authors reported changes in their learners who, at first, were reluctant to accept principles of learner autonomy. There was an unwillingness to engage in behaviour that promotes learner autonomy, such as adopting more active roles in learning, collaborating with peers and taking more control over and responsibility for their own learning processes. Another more theoretical research project with practical examples was carried out by Van Esch et al. (1999). This study focused on how to educate teachers in the theory and practice of autonomy by raising awareness of learner autonomy principles and phases and relating these to the initial training of teachers of English, French, German and Spanish.

Learner and teacher autonomy in in-service teacher training
Regarding learner and teacher autonomy in-service foreign language teacher training, Santos and Horbach (1999) investigated class management in EFL classes in Brazil with the help of questionnaires answered by teachers and students and with teacher interviews. The result showed that students and teachers disagreed on what to expect from a foreign language class, leading to serious problems in coping with linguistic content, exercises, strategies and procedures. Teachers were strict about following the curriculum and finishing the programme instead of helping the students become aware of the necessity of reflection, creating a supportive atmosphere for the acquisition of autonomy, encouraging learners to cooperate and interact and promoting student-centred learning. The study implies that teachers should promote critical reflection and active learning with their students and coach them in using cognitive and metacognitive strategies to enhance learner autonomy.

The need for teacher training was also stressed by Vieira (1999), who carried out a research project in Portugal aimed at EFL learner training in fostering autonomy and teacher training. Choosing collaborative action research as the basic training strategy for the teachers, the participants succeeded in becoming more self-confident, more able to plan and to review their projects, more flexible in their teaching approach and more inclined to reflective teaching. Learner and teacher autonomy cannot be achieved on the spur of the moment. Thavenius (1999) described how long it can take for teachers to develop awareness of their own learning processes and to become autonomous themselves. We will end this section with her quote: "We are also left with a paradox. To help learners to become autonomous, the teacher has to be autonomous, but the teacher cannot become autonomous until she has experienced the process with her learners for a substantial period of time" (Thavenius, 1999, 163).

5   Conclusions and suggestions for further research

The overview of research findings in this chapter shows us that, although learner autonomy is a relatively new concept in foreign language education, a lot of research has already been carried out. It is also evident from the overview that there is a huge need for further research. At the end of this chapter, we will summarize briefly some of the conclusions we have already drawn in the preceding sections, conclusions that may also be considered as suggestions for further research.

First, research into the construct of learner autonomy, into its development in different cultural contexts and into its political and ideological dimensions, with the help of postcritical and postmethod pedagogy, has made it clear that learner autonomy is multifaceted. Its political, cultural, ideological, philosophical, psychological and educational dimensions need to be investigated further.

Second, our review of applied research has underlined the relevance of learner autonomy to foreign language education but also indicates that more detailed investigation is necessary to clarify the ways in which it is most relevant. There is a particular need for more empirical data about important aspects of learner autonomy, like the problems and conditions regarding its implementation, the beliefs of learners and teachers and their motivation. Research into these aspects has proved that, regardless of the problems and constraints of the context, personal factors like beliefs and motivation are essential requirements in order to develop autonomy. The research we have reviewed so far, makes it clear that changes related to learner autonomy should not be introduced top-down, as has been done in The Netherlands, and that reform designed to promote learner autonomy in foreign language education needs to be well-prepared and may take many years before being implemented successfully. More research into the problems of and conditions for implementing learner autonomy in different educational contexts needs to be carried out. An example of such research might be a comparative study of the implementation of learner autonomy in different countries and settings.

Third, the research we have reviewed shows that, although strategies and interaction are essential for developing learner autonomy, we do not know much about the effectiveness of strategy use or how the quality of interaction in the target language affects language learning. More research must be done. The same goes for the day-to-day practice of learner autonomy in the foreign language classroom and for the assessment and evaluation of that practice.

Fourth, and to end this chapter, we have briefly discussed a relatively new area of research which focuses on the relationship between learner and teacher autonomy and the new roles of (future) teachers in developing learner autonomy. We can conclude that more research into this relationship and into the new roles of the teacher is called for in the near future. A final and related conclusion is that initial and in-service training of foreign language teachers has to be geared to better prepare (future) teachers to acquire the knowledge, insights and experiences they need to cope with these new roles. The project described in the next chapter seeks to apply principles of learner autonomy in initial foreign language teacher education.

6 References

Aoki, N. & Smith, R.C. (1999) Learner autonomy is more than a Western cultural construct. In   Coterall, S. & Crabbe, D. (eds) *Learner Autonomy in Language Learning: Defining the Field and Effecting Change* Frankfurt am Main; Peter Lang Verlag, 19-28.
Benson, P. (1997) The philosophy and politics of learner autonomy. In P.Benson & P. Voller (Eds.) *Autonomy and independence in language learning* London: Longman, 18-34.
Benson, P. (2002) Teachers' and Learners Theories of Autonomy. In *4th Symposium of the Scientific Commission on Learner Autonomy in Language Learning,* 19 December, 2002.
Benson, P. & Voller, P. (Eds.) (1997) *Autonomy and Independence in Language Learning*. London: Longman.
Block, E. (1986) The comprehension strategies of Foreign Language Readers, *TESOL Quarterly,* 463-494.
Carell, P.L. (1989) Metacognitive awareness and second language reading. *Modern Language Journal* 73, 2: 159-179.
Champagne, M.F., Clayton, T., Dimmitt, N., Laszewski, M. , Savage, W. , Shaw, J., Strouppe, R., Thein, M.M. & Walter, P. (1999) The assessment of learner autonomy and language learning. In Dam, L. (Ed.) *Learner autonomy: new insights, AILA Review 15*, 45-56.

Cohen, A. (1991) Feedback on writing: the use of the verbal report. *Studies in Second Language Acquisition* 13, 2, 133-159.

Cohen, A. (1999) Language learning strategies instruction and research. In Cotterall, S.. & Crabbe, D. (Eds.) *Learner Autonomy in Language Learning: Defining the Field and Effecting Change* Frankfurt am Main; Peter Lang Verlag, 61-68.

Cotterall, S. (1995) Readiness for autonomy. *System,* 23, 2, 195-205.

Coterall, S. (1999) Working with groups. Introduction. In Cotterall, S. & Crabbe, D. (Eds.) *Learner Autonomy in Language Learning: Defining the Field and Effecting Change* Frankfurt am Main; Peter Lang Verlag, 43-49.

Coterall, S. & Crabbe, D. (2002) Learners talking: Implications for teacher-Led Autonomy. In *Abstracts 4th Symposium of the Scientific Commission on Learner Autonomy in Language Learning*, 19 December, 2002, 4.

Coyle, D. (2002) Adolescent Voices Taking Control: Reconceptualising Routes to Learner Autonomy in MFI and Bilinugal Classrooms. In *Abstracts XIII World Congress of Applied Linguistics*, Singapore, 16-21 December 2002.

Crabbe, D., Hoffmann, A. & Cotterall, S., (2001) Approaches to advising for self-directed language learning. In Dam, L. (Ed.) Learner autonomy: new insights *AILA Review* 15, 2-15.

Crookes, G. & Schmidt, R.W. (1991) Motivation: reopening the research agenda.. *Language Learning,* 41, 4, 469-512.

Dam. L (1994) How do we recognize an autonomous classroom. In *Die Neueren Sprachen*, 93, 5, 503-527.

Dam. L. & Legenhausen, R. (1999) Language Acquisition in an autonomous leanring environment: learners'self-evaluations and external assessments compared. In Coterall, S. & Crabbe, D. (Eds.) *Learner Autonomy in Language Learning: Defining the Field and Effecting Change* Frankfurt am Main; Peter Lang Verlag, 89-98.

Daoud, S.A. (2002) Developing EFL Teacher and Learner Autonomy through Teacher-Initiated Action Research. In *Abstracts 4th Symposium of the Scientific Commission on Learner Autonomy in Language Learning*, 19 December, 2002, p. 5.

Deci, E.L. & Ryan, R.M. (1985) *Intrinsic Motivation and Self-Determination in Human Behaviour*, New York, NY: Plenum Press

De Charms, , R. (1984) Motivation enhancement in educational settings. In Ames, R.E. & Aimes, C. (Eds.) *Motivation in* Education. Vol. 1, pp. 275-31-. New York, NY: Academic Press.

Dickinson, L. (1995) Autonomy and Motivation. A Literature Review. *System,* 23, 2, 165-174.

Elsen, A. (due 2003) *Testing for Autonomy*. Doctoral Dissertation. University of Nijmegen.

Fernandes, V. (2002) The Discourse and the Praxis of Future Language Teacher Concerning Learner Autonomy. In *Abstracts XIIIth World Congress of Applied Linguistics*, Singapore, 16-21 December 2002, 270.

Ferreira, F.M de C.C. (2001) Autonomy in Foreign Language Teaching and Learning: Why we should look at it from a critical perspective. In *Anais II Fórum Internacional de Ensino de Linguas Estrangeiras*. Universidade Católica de Pelotas e Universidade Federal de Pelotas (Cd-rom).

Fitzgerald, S. (1999) Multimedia provision in a self-access centre. In Morrison, B. (Ed.) *Experiments and Evaluation in Self-Access Language Learning* Hong Kong: HASALD, 73-94.

Gardner, R.C. (1985) *Social Psychology and Language Learning: The role of Attitude and Motivation*. London: Edward Arnold

Giroux, H. A. (1981) *Ideology, Culture and the Process of Schooling*. Philadelphia: Temple University Press,

Hofstede, G. (1991, 1998) *Allemaal andersdenkenden. Omgaan met cultuurverschillen*. Amsterdam: Contact.

Holec, H. (1981) *Autonomy in Foreign Language Learning*. Oxford: Pergamon Press.

Holec, H. (1987) The learner as manager: managing learning or managing to learn? In Wenden, A. & Rubin, J. (Eds.) *Learner Strategies in Language learning*, 145-156. Hemel Hempstead and Englewood Cliffs, NJ: Prentice Hall.

Holec, H. (1988) *Autonomy and self-directed learning: present fields of application*. Strasbourg: Council of Europe.

Johnson, F. , Candlin, C., Harmon, M. B. , Imrie, A. & Van Moere, A. (2002) Learner Autonomy: From Concept to Curriculum - the Kanda Experiment. In *Abstracts 13th AILA World Congress,* Singapore, 16-21 December 2002, 65.

Jones, S. & Tetroe, J. (1987) Composing in a second language. In Matsuhashi, A. (Ed.) *Writing in real time*. Norwood, N.J: Ablex, 43-57.

Kanpol. B. (1994) *Critical pedagogy: An introduction*. Westort, CT: Bergin & Garvey.

Kanpol. B. (1994) *Issues and trends in critical pedagogy*. Cresskill, NJ: Hampton Press.

Kumaravadivelu, (2001) Toward a posmethod pedagogy. *TESOL Quarterly*, 35, 4.

Lai, J. (2001) Towards an analytic approach to assessing learner autonomy. In Dam, L. (Ed.) Learner autonomy: new insights. *AILA Review* 15, 34-45.

Legenhausen, L. (2001) Discourse behaviour in an autonomous learning environment. In Dam, L. (Ed.) Learner autonomy: new insights, *AILA Review*, 15, 56-69.

Little, D. (1999) Learner Autonomy is more than a Western cultural construct. In Cotterall, S. & Crabbe, D. (Eds.) *Learner Autonomy in Language Learning: Defining the Field and Effecting Change* Frankfurt am Main; Peter Lang Verlag, 11-18.

Mak, B. & Turnbull, M. (1999) The Personalised English Programme: piloting structured language learning support in a university self-access centre. In Morrison, B. (Ed.) *Experiments and Evaluation in Self-Access Language Learning* Hong Kong: HASALD, 43-60.

Martínez, H. (2002) Fostering Autonomy in the Language Classroom: Implications for Teacher Education. In Abstracts 4th Symposium of the Scientific Commission on Learner Autonomy in Language Learning, 19 December, 2002, 3.

MC Donnough, S. (1999) A hierarchy of strategies. In Cotterall, S. & Crabbe, D. (Eds.) *Learner Autonomy in Language Learning: Defining the Field and Effecting Chang.* Frankfurt am Main; Peter Lang Verlag, 51-60.

MC Laren, P. (1989) *Life in schools: an introduction to critical pedagogy in the foundations of education.* New York: Longman.

Miller, L. (1999) "Self-Access language learning in primary and secondary schools: The Malaysian experience and the Hong Kong potential. In Morrison, B. (Ed.) *Experiments and Evaluation in Self-Access Language Learning* Hong Kong: HASALD, 61-72.

Nicolaides, C. (2002) Autonomy Development en Future Language Teachers. In *Abstracts XIIIth World Congress of Applied Linguistics*, Singapore, 16-21 December 2002, 270.

Nunan, D., Lai, J. & Keobke, K. (1999) Towards autonomous language learning: strategies, reflection and navigation. In Cotterall, S. & Crabbe, D. (Eds.) *Learner Autonomy in Language Learning: Defining the Field and Effecting Change* Frankfurt am Main; Peter Lang Verlag, 69-78.

O'Leary, Chr. (2002) The development of autonomy in advanced foreign language learners on an institution-wide language program. In *Abstracts XIIIth World Congress of Applied Linguistics*, Singapore, 16-21 December 2002, 108.

O'Malley, J.M. Chamot, A-U., Stewner-Manzanares, G. Kupper, L. & Russo, R.P. (1985) Learning strategies used by beginnig and intermediate ESL students. *Language Learning* 35, 1: 21-46.

O'Malley, M.J. & Chamot, A. U. (1990) *Learning Strategies in Second Language Acquisition.* Cambridge: Cambridge University Press.

Oxford, R.L. (1990) *Language Learning Strategies: What Every Teacher Should Know.* New York: Newbury House / Harper Collins.

Pemberton, R., Toogood, S., Ho, S. & Lam, J (1999) Developing a self-directed English language learning programme for postgraduate students. In Morrison, B (Ed.) *Experiments and Evaluation in Self-Access Language Learning.* Hong Kong: HASALD, 1-24.

Pemberton, R., Toogood, S., Ho, S. & Lam, J. (2001) Approaches to advising for self-directed language learning. In: Dam, L. (Ed.) *Learner autonomy: new insights. AILA Review 15,* 16-25.

Pemberton, R. Toogood, S., Ho, S. & Tsang, E. (2002) Supporting and Developing SALL: The Need for a Core Team. In Abstracts 4th Symposium of the Scientific Commission on Learner Autonomy in Language Learning, 19 December, 2002, 6..

Pennycook, A. (1997) Cultural alternatives and autonomy. In Benson, P. y Voller, P. (eds) *Autonomy and independence in Language Learning.* London: Longman.

Pennycook, A. (2001) *Critical applied linguistics*: a *critical introduction.* Mahwah (New Jersey) : Lawrence Erlbaum Associates.

Santos, V.M.X., & Horbach, V. (1999) EFL Teacher and class management: teaching and learning strategies. In Cotterall, S. & Crabbe, D. (Eds.) *Learner Autonomy in Language Learning: Defining the Field and Effecting Change* Frankfurt am Main: Peter Lang Verlag, 143-148.

Sarig, G. (1987) High level reading in the first and the foreign language: some comparative process data. In Devine, J., Carrell, P.L. and Eskey, D.E. (Eds.) *Research in Reading Englsih as a Second Language*: 197-220. Washington D.C.: TESOL

Savage, W. & Lamb, T. (2002) Relationships Between Learner and Teacher Autonomy: Realities and Responses. In *Abstracts XIIIth World Congress of Applied Linguistics*, Singapore, 16-21 December 2002, 31.

Schmitt, N. (1997) Vocabulary Learning Strategies. In Schmitt, N. &Mc Carthy, M.J. (Eds.) *Vocabulary, Description, Acquisition and Pedagogy:.* Cambridge: Cambridge University Press, 199-227

Shaw, J. (2002) Team-Teaching as Negotiating Autonomy and Shared Understandings of What We Are Doing. In *Abstracts 4th Symposium of the Scientific Commission on Learner Autonomy in Language Learning,* 19 December, 2002, 7.

Sinclair, B. (2002) Multiple voices: Negotiating Pathways Towards Autonomy. In *Abstracts XIIIth World Congress of Applied Linguistics*, Singapore, 16-21 December 2002, 185-186.

Smith, R. (2001) Group work for autonomy in Asia: insights from teacher-research. In Dam, L. (Ed.) Learner autonomy: new insights, *AILA Review* 15, 70-81.

Thavenius, C. (1999) Teacher autonomy for learner autonomy. In Cotterall, S. & Crabbe, D. (Eds.) *Learner Autonomy in Language Learning: Defining the Field and Effecting Change* Frankfurt am Main; Peter Lang Verlag, 159-164.

Trebbi, T. (2002) Freedom, A Prerequisite for Autonomy. In *Abstracts 4th Symposium of the Scientific Commission on Learner Autonomy in Language Learning*, 19 December, 2002, 2.

Usher, R. Edwards, R. (1994) *Postmodernism and Education*. London: Routledge.

Van Esch, K., Schalkwijk, E. Elsen, A. Setz, W. (1999) Autonomous Learning in Foreign Language Teacher Training. In Faber, P., Gewehr, W., Jiménez Raya, M. & Peck (Eds.), A. *English Teacher Education in Europe. New Trends and Developments*. Frankfurt am Main: Peter Lang Verlag, 15-30.

Van Esch, K. Schalkwijk, E. & Van Summeren, Ch. (2000, 2001) Zelfstandig Leren van Moderne Vreemde Talen,. In *Levende Talen Magazine*, 2000, 87, 8, 5-7 (1), 2001, 88, 9-11 (2), 2001, 88,8-11(3) and 2001, 88, 12-15 (4).

Van Esch, C. & St. John, O. (Eds.) (2003) *A Framework for Freedom. Learner Autonomy in Foreign Language Teacher Education*. Frankfurt am Main: Peter Lang Verlag.

Van Lier, L. (1996) *Interaction in the Language Curriculum. Awareness, Autonomy & Authenticity*. London: Longman.

Vieira, F. (1999) Pedagogy for Autonomy: teacher development and pedagogical experimentation -an in-service teacher training project. In Cotterall, S. & Crabbe, D. (Eds.) *Learner Autonomy in Language Learning: Defining the Field and Effecting Change*. Frankfurt am Main; Peter Lang Verlag, 149-158.

Wenden, A. & Rubin, J. (1987) *Learner strategies in language learning*. New Jersey: Prentice Hall International.

Wenden, A. (1995) Learner training in context : a knowledge-based approach. In *System*, 23, 2, 183-194.

Young, C. (1996) *Listening strategies* Unpublished PhD thesis, University of Essex

Learner Autonomy in Initial Foreign Language Teacher Education
Socrates Lingua Learner Autonomy Group[1]

1 Introduction

In this chapter, we will describe a project in which notions and principles of learner autonomy are applied to foreign language learning and teaching. Teacher trainers from Germany, The Netherlands, Spain and Sweden participated in this Socrates Lingua-A project on Learner Autonomy in Initial Foreign Language Teacher Education. The project aimed to establish common views of autonomy-oriented foreign language learning methodology and to develop modules in which future foreign language teachers are trained in fostering learner autonomy in the learner. At the end of the first year (1998-1999) we published *A Comparison of School Systems, Framework for Freedom* – a theoretical framework for our work, illustrated by a video animation *In the Driving Seat* – and six modules on listening, reading and speaking in a foreign language. In the second project year (1999-2000) we concentrated on the development and publication of five modules related to intercultural competence and learner autonomy. In our final year (2000-2001) we developed three modules on foreign language writing skills and a web site. All these materials (the theoretical thinking, video animation, modules, background materials and web site are described extensively in Van Esch & St. John (2003).

We start the first section of this chapter with a metaphor that illustrates how we view the complexity of learning processes. From this analogy we abstract four stages: *engagement, exposure, integration* and *transference*. The stages are interdependent and related in a learning cycle. They fit in with our views of communicative foreign language learning and teaching. Our perspectives and approaches are rooted in social constructivism and cognitive psychology. Insights from these disciplines helped us to define and theoretically underpin our concepts of learner autonomy. Applying these concepts led to the formulation of important pedagogical principles which are summed up here, but described and explained in more detail in Van Esch & St. John (2003).

In the second section of this chapter, we will focus on the actual teacher training modules and present samples of the goals and objectives, structures, procedures and tasks of the modules. We will end with a brief conclusion.

2 A Framework for Freedom
In the Driving Seat

My father was an excellent driver. His handling of our VW van and remarkably fast reactions had been fine-tuned by the unpredictable occurrences

---

[1] The Socrates Lingua Learner Autonomy Group who contributed to this chapter consisted of: Ragnar Aagard, Helga Deeg, Adri Elsen, Marion Friedrich, Gloria Jover, Oliver St. John and Kees van Esch.

and surging crowds of the Tangier Kasbah streets. I dearly wanted to learn to drive and asked my father several times whether he would teach me how to. When I was ten, I was given my chance. On a lonely stretch of road, I opened the driver's side door and clambered onto my father's lap behind the wheel with the open road ahead. I was engaged to the (driving) learning process.

As the car began to move, I focused on the steering wheel, gripping it with all my might. His hands were also on the wheel with mine as we began to drive together. At this stage, my father's control was fairly comprehensive although I was not aware of it. I thought all there was to driving was steering and I was in the middle of it! Gradually, I began to get the "feel" of handling the controls as he (literally) handed over more and more control to me and progressively allowed me hands-on experience of driving. I was exposed to new territory in close co-operation with my father and my experience was extended beyond what I knew and was able to do.

Things started to come together mentally too. Take the gears for example: When I first moved the gear stick under my father's hand, the path I took seemed haphazard and incoherent. However, as he drew back from guiding my attempts to change gears, I became more actively involved in trying to make sense of the new experience and an inner pattern began to emerge. Engaging the gears on my own was key to mastering the movement. I advanced from focusing on the gear stick to shifting gear, at first without looking at the stick, and then with the growing awareness of which gear I was in. My efforts to synchronise the clutch and gear movements with increasing independence resulted in making the patterns a part of me and understanding the principles.

Another example was the focus. At first I looked at the controls and the stretch of road immediately in front of the car and, as a result, drove rather slowly with a tendency to veer from one side of the road to the other! My father explained the importance of focusing on the road ahead: "It's a bit like someone trying to walk straight when they're staring at their toes". I saw his point but still my horizon was the dashboard and the immediate stretch of road beyond the bumper! As I improved, my father steadily widened the perimeters I was able to practise and make choices in. As a result, I took over fuller control of the car, my confidence grew and my gaze began to lift onto the road far ahead. My progress continually brought me within reach of new challenges which, with my father's help, became opportunities to use what I'd learned as a platform to build further on. They made it possible for me to integrate the action of handling the controls and my immediate environment with what I already knew and could already do. The more I internalised the outer activity in the car, the more I was able to focus ahead, beyond my immediate surroundings. The results were impressive: I became a much better (and faster!) driver. In short, I took greater responsibility for reaching my destination efficiently since I had integrated the operations involved in driving a car with knowledge systems I had already built internally and used in the process.

I remember on one occasion, my father was asked to drive someone else's car – a Studebaker. I was at a loss to understand how he would be able to do it. He could drive our car, but he hadn't learned to drive theirs. Before long I too was able to drive other cars – bigger cars, smaller cars, faster cars, cars with automatic gears etc. – and handle these cars in different driving conditions, different geographical settings, on different road surfaces, terrain, etc. I learned to transfer and implement the principles I had learned in our Volkswagen to other vehicles. I could drive.

Four stages

The learning process is a vastly complex one. The interrelationship between the cognitive and the mechanical can still be only inadequately described. However, from this simple analogy, at least four stages can be abstracted which we believe are essential to learning a skill and which can be discerned in many other learning experiences (e.g. riding a bicycle, swimming, mountaineering, etc.)

1. *Engagement* – a condition in which a learner, because of factors such as personal motivation or teacher intervention, is willing and able to embark on an agreed course of action towards certain learning objectives. It is the point at which a student initially connects with a learning process and is in a position to learn.
2. *Exposure* – involves extending the student's learning environment by exposure to new knowledge and experience. It is a passage from where the student is at (his/ her world, previous experience, etc.) to a destination beyond a student's personal frontier of knowledge and familiar experience.
3. *Integration* – the operation whereby new experiences and external actions are cognitively digested, resulting in the construction of new knowledge and conceptual systems on the basis of what has already been learned. At this stage, learners are engaged in the two-way task of:
   - using their prior knowledge and strategies actively to make sense of new experience;
   - incorporating new information and learning challenges into existing knowledge and ability stores.

   This process involves reflection (on the part of the learner), abstracting principles or concepts and a new synthesis of knowledge. The result of this process is perception, understanding and improved (mechanical) performance.
4. *Transference* – the application of one's skills to a wider field of activities or to other areas. This entails using learned skills to reach a greater variety of goals and so expanding a student's learning environment and

opportunities. As transference is achieved, challenges are redefined and new learning tasks can be accepted.

Learning cycle and learning spiral

Each of the stages mentioned above are interdependent and are related in a learning cycle (Fig 1). Learning takes place as a student passes through these stages and the omission of any stage is to the detriment of the learning experience.

Cycles build on one another progressively in a learning structure which might be represented by an expanding upward-moving spiral as learning grows outward and upwards on the strength of each cyclic coordination. (Fig. 2) After transference has been achieved at the end of a cycle, engagement can take place at a higher level in a new redefined learning environment. It is the teacher's job to facilitate this cyclic momentum which the student is learning to take responsibility for.

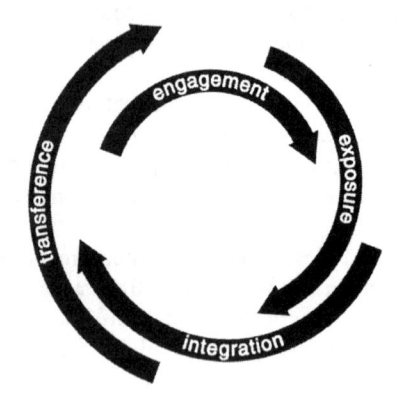

Fig. 1 Learning cycle   Fig. 2 Learning spiral

Communicative Competence, Social Constructivism and Learner Autonomy

Learning how to drive and the four stages abstracted from the learning process have social and cultural dimensions. Learning does not take place in a vacuum. In learning we interact with physical and social environments that are largely determined by the culture we live in. The physical environment in our driving metaphor shifted from the VW van, its controls and the Tangier Kasbah streets to other cars, controls and surroundings. In the social dimension the roles of the father and the son are prominent. The way they interacted was essential to the positive learning experience. At this stage two questions beg to be answered. As language learners, language teachers and teacher trainers, we wonder how our ideas on learning relate to the learning and teaching of foreign languages? In addition, we wonder whether there are any theoretical and empirical grounds to justify a choice of pedagogical principles that can be applied to the process of language learning and language teaching. In our efforts to answer these questions, we refer to the concepts of communicative competence, social constructivism and learner autonomy.

Learner autonomy and social learning have become key issues in communicative language learning and teaching. Foreign language teachers and researchers around the globe are becoming more and more interested in studying and applying aspects of learner autonomy and social learning. Developments in these areas seem to corroborate our views of the learning cycle and the learning spiral. Approaches to foreign language learning have moved from orientations almost exclusively directed to grammar and translation to more eclectic approaches geared to learning how to communicate in a second or foreign language. (Van Els et. al., 1984). Communicative foreign language learning is about acquiring knowledge and skills that first of all help you to understand information in a language different from your mother tongue. You gradually learn to successfully interpret what you see, what you hear or what you read. In addition, you learn to verbally react to or interact with what you see, feel, hear or read when given the proper incentives. You gradually build up knowledge and skills that help you to speak and write. In short, by interacting with your physical and social environment, you are building up both the confidence and the competence to interact and communicate in a foreign language. A useful discussion of the theory and classroom practice of communicative competence can be found in Savignon (1997, 2002 and in this volume).

Our ideas on learning and communicative language teaching are rooted in a theory of learning commonly referred to as social constructivism. Constructivism applied to language learning is basically the notion that language learners construct their own knowledge from their experiences (Wolf, 1994, 1999). From a constructivist perspective, we consider language learning as a self-regulatory process of integrating new insights, representations and models of what aspects of a language to learn and of how to learn these with existing insights, representations and models. This is done with culturally developed tools and symbols, such as language. The processes used to learn new language are negotiated and made explicit in cooperative interaction with others.

We believe learner autonomy can be realised as teacher control and management is progressively relinquished and transferred in cooperation with the learner. Development can only be sustained through a process in which control over and responsibility for the learning situation is gradually shifted from teacher to learner. This transfer implies widening scope for learners to take charge of their own progress. Although far from a neat and automatic operation, this process can be achieved through a co-operative teacher-learner venture which might be illustrated by the figure below:

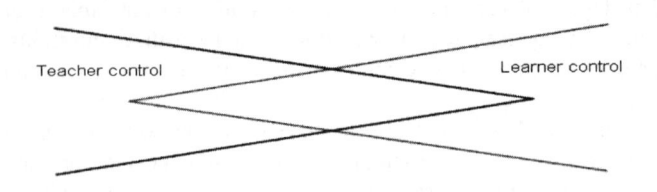

Fig. 3 Teacher and Learner Control in Learner Autonomy

The process described here highlights several aspects of learner autonomy which we believe to be significant and which, in our opinion, are not always recognised as integral to this approach . These include:

1. a sustaining framework created by both teacher and learner in which the perimeters of operation widen on the basis of a learner's progress in managing the dimensions of the learning situation.
2. a learner's willingness to personally invest in the process as well as the product of learning and to use what is learned along the way to redefine learning targets and directions.
3. a learner's commitment to both consent to and carry out actions that fulfill learning obligations.

Gathering these strands of thoughts together, we can say that learners develop autonomy progressively as they become empowered and free to choose, perform and carry through independent actions which are conducive to and necessary for supporting the processes as well as the products of their own learning.

From a trainer's point of view, learner autonomy is conceived not as a methodology or method, but rather as an approach guided by a set of pedagogical principles towards the goal of developing autonomy in the learner.

Implications of Learner Autonomy on Foreign Language Learning and Teaching

Applications of learner autonomy influence teaching methodology and dramatically change the roles of the language teacher and the language learner. In order to help future teachers cope with these changes effectively, they have to be prepared practically and academically in initial teacher training. We focus primarily on the learner's awareness of a variety of learning strategies and processes leading to proficiency in a foreign language. Learner autonomy has important and challenging implications for what is learned in a foreign language and how this is learned. Learner autonomy implies learner involvement at every successive learning stage by the creation of opportunity for independent choice and platforms on which learners can take responsibility for their own learning. This aim led us to formulate pedagogical principles that guided, and continue to guide, our work as foreign language teacher trainers. The principles are clustered around the following key areas: 'Learning by doing', 'The Role of the Learner', 'The Role of the Teacher', 'Cooperative Interaction', 'Learning to Learn' and 'Assessment and Evaluation'. For a more detailed description of these principles see Van Esch & St. John (2003). If learner autonomy is to be realised, then we need to consider how these principles can be applied so that they impact and permeate each stage of the learning process in ways that are optimal for the learner. A learning model underpinned by such principles provides us with a framework for practical teaching modules that aim both to develop learner autonomy and support successful language learning.

We believe it is important to implement these pedagogical principles in foreign language learning and teaching because foreign languages have become everyday features of our communities. Sources of input and authentic materials are easily accessible and are regularly updated. In addition, travelling opportunities widen the possibilities of coming into contact with speakers from foreign language environments and the needs for learning languages have broadened to many different social layers and fields.

On the one hand, we have a deeper insight into learning and the learning of languages. On the other hand, we have better informed learners. This implies that the teacher is no longer the only provider of language and communicative situations; no longer the only possible organiser of the learning process, the only selector of material or input, the only person who decides the appropriate level of difficulty etc. The student does not have to depend solely on the teacher as the source of language input or language learning opportunities. Difficulties may arise precisely from the fact that the foreign language is invading the learner through many other channels of information and he/she lacks the tools and criteria to profit from this situation autonomously.

3 The modules

3.1 Goals and objectives

Formulating common goals was an important first step to shape the initial ideas we used in the modules. The aims were supposed to be achieved in our educational settings and we tried to design our modules in accordance with the goals as efficiently as we could. Given the theoretical framework and our belief in the pedagogical principles we mentioned in the previous section, the following goals, developed in the first year of the project, provided a common pedagogical basis for our modules:

1 Learner Development
   - to apply the principles of learner autonomy to the learning process as a framework for developing autonomous learners.

- to help students build linguistic, strategic, pragmatic competence for effective communication.

2 Language Acquisition
- to enable students to acquire language skills by means of the conscious use of strategies.
- to involve the learner in defining his/ her own learning objectives and choosing techniques to achieve these.

3 Cooperative Learning
- to create an environment in which learners can take responsibility for the learning situation and teachers are willing to be co-learners.
- to help students realise the value of and create opportunities for collaboration between peers as an integral part of the learning process.

4 Methods of Evaluation
- to encourage an awareness of learning as a process as well as a result.
- to foster an ability to be critically and constructively reflective.
- to incorporate teacher, peer and self-evaluation as a basis on which to proceed with further planning and learning activities.

5 Teaching Competence
- to enable our teacher trainees to develop a pupil-learner focus and to transfer their pedagogical perspectives and teaching skills over to the school classroom and milieu.

We also formulated general aims for the competences and skills we focused on, as well as setting objectives for each module, which, for practical reasons, we do not list here.

3.2 Target group and focus

Each module identifies the target group and focus. The target group is the same for all modules: foreign language teacher trainers and trainees. But the focus is different for each module depending on the strategies and skills which it has been designed to develop, its context and approach. In comparison with the first-year modules on listening, reading and speaking, the second-year modules on intercultural competence and especially those developed in the third year on writing skills show increasingly clear differences in focus. In the following paragraphs, we outline the writing modules in order to illustrate these differences:

> The structure of each module in this chapter is built on the four core stages of the learning model. All the modules emphasise the importance of

analysing learner needs, reflecting on various approaches to writing, setting relevant goals and generating intrinsic motivation for writing. All seek to enable learners to achieve these goals independently by taking increasing levels of responsibility for their personal progress as writers and as trainees learning to teach writing. In short, they are all informed by the principles of learner autonomy, such as learning by doing, cooperative interaction, self-evaluation and learning strategically how best to learn.

How one module differs from the other two becomes apparent from this description. The first module, 'Profiling for Progress', begins with a Writer's Profile designed to help trainees survey their writing experiences, evaluate the potential of unexplored writing aspects and to set their sights on new horizons. One of the central guiding principles is that of maximising opportunities for trainees to customise their own learning routes aligned with the priorities and personal goals they initially set. The authors have tried to realise this aim by providing a wide range of writing tasks and open-ended options followed by specific suggestions, which offer guidance while still leaving room for individual choice and direction.

The second module, 'Learner Autonomy in Initial Foreign Language Teacher Training: Writing Skills', builds on the central idea of a real or virtual exchange project bringing together groups of trainees and pupils from different countries for purposes of social contact, cultural insight, language learning, etc. The tasks of the module are intended to capitalise on all the writing opportunities a co-operative international venture of this kind supports. The module underlines the importance of motivation for writing and offers the international exchange project as a context in which trainees and pupils have real reasons to write. When, for example, the purpose of writing is to build relationships and prepare for a forthcoming meeting with a group of partner participants from another country, trainees and pupils will be motivated to write e-mails to their colleagues abroad and produce a written brochure presenting their school/town/municipality/country in a foreign language. At the same time, the products and activities which the exchange project generates provide an opportunity to experience and examine writing as a process as well as to develop guidelines for learning and teaching writing skills.

The third module, 'Learner Autonomy in Developing Writing Skills', starts by experimenting with two different procedures for writing a sketch as a way of exploring co-operative and creative writing. From this immersion experience, previous writing experiences are examined, attitudes to writing discussed and trainees are encouraged to set individual writing goals. The hallmark of this module is the progressive production of a variety of text types. At every stage of the module, trainees are invited to produce and reflect on a new text type that represents a greater challenge than the one chosen in the previous stage. The writing process, self-evaluation and the successive resetting of personal learning goals play important parts in the development of individual writing skills.

Finally, two appendices are included that provide practical tasks that can be used in the development of writing skills. One is 'Writer's Profile' belonging to the first module of this chapter. The profile can be used independently in writing classes as it is or in a modified form. The other one is 'A pool of writing tasks' possible to use with students of almost all ages.
(Van Esch & St. John, 2003, pp. 180-181)

3.3 Rationale

The rationale of each module explains the reasons and ideas behind the development of a particular module. As an illustration, we insert the rationale from the module of Friedrich 'Meeting for meals':

> Eating is an essential part of our lives. In this context, it is not only *who* eats *what* that is important, but also how food is prepared, served and eaten in different cultures. Therefore 'eating' culture is understood not only as a collection of different recipes but, in a broader sense, as part of a way of life. As there has always been an interest in eating habits between cultures, the topic of this module was chosen as one possible starting point for the development of intercultural competence.
>
> The learning process of becoming interculturally competent is not dependent on modern technology, although the latter can be very useful to intensify the process and to motivate teacher trainees or students. Principles of learner autonomy are assumed throughout the module. Teacher trainees are intrinsically motivated and the work of acquiring new knowledge is organized, structured and controlled by themselves. Social and language problems are spontaneously solved independently or with the help of the teacher trainer or teacher. Cooperation is intended to be part of their working strategy.
>
> Consequently, the role of the teacher trainer/ teacher changes. He/ she introduces different ways to learn, helps trainees to find or provides information, negotiates with trainees in the learning process, suggests strategies (e.g. for solving problems), and advises the teacher trainee or groups of them.
(see Van Esch & St. John, 2003, 135)

3.4 Structure

The structure of each module is built on the four core stages of the learning model developed as part of the theoretical framework and described above (see also Van Esch & St. John, 2003). We believe that these stages are essential to learning a skill and can be used as a productive theoretical basis for the development of language proficiency and teaching competence. Each of these stages can be realised in various ways. The modules often have different starting points and take the learner through distinctive sequences of learning opportunities. That is because the authors' views and ideas were often formed by different experiences. In the course of the project we greatly benefited from sharing each other's views and ideas.

3.5 Tasks and activities

In the paragraphs below, we present sample tasks and activities developed in this project to illustrate each of the four stages we have distinguished.

1 Engagement

The *Engagement* stage is designed to help a learner become willing and able to embark on an agreed course of action towards certain learning objectives as a result of factors such as personal motivation or teacher intervention. It is the point at which a student initially connects with a learning process and is in a position to learn. The *Writer's Profile* from Elsen & St. John's 'Profiling for Progress: Learner Autonomy in Writing skills Development' (see Van Esch & St. John, 2003, 181-199 and 217-218) is an example of an *Engagement* task.

> The *Writer's Profile* (shown in this section) is a questionnaire outlining seven writing 'dimensions' which represent the following aspects of writing: attitude, ability, need, process versus product, cooperation and feedback, creative writing and the relationship between writing and thinking. The dimensions provide an opportunity for trainees to rate themselves as writers on these writing variables. Each dimension is supported by a set of four questions designed, as a further aid, to extend and focus thinking. The overall result of responding to this questionnaire is a 'profile' which, we hope, will be useful as a way of personally taking stock of where a writer is 'at' and of moving purposefully forward through a writing course.
>
> On their own, trainees respond to the questionnaire by rating themselves on a scale of 1 – 5 with regard to each aspect. They basically rate themselves as they see themselves as writers in the present. This rating should result in a concrete set of marks which can then be connected by straight lines to build a 'Present Position' profile. In addition, trainees are encouraged to reflect on whether they would like to move along some of the dimensions one way or another. We have suggested the use of arrows in order to indicate a general aspiration or wish with regard to the aspect under consideration. It may also be possible to connect up these indicators (e.g. the arrowheads) with lines as a way of representing a position they would like to reach by the end of the module/ course. In this case, the use of a different colour or dotted line would make this 'Potential Position' profile stand out more clearly.

After filling out the questionnaire, the teacher trainees consider the significance and implications of their profiles by comparing their two profiles and reflecting on what they indicate about, for example, their present positions and priorities as writers. Then, groups are formed on the basis of different profiles and trainees compare, explain and discuss their personal profiles with one another. They are encouraged to reassess their personal writing goals in the light of these discussions. Finally, each group gives a short report to the whole class of the most important points and conclusions of their discussions.

The Profile Questionnaire

In view of yourself as a writer, how would you rate yourself on the 1 to 5 scale of each dimension below?
(1 + 5 = very much; 2 + 4 = a lot; 3 = Can't decide)

A. I love writing   I don't like writing

1	2	3	4	5

What are the reasons behind your rating?
What have you found difficult about writing so far?
What examples can you give of successful pieces of writing you have produced?
Why were you successful with these pieces of writing?

B. I'm a (very) good writer   I'm a poor writer

1	2	3	4	5

1) How do you justify your rating?
2) How do you relate this rating to your success or lack of success as a language learner?
3) What advantage(s) or disadvantage(s) has this rating led to in your life? Why?
4) How do you think moving along this dimension would affect your language learning or any other ability you have/ would like to have in you life?

C. I usually write   I usually write
    because I want to   because I have to

1	2	3	4	5

Can you give examples that illustrate your rating?
How do you think your rating has affected your attitude or motivation with regard to writing?
Would you like to move along this dimension one way or another? If so, which way and why?
(You can indicate the direction with an arrow next to your rating)

Can you give examples of the kinds of writing/ texts you'd like to try producing?

D. I focus mainly on					I focus mainly on
    the process of writing				the product of writing

1	2	3	4	5

What are your reasons behind this rating?
What do you presently do, if anything, to plan and/ or revise your texts?
What would happen to your writing production if you took a position at the other end/one of the ends of the scale?
If you would like to move along this dimension one way or another, indicate the direction with an arrow next to your rating. Why do/ don't you want to move in this way?

E. I write best in					I write best
    co-operation with others				on my own

1	2	3	4	5

How would you explain your rating above?
What advantages or disadvantages can you see in co-operating with others to produce a piece of writing?
Can you give any personal examples which illustrate the positive and/ or negative effects of feedback from others on a piece or your writing?
If you would like to move along this dimension one way or another, indicate the direction with an arrow next to your rating. Why do/ don't you want to move in this direction?

F. I write best when guiding				I write best when
    my own creative processes				given guidelines

1	2	3	4	5

How do you account for your rating?
What do you see as the benefits and/ or difficulties of the writing focus your rating represents?
In what ways would the quality of your writing be affected by moving from your present position on this dimension towards the other end of the scale?
Why would or wouldn't you like to move along this dimension one way or another? (Please indicate your move if you would like to make any)

G. I write to learn					I learn to write

| 1 | 2 | 3 | 4 | 5 |

What factors does a writer's rating on this dimension depend on?
How would you change the formulation of this dimension's poles to make it easier for writers to rate themselves? Why?
How would you describe the relationship between writing and thinking when you are producing a written text?
Why would or wouldn't you like to move along this dimension one way or another? (Please indicate your move if you would like to make any)

2 Exposure

The second stage, *Exposure*, involves extending the student's learning environment by exposure to new experience. It is a passage from where the student is at (his/ her world, previous experience, etc.) to a destination beyond a student's personal frontier of knowledge and familiar experience. The example we offer here is a sequence of tasks taken from the *Exposure* stage of a second-year module on intercultural competence 'Home and Horizon'by Aagård & St. John. (see Van Esch & St John, 2003, 107-129). After having analysed the differences between Swedish / Spanish / Dutch / German homes in the *Engagement* stage, teacher trainees turn to the *Exposure* stage and organise an international home event:

Tasks and procedures
Each group chooses a foreign home (e.g. The French/ Spanish/ German home) to present and display to the entire class as part of an international home event. The following phases are suggested:

Research
Groups plan, gather information, collect materials and prepare their presentations/ exhibitions. Research will include tapping into sources such as the Internet, library materials, foreign press, national magazines, furniture catalogues, group members' personal experiences, interviewing foreign nationals who live in the area, visiting restaurants, travel agents, the embassy, etc.
Representation
The presentation of the foreign home could take many different forms such as, displaying pictures, posters, printed materials, objects, a model of a home, a sketch of an indigenous family engaged in a typical 'home' activity, building a life-size replica of a room in the home as a 'stage' backdrop, a video/ audio presentation of the sketch, etc.
Reception
The event is officially opened and trainees visit it to observe and experience everything on show. The logistics of group members being involved

dramatically in representing cultural aspects of *their* 'home', might mean that different events are visited at different times.

As they go round the show, trainees can use the survey tool they have developed (see Engagement) to make notes about and profile each foreign home they are exposed to. This should help them collect relevant data and organise their observations.

Reflection

Back in their groups, trainees reflect on, discuss and draw conclusions through the following questions:

What struck you as different or distinctive about each home? Share any features or factors that you noticed were special or typical about the homes you visited?

What do these indicate about the culture of the country?

How sufficient was your survey tool to cover other homes? i.e. What dimensions or aspects were lacking (if any)?

What does this show about Swedish homes and culture?

What did you learn about Swedish culture that you hadn't thought of or been aware of at the beginning of this module?

Why do you think you became aware of this aspect?

During this stage, trainees should be encouraged to exchange personal experiences of visiting or hearing/ reading about foreign homes and cultures. These would probably include experiences of hospitality, social behaviour, food, entertainment, etc. as well as cultural surprises, shocks, 'mistakes' and misunderstandings.

3   Integration

The third stage is *Integration*, the operation whereby new experiences and external actions are cognitively digested, resulting in the construction of new knowledge and conceptual systems on the basis of what has already been learned. At this stage, learners are engaged in the two-way task of using their prior knowledge and strategies actively to make sense of new experience and incorporating new information and learning challenges into existing knowledge and ability stores. To illustrate this stage, we include a series of *Integration* tasks from Jover's module 'Cognitive and Attitudinal Development in Intercultural Learning' (see Van Esch & St. John, 2003, 90-107). In order to develop both cognitive and attitudinal intercultural capacities, this module focuses on the need to become interculturally aware for foreign language communicative competence, on developing criteria for selecting suitable cultural content and on evaluating students' intercultural achievements. There are two basic objectives to the *Integration* stage of this module. The first is to enable trainees to share their learning experiences through group presentations. The second objective is to help trainees evaluate the degree of intercultural learning they have achieved in terms of cognitive and attitudinal development.

Tasks and procedures

The aim is that the trainees should actually acquire knowledge and develop as individual users of the second language. They also need to take culture into account as a very important part of their learning and, consequently, of their own conceptions of learning-teaching a second language.

This stage of the module consists, to a large extent, of a series of evaluation activities at different levels and from different points of view. It includes:
- the presentation of research work
- observation and evaluation of the presentations by peers
- self-evaluation
- evaluation by and feedback from the trainer
- collective evaluation of the group's cognitive and attitudinal development regarding culture and communication.

Presentation
1. Each group reports to the whole class by formally presenting their products. They should all receive a written report of the topic dealt with. This material can be copied and distributed to the others before or after the presentation.
2. The idea of using a common structure for this report may help in several ways: a) trainees learn how to structure their learning not only for themselves but for sharing or presenting it to others; b) listeners can follow and process the information more efficiently if they have some prior knowledge of each presentation's structure; and c) the trainer receives a more systematised final product which will make evaluation easier.
3. Discussion around each topic presented will follow naturally.

Evaluation

Evaluation can and should measure the process of learning and the degree of achievement reached. This is especially important in the field we are dealing with where so many aspects are really difficult to be objective about. Nevertheless, if the stages outlined so far have worked, our trainees will have been reflecting on, analysing, verbalising and pinpointing ideas which will have given them a frame to learn in. They will have succeeded in finding a topic to research into and should have profited both from the process and the outcome of their investigations. They will have been engaged in discussion and debate. They will have contributed to a collective effort. This activity should certainly have resulted in considerable learning.

Our proposal for evaluation aims specifically at examining what has actually happened, namely, how far our trainees have got in the construction of new knowledge about cultures and interculturalism and in the development of positive attitudes towards the target culture.

We suggest 4 levels of evaluation:

A. Peer-evaluation. As a complement to the discussion, the group can formally evaluate each presentation with a simple instrument in which to collect their views during or after the report. Appendix 5 shows an example of an evaluation sheet.

B. Self-evaluation. Individually, the trainees answer a questionnaire to be discussed with the trainer later. Appendix 6 gives an example of an individual questionnaire.

C. Evaluation by the trainer.
- Evaluation of presentations: the presentation in itself may turn out to be a perfectly suitable activity to evaluate and, to aid this task, the trainer can note down responses in a previously designed table of questions. Appendix 7 shows a tool for evaluating presentations.
- Individual trainees write an essay on any given topic. Topics may be selected from those on the 'study' list. Offering a choice is always a prerequisite for learner autonomy processes. It should be noted that we are not specifically testing language, although, of course, we are always observing learners' linguistic performance and will have decided when and how to provide feedback if necessary.

D. Group's self-evaluation:

Because learning has been carried out cooperatively, we propose the following ideas to give the group the opportunity to check its collective progress. The first involves *revising the mind map*. Trainees are asked to review the mind map they produced at the beginning of this module. They will, most probably, have some changes to make, items to add or may want to reformulate certain ideas and categories. They might even decide to produce a new one and, after comparing it with the original one, display it in the classroom in order to profile the new level of knowledge and awareness they have reached. The second idea involves *summarising their learning achievements*. Using the four categories established as aspects of intercultural competence (cf. *Modern Languages: Learning, Teaching, Assessment. A Common European Framework of Reference*. Council for Cultural Co-operation, Strasbourg, 1998) the group may benefit from the following instrument to check the levels of their learning and acquisition in this area:

		NO	YES	WHAT
SAVOIR	**Do we know more about:**			
	culture?			
	cultures?			
	some cultures?			
	interculturalism?			
	communication?			
	...			
SAVOIR FAIRE	**Have we deepened our understanding of:**	NO	YES	WHAT
	how to behave?			
	social norms?			
	others' behaviour?			
	...			
SAVOIR ÊTTRE	**Have we learnt to be more:**	NO	YES	WHAT
	respectful?			
	tolerant?			
	open-minded?			
	understanding?			
	...			
SAVOIR APPRENDRE	**Did we learn to learn about:**	NO	YES	WHAT
	our culture?			
	other cultures?			
	intercultural communication?			
	...			

4   Transference

As we have already stated, the *Transference* stage refers to the application of one's skills to a wider field of activities / other areas. The following is an example of a *Transference* stage from Deeg's 'Intercultural Learning: Celebrating Christmas as an example of a religious celebration in a multicultural group of learners'. (see Van Esch & St. John, 2003, 133). This module explores the meanings of Christmas traditions from different cultures in order to involve learners in the process of understanding the values and beliefs that lie beneath the surface. The objectives of the module's *Transference* stage are to enable trainees to present and discuss an aspect of the way Christmas is celebrated in the world, as well as to evaluate this group work.

Task and procedures
1. The groups give the presentations they have prepared to the whole group and participate in discussing the group work. A trainer can chair the discussion or the trainees can decide to appoint a trainee chairperson. If a trainee is the chairperson, the trainer will observe the presentation and discussion of the group work and intervene when necessary or even participate.
2. Trainees evaluate the presentations with questions such as:
   * Did trainees stick to what they agreed on with regard to the presentations?
   * If any changes were made, what were the reasons for them?
   * Were the subsequent changes helpful for the task of evaluating the presentations?
   * The exchange of perspectives and opinions (including any prejudices) in the discussion also needs to be examined and evaluated.

3.6   Background materials

During the project we selected and/or developed background materials to provide useful support information on aspects of our modules and areas that we felt deserved further explanation. We included these background materials as appendices to the modules but, for the sake of brevity, we will only sum up the types of materials here. The items vary and may consist of additional information about tasks, pools of additional tasks, background literature, questionnaires for helping teacher trainees encourage learners to develop tasks or to evaluate tasks, reference texts on organising the process of e.g. writing or on developing intercultural competence and sets of 'descriptor' scales for communicative language competence and intercultural competence, taken from the Council of Europe's *Common European Framework* (2001).

4 Conclusion

In terms of an overall conclusion, we can say that the project has been challenging and productive. It led to reflection on and the formulation of a firm theoretical basis for developing materials for initial foreign language teacher training. In addition, it taught us how teacher education was organised in different European countries. In this light, we were able to understand and discuss the various benefits and problems of the different systems. The project gave us a lot of opportunities to cooperate and to learn from each other about applying learner autonomy to our teacher education courses and at the schools where our trainees were teaching. The project led to a real exchange of ideas and experiences and changed our views on teacher education and on learning foreign languages at school.

But we also had to face problems. One problem was related to dissemination, that is, to sharing our ideas and tasks with others so that the results our work could contribute to discussion and development in these fields. Because of our preoccupation with developing the theoretical framework and the modules, we did not manage to disseminate our work beyond our institutions. As a result, dissemination is one of the main goals we are now trying to achieve. A first step was the development of a website featuring our theoretical framework, tasters of the modules and a discussion platform. The website address is: www.learnerautonomy.com. Another step involved publication of the materials in a book with the support of a video (see Van Esch & St. John, 2003). A third step was a three-year Comenius project on *Learner Autonomy in In-service Foreign Language Teacher Training* which is aimed at carrying out action research in order to improve teaching practices for fostering learner autonomy and intercultural competence in the foreign language classroom. A fourth step is organizing courses on learner autonomy to be given to and discussed with teachers from different European countries over the coming years.

5 References

Council of Europe, Council for Cultural Co-operation. Education Committee. Modern Languages Division (2001) *Common European Framework of Reference for Languages: Learning, Teaching, Assessment.* Cambridge: Cambridge University Press.

Savignon, S. J. (1997). Communicative competence: Theory and classroom practice. Second Edition. New York: Mc.Graw-Hill.

Savignon, S. J. (2002). Communicative Language Teaching: Linguistic Theory and Classroom Practice. In: Savignon, S.J. (Ed.) Interpreting Communicative Language Teaching. New Haven & Londen: Yale University Press, 1-29.

Van Els, T. Bongaerts, T., Extra, G., Van Os, Ch. & Janssen- van Dieten, A. (1984) *Applied Linguistics and the Learning and Teaching of Foreign Languages*. London: Edward Arnold

Van Esch, K. & St. John, O. (eds.) (2003) *A Framework for Freedom. Learner Autonomy in Foreign Language Teacher Education*. Frankfurt am Main: Peter Lang Verlag.

Wolff, D. (1994) Der Konstruktivismus: Ein neues Paradigma in der Fremdsprachendidaktik, *Die Neueren Sprachen* 93, 5, 407-429.

Wolff, D. (1999): Zu den Beziehungen zwischen Theorie und Praxis in der Entwicklung von Lernerautonomie. In: Edelhoff,C., R. Weskamp: *Autonomes Fremdsprachlernen*. Ismaning: Hueber, pp. 37-48.

Foreign Language Teaching in Europe

Edited by:
Pamela Faber, Wolf Gewehr, Manuel Jiménez Raya and Terry Lamb

Vol. 1 Pamela Faber / Wolf Gewehr / Manuel Jiménez Raya / Antony Peck (Eds.): English Teacher Education in Europe. New Trends and Developments. 1999.

Vol. 2 Stephan H. Gabel: Über- und Unterrepräsentation im Lernerenglisch. Untersuchungen zum Sprachgebrauch deutscher Schülerinnen und Schüler in interkulturellen Telekommunikationsprojekten. 2000.

Vol. 3 Winfried Bredenbröker: Förderung der fremdsprachlichen Kompetenz durch bilingualen Unterricht. Empirische Untersuchungen. 2000.

Vol. 4 Manuel Jiménez Raya / Pamela Faber / Wolf Gewehr / Antony J. Peck (eds.): Effective Foreign Language Teaching at the Primary Level. 2001.

Vol. 5 Yvette Coyle / Mercedes Verdú / Marisol Valcárcel: Teaching English to Children - Interactivity and Teaching Strategies in the Primary FL Classroom. 2002.

Vol. 6 Markus Kötter: Tandem learning on the Internet. Learner interactions in virtual online environments (MOOs). 2002.

Vol. 7 Manuel Jiménez Raya / Terry Lamb (eds.): Differentiation in the Modern Languages Classroom. 2003.

Vol. 8 Kees van Esch / Oliver St. John (eds.): A Framework for Freedom. Learner Autonomy in Foreign Language Teacher Education. 2003.

Vol. 9 Kees van Esch / Oliver St. John (eds.): New Insights into Foreign Language Learning and Teaching. 2004.

www.peterlang.de